Manchester must dance

Manchester University Press

Manchester must dance

A life of music, madness and moving on up

MIKE PICKERING WITH
PAUL MORLEY

Manchester University Press

Published by Manchester University Press
Oxford Road, Manchester, M13 9PL

www.manchesteruniversitypress.co.uk

British Library Cataloguing-in-Publication Data
A catalogue record for this book is available from the British Library

ISBN 978 1 5261 9056 7 hardback

First published 2026

EU authorised representative for GPSR:
Easy Access System Europe, Mustamäe tee 50, 10621 Tallinn, Estonia
gpsr.requests@easproject.com

MIX
Paper | Supporting responsible forestry
FSC® C013604
FSC www.fsc.org

Typeset
by Cheshire Typesetting Ltd, Cuddington, Cheshire
Printed in Great Britain
by CPI (UK) Ltd, Croydon

Contents

Forewords

MARTIN FRY

I've known Mike Pickering since 1976, when I was about 17. He was older than me, but I recognised a kindred spirit when I saw one. We went to the same school, but our meeting was accidental: we used to walk the streets where we both lived – a slow, unexciting part of Stockport that really needed something like punk rock to give you something to aim for. Nothing much lay ahead of us, and whatever jobs were around at the time didn't seem enticing. There had to be more.

Luckily Manchester, a short train ride away, was quick to become a punk city. That's where we got our education – in music, books, television, clubs, clothes and seeing the Sex Pistols. We would end up using it for the rest of our lives. We started using it when I put together a fanzine called *Modern Drugs*. Mike would write for it.

We took from punk the idea that we could do something for ourselves and that music in some form was our future. When I left for Sheffield University we saw each other less. The education that counted in Sheffield still meant music and going to the same clubs as The Human League and Cabaret Voltaire. Eventually Mike left Manchester on his own travels, learning things on the road that he would bring back to the city and use. An intermittent series of phone calls began that would map out what happened to us over the years, two no ones from nowhere with this dream of becoming something, who loved making plans and looking for opportunities and other like-minded people.

This was decades before the internet and mobile phones. To keep in touch meant a certain effort and even love, and as male northerners brought up in the sixties and seventies, when emotions seemed scary, we weren't necessarily very communicative on the phone. Just the basics. Even when I was seriously ill a couple of times, when there were marriages and the adult stuff, it was still just business as usual.

It was a way of maintaining contact, of reminding ourselves through thick and thin of the afternoons we used to spend in bookshops or playing records, taking control of our destiny. Mike was worth keeping in touch with even if he always used to deliver his news, whether mundane or life changing, in the same dry, unexcited Manchester voice.

I was always a bit more dramatic. I guess of the two of us I was the romantic and he was just getting on with things that he found he was good at, never really expecting anything to happen. When it did, he started to think: what was he going to do next?

I went to university, he went to Holland, which had a certain social freedom he made good use of. It was hard to keep up with him, because international calls didn't make life easy. Sometimes months went by without contact, but then a quick call would bring us up to date with our news. His was delivered as if everything he did was what it was. He was cleaning dishes in a cafe. He'd started promoting bands. He was playing records in bars. He was working as a roadie for international bands. He'd met Kraftwerk. 'What were they like?' 'Quiet ...' 'Have you heard the new James White and the Blacks record?'

I had found myself in a band, a punkish electronic band, and Mike said, 'Oh yes, I'm in a band, a punkish dance band.' He got us over to play at this club he'd started organising. While we were there we started to think of changing our name from Vice Versa.

Another phone call and he's back in Manchester working with the mysterious Factory Records label and living with Rob Gretton, the manager of New Order. Rob wants to start a club. 'Sounds great', I say. 'It's interesting', he says, as if he's surrounded and can't speak. 'Yeah', he tells me, 'I met Tony Wilson off the telly. Smokes a lot of weed.' 'OK, talk later.'

The band I was in, now named ABC, got a record deal and became a successful pop group that played on *Top of the Pops*, when that could mean you'd become a household name, sometimes overnight. I got busy, but we'd keep in touch. He was busy as well, but he never said much about what it all involved. He was in New York with New Order. He was making records with his group. He'd got married. Rob's club had opened, which was now as much Tony's club, and it looked great – but they were having a bit of trouble. He'd met Madonna. 'What was she like?' 'Rude ...'

I had some hits in the eighties, which kept me even busier, but there were always the phone calls. He'd signed a group called James to Factory who sounded promising. Then another one, a rowdy bunch from Salford called Happy Mondays. 'Yeah', Mike said, 'I might be producing their first record. Tony thinks it's a good idea. He might be pulling my leg.'

He'd started DJing at The Haçienda. That seemed to go well, and then not so well. Around 1988 or 1989 he seemed unusually happy about things. I would go and see him DJ at The Haçienda, and I could see why. By 1990, Mike mentioned drugs and guns and needing a change of scenery.

Then in the nineties, when I wasn't having hits anymore with ABC, he was the one having hits with a group he'd put together called M People. I'd made quite a fuss of being in ABC, wore the gold jacket, but Mike was still just taking everything as it came. 'Hey Martin, yeah, we won the Mercury Prize. Beat Blur, Pulp and Take That. Should have seen the look on the faces of those who thought we were just a shallow dance group.'

M People had their time, and then we were in the twenty-first century and he was working for Sony as an A&R consultant. Another phone call: 'I've just signed this kid from Dumfries called Calvin Harris. Reminds me of a young me.' He'd keep in touch, sometimes calling when he was with Calvin in Las Vegas or Los Angeles. Communication was a lot better now. He was calling from a private jet. I could tell it was going well. Still not too much detail, though. A call from Los Angeles in 2009: he's having breakfast with the legendary American producer Rick Rubin just off Santa Monica Boulevard, talking about wrestling. Of course he is.

More years passed, and we still checked in with each other regularly. I was making a decent living singing ABC songs around the world. Mike had been very keen in the late nineties, when it seemed like it was worthless, that I buy the ABC name. I wasn't so sure. But he insisted and I sold my car and paid what seemed like a small fortune for it. He turned out to be right. People still loved to love.

A call in the 2020s, when we'd decided we weren't the type to put our feet up. Mike says, 'I'm thinking of writing a book. What do you think?'

I say, 'I think it's a good idea. It'll be great to find out what you've been doing all these years.'

JOHNNY MARR

The first really vivid memory I have of meeting Mike, early 1982, I was just this teenage lad who worked at X Clothes in central Manchester. It had been open for a few months, but quickly became the place to go. It had come from Leeds, but I soon put a Manchester spin on it.

I'd been in a few bands but had just formed this weird new band with a singer called Morrissey. Hardly anyone knew that at the time. Mike had been into the shop a few times and I'd got to know him as a customer, one of those who had a good eye for clothes. He knew what was good and what wasn't, especially for someone in their late twenties. He was into all the stuff I was picking up on trips to London from the King's Road, and even had me order a jacket from Johnsons where people like Elvis Costello and Blondie were getting their clothes.

I was also impressed that he got that my look then was very much based on Theatre of Hate, sort of goth rockabilly, which my Wythenshawe friend Billy Duffy, later of The Cult, was in. Some of – let's say the older guard – weren't so knowledgeable.

Mark E. Smith of The Fall, for example. He could always be trusted to buy the wrong thing. He always called me 'son' and 'pal', and treated me like a lowly shop assistant, which used to annoy me. I would think, I'm a better fucking guitarist than your guitarist, and I'm going to knock you off your perch one day. I acted like a cocky so and so, but it was all a front.

Mark would buy the cheap, generic shit, and I'd let him. He'd try something on. 'Wow, you look great', I'd lie.

Mike just naturally treated me as an equal. I wasn't yet Johnny Marr of The Smiths, I was just Johnny X Clothes, someone who happened to play guitar, but Mike helped me from the very beginning.

We didn't know each other that well at first, but we'd talk about music and what was happening. Mike was cool, and I had respect for that. For some reason, I knew instantly that he was a dance guy, into soul and funk, and that before punk he wasn't one of those rock guys with long hair that suddenly cut it off when Johnny Rotten came

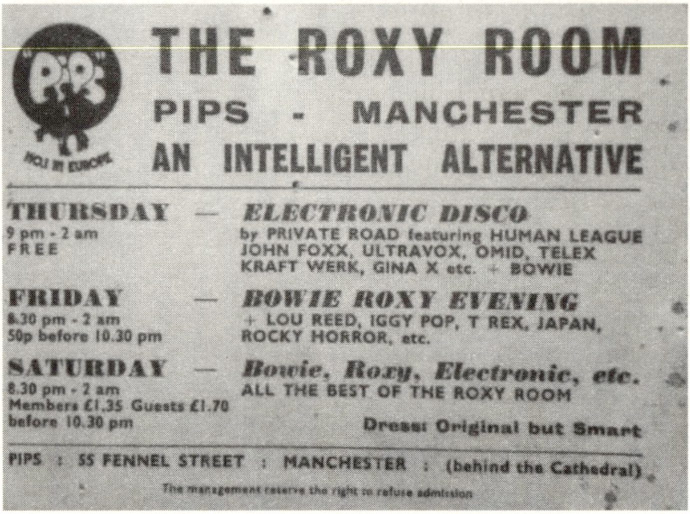

Pips Roxy Room Manchester Flyer mid-seventies

along. He would be in the shop with records that he'd bought from Spin Inn on Cross Street, which was where you'd go to buy the best soul and funk.

I saw Mike as being someone who'd always had short hair and never wore flares and hippy clothes. I'd suss people out; it seemed part of the job. The details were important. It was the same when I was playing the guitar – the small details are important, they're a vital part of the whole thing.

He had a Perry Boy vibe, and it seemed like he'd been to the Bowie/Roxy Room at the Pips nightclub near the cathedral. All would become clear, of course.

He came in this time with Peter Saville, who I knew very well as the designer of the astonishing Joy Division sleeves for Factory Records, but not to talk to. He'd never been in the shop before. Mike was better connected than I thought.

He was carrying these cardboard tubes, and I'd never seen anything like them. They had blueprints inside, and Mike was really excited, and said, 'Check these out.' Mike unrolled them on the shop counter, and they were the blueprints of the new club Factory were going to open: The Haçienda.

There were all sort of rumours spreading around town about the club famous Tony Wilson and Factory were planning, and here was Mike with the actual blueprints, right on the inside of the latest thing that was happening in Manchester. We were staring at them, not knowing what it all meant, but just the fact there were blueprints made you think it was going to be something special.

Mike always seemed to be on the inside, always around when things were happening, but never made a big thing of it. He kept himself to himself as others would claim they were there, when often they weren't and he was. He got to things early, but he didn't want to necessarily stand out as the leader of something. He was happy to be part of the community, but he just had this instinct to get to something first and then move on when it got crowded.

Mike was a very Manchester person, but not old school, looking inward all the time. He was a modern Manchester person. The fact he talked about Chicago, New York, Detroit, Europe made him more Manchester to me. Manchester at its best is never just Manchester and nothing else. And he was always very positive. Manchester can be brilliantly moany and glass half empty, and sometimes no one more than Mike, but it always needed the positive and encouraging as well. He could make a half full glass seem full to the brim, and back then it took a lot to test his enthusiasm for music and fashion. Tony, Rob, Peter, the Factory set – they needed someone like Mike.

When the club started, he'd invite me over in the early afternoon – and it would be one o'clock, and you're smoking a spliff inside this club that actually looked great in the daylight – and shooting the shit with Tony Wilson. Tony could be very pompous and patronising, and was the worst dressed ever, especially in the early 1980s, which always amused me. He could never work me out, but he definitely believed in Manchester – and he could see that Mike did as well.

Everyone had their roles at Factory and The Haçienda, some clearer than others. It was never clear what Mike's exact role was – perhaps because it wasn't exact – but in those early days, when it was in its first few months, and there were those who thought it was too trendy, whatever that means, Mike was like the ambassador for it around the city. He stood up for it when it was struggling and people didn't give it much of a chance. In a way, when he was DJing and making the noise that helped make the club, it was a continuation of that ambassadorial role.

He put The Smiths on at The Haçienda when they were just my little band. I'd found the singer. I'd found the drummer and bassist. I found the first gigs. I found the rehearsal rooms.

We were no one, and I asked Mike if he could get us a gig at the club – and the thing was, it was another of his invisible roles, but he booked the bands. He put us on supporting a Factory group, 52nd Street, who were much bigger than we were, and it was a great help to us. I'm not throwing shade at anyone, but history has it that it was all because Morrissey knew Tony Wilson, and Wilson gave us that break. It was Mike.

He took the gamble – he just assumed we'd be good because he knew me and we'd talk about music. There was no sense we'd be 'The Smiths'. To him, it was Johnny's new band. I remember in the shop, I'd played him a cassette of some of our songs. 'Here, you'll like this one, it's about the Moors Murderers. We recorded it slow and it's in the wrong key – check it out.' I'd stick it on in the shop sometimes – after The Human League or The Associates there'd be this really bad hiss and through the gloom someone singing about digging a shallow grave. It didn't seem immediately promising.

And Mike put us on. And our name was on the poster – an actual Haçienda poster – and not all bands got their name on the poster. Which was almost better than the gig itself because that meant you must be something. It meant you were a real band.

We were never going to be a Factory band, but The Haçienda was different. We were back there a few months later on Thursday 24 November 1983, and it was the same day as we made our debut on a live *Top of the Pops* show, Morrissey using a bunch of gladioli as his microphone. Mike had us booked into The Haçienda for weeks, and it would usually have been ok because *Top of the Pops* was recorded on a Wednesday, but this edition was live.

We couldn't bring ourselves to cancel under any circumstances. It wasn't any grand gesture. It felt like the first Haçienda show had been an important steppingstone to being on *Top of the Pops* in the first place, and we'd had such a great year, it felt like our triumphant homecoming. It didn't occur to us we could do it anywhere else.

As soon as we finished this great experience, *Top of the* bloody *Pops*, we raced to Euston Station and caught the train to Manchester Piccadilly. We were so high on it we were racing up and down the aisles telling everyone we'd just done *Top of the Pops*. We still had a job to do back in Manchester.

At the station, there's a frantic-looking Mike waiting for us, racing towards us shouting, 'There's two thousand inside and a thousand outside!' It was like being in a Beatles film, and we all squeezed into this tiny yellow Morris Metro van, and Mike drove us to The Haçienda. I remember thinking, a yellow van isn't very Factory! It stunk because someone had spilt some milk in there.

There's The Smiths squashed into this little van making its way down Whitworth Street, pushing through hundreds of fans who've turned up but can't even get in. At that point, let's be honest, we had just become the most important band in Britain, and we'd made this explosive debut on *Top of the Pops* – and Mike comes to get us in a crappy yellow van that smells like sick.

We had to make our way through this screaming crush of people trying to get at us, and Rob Gretton literally picks me off the ground and drags me through. I only weighed about seven and a half stone, but still.

The stage was all set up for us, and we went straight into 'Handsome Devil'. There were hundreds of sweaty bodies with their hands in the air. and the Manchester energy is amazing. We're amazing, even if we sound like shit. It was our first really proper live pop star moment.

There was a lad on some other lad's shoulders about three rows back, and he was shouting 'Johnny! Johnny!' and reaching out to me with a mad look in his eye. He had no shirt on, and I realised it was someone I had quite looked up to at school. I thought, put your fucking shirt on and get off his shoulders. I still thought of him as one of my mates, and he was screaming at me, completely losing his mind.

It was the first time my mum and dad had seen The Smiths play, and I saw them near the sound desk, a bit in shock, while the sound man was passing a smoking pipe across my dad's face and handing it to Mike.

Mike was there. He was always there.

NOEL GALLAGHER

I was wondering if Mike was going to call this book *Search for a Hero*. I think he should have. Or there was that time we were together with a few friends and family at the FA Cup Final to see Man City against United, and a bunch of United fans spotted us walking up Wembley Way. They got a bit lairy and entitled, and pressed against us, trying to provoke us. All very unnecessary. One of them shouted right in Mike's face, 'You Blue Haçienda cunt.' That could be the title. Best insult ever. 'Blue Haçienda cunt.' Maybe a special edition.

We first met properly, shaking hands and all that, at a Manchester City game. I think it was against Watford, at Maine Road in the last years of its life before we moved to what became the Etihad. I'm not sure if we were in the Second Division or had made it back to the Premier League. Things were a bit fuzzy back then. No signs at all of what would happen to City when Sheikh Mansour and Khaldoon took over a few years later.

We won one nil, and Shaun Wright-Phillips scored. He'd just broken into the side and his kit was too big for him.

It was pissing down with rain of course, the roof was leaking, it was fucking freezing, and my lot were stood at the back of the stands. I was with Phil Smith, Oasis tour DJ, and our kid, Liam, when he still used to go, and probably our Paul as well.

And Mike strolled up with a drink and took one look at us miserable sods in the cold and wet and said, 'Ah, so this is where the fucking celebrities are.'

We might have passed in the night at The Haçienda, but when Mike was having his time, I was just a face in the crowd. I was never really part of The Haçienda scene. It took me ages to find it the first time I went because there was no sign outside. It was dark down there.

I walked right passed it, and then missed it again. The first thing about The Haçienda was you had to find it. You'd be wandering up and down Whitworth Street thinking, somebody must know where it is. You couldn't imagine an organisation that advertised themselves less, considering they were so full of themselves. When you found it, you went through these bloody plastic curtains, and you asked someone, 'Can I come in?' 'If you want.' 'Is this where the Railway Children are playing?' 'Yes. Do you want to come in?' 'Go on, then.'

This is the thing about The Haçienda – loads of people think they must have met me there because of who I am, but back then I was a nobody, I was just a geezer. Loads of people will say, 'I'm sure I met you there.' No – you wouldn't have recognised me. I wasn't Noel Gallagher then, not in the way I would be later.

There was definitely an incident where me and Mike bumped into each other, without being formally introduced, and that might count as a first meeting.

I would go to a lot of raves held around the North at the end of the eighties, early nineties: Sheffield, Huddersfield, Blackpool. Thousands of kids dancing off their heads in fields in the early hours, defying the police. Fucking fantastic. There was a great one in Blackburn, and I remember Mike played one night. There were two tents. The one he was playing in was packed. Then he finished around half midnight and said, 'I'll be over in the next tent in half an hour', and everyone from that tent moved over to the tent next door. No one was there when the next DJ came on. Mike was the man.

There was an illegal rave being thrown in Leeds, just off the motorway in a big fucking field, obviously. I never actually got there. I was working for the Inspiral Carpets, so it was 1989, maybe 1990.

The police were ready for it, and they were pulling cars over with likely looking people inside. We were so high in our car we thought, oh look, they're wearing a hi-vis jacket. Let's pull over. And they'd been waving to us, and we thought, this is well-marshalled for a rave.

The hi-vis guy asked, 'Where are you off to?' And we thought he was being helpful and told him, 'We're off to the rave.' I don't know how we missed it, but he was a cop. 'Can you get out of the car please?' We got out and thanked him for helping us, and before we knew it, we were hooked.

We got taken to the station, but there were so many other people that had got arrested we got put in the basement of the town hall. People can't comprehend now heavy-handed the police were then, raiding the raves like military operations, but also arresting people five miles out from a field on the off-chance they were going. True, some of them were hiding something, but the cops didn't know that.

We were in this basement for hours, slowly coming down, waiting for something to happen. And Mike rolled up at about four in the morning, with some social commentary about how this was fascist Britain, and everyone stood up and cheered. It was fucking Mike Pickering of The Haçienda and he was carrying his records! It was like he didn't want to get them confiscated, he wasn't letting them out of his sight. For a DJ like Mike, your records were everything.

Had he come to save us? Had he hell. We were all in court in the morning.

There were loads of us in the dock, and we couldn't afford legal counsel, so we were given a court-appointed solicitor. She was really on it and claimed we were all the victims of acid house culture. I was with her all the way – yes, we're the victims here!

She said, these are just normal kids who read about it in the newspapers and they see it on the TV and they're enticed into this world. It's not their fault. I was cheering her on – it's not our fault! We're the victims! We're fucking innocent!

Didn't see Mike. He got off. Maybe he paid a fine.

He claimed he wasn't booked to appear, but the organisers had put his name on the flyers, which was what these illegal raves often did – put the big names on their flyers to get kids to come along. He was definitely due to play this rave.

When they asked him why he had his records with him, he said, 'I came from another legal gig to confront the promoters for putting my name on their flyers without my permission.' He wasn't having his name bandied about like that.

I spent the night in jail and I can still feel how cold it was as we waited to be let out, a great night out lost forever. Four in the morning I'm wandering the godforsaken streets of Leeds, wondering how the hell I'm going to get home.

I blame Mike Pickering, although he should be given a knighthood for services to clubbing.

Enjoy the book.

CALVIN HARRIS

I wasn't even born when The Haçienda opened. I was about 5 when Mike was at his Haçienda peak as a DJ, so I've absolutely no memory of that. When I first met him in 2007, I didn't really know anything about him. It was before my time. Even rave or acid house was something that had happened and was over. It was history. It wasn't on my radar when I started making music as a 14-year-old at the end of the nineties. I was thinking Jamiroquai, Klaxons, LCD Soundsystem, that was what I was listening to.

He was working for Sony Records, and he was very interested in signing me, saw something in my music few others were seeing, and talked differently from other people I'd met in the record business. More conceptual, although I wouldn't have put it like that then.

I vaguely knew that he'd been in M People and they had big hits in the nineties, but nothing I was particularly paying attention to. My manager and lawyer told me he had lots of experience in making music and had been an influential, inspirational DJ, but I had to piece together what he had done once he'd signed me to Sony. As we got to know each other and worked together, I realised, God, he's done this, and he's been that, he's been part of this scene, he's worked in studios, he's played to huge audiences around the world as a DJ, and he's sold millions of records as a musician.

He's the last person to tell you all of this himself. He definitely didn't go out of his way to tell me. I really did have to figure it out for myself.

When he was wanting to sign me there was no hard sell about his exploits, no ego, no CV he was shoving in my face. At first, I just trusted his instinct – I didn't necessarily need to know what he'd done. But when I started to find out, it was amazing how much he'd done.

You'd never see him all over those nostalgic talking head TV shows banging on about how great it all was back in the day. He never looks for credit. It must have come from his DJ background. He was only interested in the next record he was going to play, and in his life he was only interested in what was coming next, in learning something new.

It was like he was always starting from scratch, and what interested him was what he was going to do next, which he hoped would be working with me. I was the next record he was going to play. He was looking to learn as much from me as I might be learning from him.

We started working together, and it went well. We both believed in dance music, the sound of it, where everything was possible. He was a great sounding board for new ideas. I could send him work in progress and he knew just when to suggest something and when to just let me get on with it. I liked to work quick and he was happy to keep up with me.

When I made a huge decision, say, not to work with a band anymore but perform my own songs as a DJ, he didn't turn a hair. As far as he was concerned, it made total sense, and it did to me, so there were never any intense meetings about it or anything. He might have been having battles inside Sony when my first album didn't meet its sales target or whatever, but he never let on to me.

His excitement at what I was up to and openness to it was always encouraging, which sometimes as a musician is all you need. In hindsight it made sense that he identified with how I approached being a performer, because he had been one, but as he was the only A&R guy I'd ever worked with, at first I pretty much took it for granted.

We just got on with it, and if he said my new songs were shite, I wrote some others, even if I disagreed with him. You couldn't really argue with how we worked together, because I was having international hits, and they were getting bigger, the singers I was working with were getting more famous, the stages I played were getting bigger and the streaming numbers were climbing and climbing into the tens of billions. My world was changing pretty fast, but there was always Mike, always solid and down to earth in how he talked to me, always good with some advice, however crazy things were getting.

He loved it when things went a bit mad. When I came up with 'We Found Love' in 2011, which was the song that changed everything for me, the absolute breakthrough, it was originally going to be released by Leona Lewis, who had won the *X Factor* talent competition. She was on the Syco label of *X Factor* boss Simon Cowell, king of the pop world and all that, a huge part of Sony's success at the time.

I'd done a demo, with my shaky falsetto, and that was shite, so we got a girl singer in, and then Syco heard it, and it was all set for Leona. It was going to be her big return song after a break, and it all seemed great to me. Who could be bigger than Leona at the time? I wasn't thinking internationally at all.

Meanwhile, my manager Mark Gillespie had sent the demo to Rihanna's manager, and when Rihanna heard it she really liked it and wanted to do it. She saw something even when her own label didn't. Knew exactly what she was going to do with it. They couldn't hear a chorus, they didn't get the club side of it, they thought it had an odd structure, because of a little trick I'd learnt from deadmau5 that was a step up for the sound of my tunes. They thought it would bomb, which you just didn't want at that time with Rihanna.

She'd already had ten Billboard number 1s, so this was absolute royalty, the dream collaboration. Rihanna really campaigned for it. She had said to her manager, I totally want this song, you have to get me this song. When I heard, being the impatient artist, I was like, 'Yes, but when is she going to do it?', because I had got myself on this schedule where I wanted a song out every two and a half months, boom, boom, boom. I've recorded it with Leona, it will be a hit with her, I want to put it out now, no fucking about.

Mike and Mark couldn't contain their excitement, and Mark said, 'Well, when the Rihanna camp like something, these people move quick.' And they did. Rihanna completely transformed the song with her voice, but gave me all of the publishing, and a collab credit, which was amazing, and it was absolutely massive and helped take me into a different dimension.

Mike told me later that obviously someone had to tell Simon Cowell that there was a bit of a problem and we were going to give the song to Rihanna, and take it away from Leona. Mark lost the toss, and he nervously goes in to tell Cowell in the Sony offices, Mike hiding around the corner listening in waiting for the bomb to explode. After a few seconds, Mark comes racing out of Cowell's office, with a furious Cowell screaming at the top of his voice, 'I'll make sure you never work in this business again. Tell Calvin he's finished. And tell Pickering he can go to fucking hell.' Mike found the whole thing hilarious, all part of the strategy of how to get a hit record.

I don't think I ever found out all that Mike had done before we worked together. I'm excited for this book, but I hope he isn't too humble. I hope he speaks up a bit.

When he won some legends award at a ceremony in Ibiza which I'd gone to as his plus one, they showed a film about his career before the award was given. It was meant to show everything he'd done, but it barely touched upon M People. There was a lot of The Haçienda, but M People was almost glossed over. It was like somehow being in such a successful band throughout the nineties wasn't why he was getting the award, like it was some sort of embarrassment, like it wasn't cool. I was angrier about that than he was.

When I got up to give a little speech, I said, 'Yeah, nice film, but next time, can we have more about M People? They sold millions of albums, had numerous hit singles, won loads of awards, they put dance music into arenas and were a big part of what made dance the biggest selling genre in the world.'

What's wrong with that? If he doesn't speak up about that in his book, I'm going to ask for my money back.

Part I

Learning

1
A different world

On the afternoon of Wednesday 20 November 1963, I found myself brushing against history and in a desperate race against time. I was an eager, fresh-faced 9-year-old living in an ordinary part of north Manchester a fifteen-minute bus ride from the centre of the city. It was two days before the assassination of J. F. K. in Dallas, Texas, and three days before the startling first episode of *Doctor Who* was broadcast in black and white on the BBC's only channel. This addictive new time-travelling adventure had an electronic music theme tune that seemed to be in full colour, warping backwards from the future at a time when the past was having trouble letting go. Sometimes it was as though it would do anything to hold you back.

Manchester, more than most places, was struggling to leave behind its immense, dirty industrial history, its once grand civic buildings not yet fully cleansed of the soot and grime that was a hangover from its decades as a wealthy, pioneering world-famous industrial city. The original nineteenth-century modern city now seemed mired in the past. After the Second World War and the Blitz that scarred much of Manchester, as its once dynamic world-changing mills and factories shut down, buildings blackened by years of filthy smoke pollution were slowly cleaned up as part of a weary post-war rejuvenation.

Despite determined attempts to renew itself, the city seemed resigned to a new era of energy-sapping post-industrial decline, its once revolutionary vigour replaced by a pervading sense of lifelessness. It would take a miracle to bring life back to the city, and who knew where that life would come from. Who knew how much a part of that life would be music, from outside the city, and then because there was nothing else for it, and Manchester could not turn its back on being modern, within the city.

The Clean Air Act of 1956, giving local authorities the power to create smoke-control areas, had limited the burning of coal to help Britain's towns and cities emerge from its toxic gloom. Seven years later, even as the once ever-present thick smoke dwindled, steam trains still huffed and puffed under bridges and across viaducts, and masses of houses still burnt coal that spewed from thousands of chimneys. Manchester was prone to days when an unforgiving smog would suddenly appear out of nowhere. The streets, houses, pavements and lampposts melted away into a thick grey dampness hiding the light of day.

It was as if it was something the locals were perversely nostalgic for, a reminder of when Manchester was great. It spilled over from a time when the production of cotton and associated material led to smoke hanging over the landscape with menacing purpose. The blank mist blocked your nose with black tar and left an acrid smell that would take days to disappear. You couldn't see more than a few feet ahead and you would be stuffed by your mum into an itchy balaclava wiping the filth off your exposed face.

Cars moved slower than walking pace. Bus conductors would need to walk along in front of their buses making sure they didn't hit anything, or anyone, as they crawled along the road, inching forward towards the invisible next bus stop. If you wore any brightly coloured clothes, even just your socks, they would quickly turn black.

On that Wednesday morning in historic November 1963, I was looking forward to something so exciting and unknown I was jumping up and down with excitement. A couple of years earlier it had been a world before The Beatles, which meant a world that still seemed more statically, hopelessly Victorian and Edwardian, beaten back by war and rationing, than bravely new and exciting and full of possibility.

That was slowly changing, as The Beatles, from nearby Liverpool, the other end of the Manchester Ship Canal, played shows around the country and started to release fast, modern-sounding records and make headlines. They were coming to life, as though their magical presence alone could restore colour to the world and clean up the lingering smoke and forever dirt, and they were now on their way to my hometown. Fog was a ghostly thing from the past. I was on my way to see the fabulous tomorrow.

I wasn't so much excited by the idea of The Beatles, still too young to fully appreciate who and what they were, to understand the transformative nature of their imagination, but by the idea of spending a Wednesday afternoon doing something different from usual. Something that did not involve going to school, which was mostly boredom, fear and bullying – in the schoolyard and from the teachers, most of whom seemed creatures that came from the same place as the fog.

Something that didn't mean having to make up my own entertainment playing football with pals on the street, often until it was dark, when mum would drag me inside and roughly scrub the dirt off me. I'd mess about in the tiny back gardens of friends. The grubby park, a few hundred yards away, seemed an enchanted playground, and the nearby woods the dangerous, thrilling edge of the world, where you could run wild for a bit, forget about your parents and school for a while.

The Beatles, when they were still a hard-working live band, were on a winter tour playing two shows in the afternoon and evening at the Manchester ABC (also known as the Apollo), in Ardwick, in the weeks after their explosive-sounding, chart-topping second and third singles, 'She Loves You' and 'I Wanna Hold Your Hand', and their second album, *With The Beatles*. My mum was taking me to the early matinee show, along with our next door neighbour, Jean Sullivan, and her friend, all of us crammed into my dad's sky-blue Ford Anglia van, his pride and joy, bought new for £500, parked in front of our house like it was part of the family. He stopped smoking and saved the money he would have spent on Woodbines to afford it. When we got it – a new car was still such a novelty – all the kids, and some of the adults, along the street came running to have a look at it.

There was always music in our house. My mum had a real Irish spirit and loved all sorts of music, but was quite square. Sinatra had been her first musical crush, and she particularly loved the soundtrack to *South Pacific*, one of those bright, uplifting albums signifying nothing that all parents seemed to have in their house before the arrival of The Beatles and everything that followed. Her younger sister Brenda lived with us and was a little more adventurous, religiously playing the rhythm and blues of The Drifters and Sam Cooke, the latter credited with inventing the idea of soul music, his music of empowerment paving the way for Aretha Franklin, Al Green, Marvin Gaye and Curtis Mayfield. A whole new order of things.

Sam's songs of solace and stimulation that Brenda loved to bounce around to in our cramped, very northern front room, setting her pulse racing, seeped into me more than the stiff-sounding songs from *South Pacific*. His smooth clear voice cut through the bleakness of a grey Manchester afternoon more than Frank's. Sam seemed modern, young and fresh. Words like 'where there's light there's hope' and 'a change is gonna come' made you feel ready for a brand-new day. Old, staid Frank tugged you back to a time before The Beatles, who were bringing the contagious beat and joy of Sam's soul sound into England, exuberantly thinking of ways to make it their own. Across the ocean from Chicago, via Liverpool, into Manchester, hard, working cities that desperately needed entertaining and lifting out of the doldrums. It was all ours if we could only find our way through the fog.

The smog dropped as soon as we set off, mocking our naive enthusiasm. We would have to fight our way through Manchester towards Ardwick, just outside the centre. Along the way, the traffic came to a standstill in the murk. Everything seemed to stop. Jean, our neighbour, was getting so agitated at the thought of missing the show, she abruptly got out of the car, with no idea where we were, and walked off, shouting a bad-tempered goodbye, disappearing in seconds. Mum had to pin me down to make sure I didn't follow her.

Seeing how crestfallen I was, she was determined to get us there. Mum wasn't the type to give up, and after what seemed like an eternity, sheer will power forcing the plucky Ford Anglia through the day's darkness, she got us to the Apollo.

We had no idea whether Jean had made it, but we'd missed the matinee and were met with chaos – people milling aimlessly outside the theatre, beside themselves at having missed the show. There were dozens of policewomen and St John's Ambulance attendants on duty because of the hysterical crowds – who would have been hysterical even if they'd made it on time – and one of the policewomen calmly said to my mum, who was making it her business to see if we could get into the second show, that because people were coming from all over the northwest, some were not going to get there in the fog.

We hung around in the foggy chill, and a few minutes before the evening show began they started letting us use our tickets to go in. I doubt that that would happen now, but there was a wartime spirit to it all – everyone getting together to say, 'let's make this work', and mum, fighting all the way, got us on the balcony with a great view of the stage, and a seething mass of uncontrollable, mostly female, excitement in the stalls below us.

It was mayhem. Screaming girls all over the place, screaming as one – this big, frightening noise that kept coming. I'd never heard anything like it, and never would again. Right across the front row of the balcony where we were sitting were members of St John Ambulance, on alert for fainting girls. A line of nervous policewomen linked their arms to form a chain so that no one jumped off to get closer to the four jerky figures on stage – all smiles, suits and hair.

Police*men* were mostly in the stalls, engaging in what seemed like a pitch battle against a fearless enemy as they struggled to contain the collective urges of teenage girls tasting for the first time the freedom of pure, raw desire. Any expected feminine decorum was abandoned. There were police everywhere, out of their depth among girls out of their minds, their silly hats being knocked off, their impractical ill-fitting uniforms clutched at as the audience let rip. The audiences relentless screaming was a performance in itself.

There was no PA; the group simply played through basic amps. There were five or six acts on the bill, because this was closer to brisk, no-nonsense variety shows than the rock gigs to come. So The Beatles can't have played for very long once all those singers and groups had got out of the way – of little use to this audience who only wanted ecstatic Beatle energy.

They played ten songs, starting with 'I Saw Her Standing There' and ending with 'Twist and Shout', but I had no idea about that at the time, or how it all had a furious, punkish speed I wouldn't come across again for thirteen years. The group seemed in a hurry to get somewhere – which turned out to be more fame, more history – but, first of all, safety. A few dishevelled local bobbies holding back an explosion of lust and longing was all that separated the group from being eaten alive.

It was a strange little bill, not that I understood that at nine, where you could see that pop music hadn't quite taken off yet and rock music was still in the distance – Peter Jay and the Jaywalkers, The Vernons Girls, The Brook Brothers (who were complete clones of the Everly Brothers), The Kestrels, The Rhythm & Blues Quartet and then, finally, bursting out of themselves, doing something only they knew to life – The Beatles, in a different world from the others.

In their now classic collarless suits, they were pure Beatle, pure John, Paul, George and Ringo, something that existed to absolutely idolise, and it was all absolutely wild. I got caught up in it without having the vaguest idea what was happening. It was the excitement that was amazing because you couldn't hear them. It wasn't music. It was sensation.

You could just about hear them in between songs shouting something into their microphones, but as soon as another song started, with that fierce punk suddenness, the shrieking began again, louder than before, rising to a manic pitch that eventually chased the group from the stage.

After they'd gone there was a shocked silence, everyone waking up from a fever dream having got something out of their system that would take some explaining, and then the anticlimax of getting out of the theatre, into the dark outside. The fog had gone, it's job done, but as we made our way to our car which we'd left behind in a panic a few hours before, even in the dark you could feel there was now new light in the world.

The next morning, I flicked through the flimsy show programme my mum had bought me, but rather than keeping it, having no idea it would become a piece of valuable treasure, I cut it up. I stuck the photos all over my bedroom wall, even of the forgettable faceless acts that weren't The Beatles.

I'd seen the light. It didn't mean I was necessarily going to be a Beatles fan. I would find my own source of revelation, but now I knew I always wanted to see gigs. Whatever it was, I was in. I wanted to be part of it. Eventually, I wanted to try anything to do with a pop concert or a gig. I was no singer, so that was out. I couldn't play an instrument, so that seemed remote. What about behind the scenes? Even the life of a roadie moving things around a stage seemed exciting – getting things ready, making things go smoothly, shining lights on the lead singer, untangling guitar leads. It looked a great life. You could do whatever you wanted when you weren't working, and you'd go to so many different places. It seemed a fantastic way to see the world.

2
A northern soul

I kept badgering my mum to take me to more gigs, but she was only interested in taking me to see Tom Jones. She loved him. That was where she went after The Beatles, but I didn't. I started to like The Rolling Stones, not least because they seemed dangerous and my mum and dad really didn't like them. There was a six-year gap before I started to go to gigs, and by then The Beatles had broken up. Music for me was records, and the radio, and getting recommendations from friends and relatives. Jean Sullivan, who made it to The Beatles matinee show with a face covered in soot, became a wonderful source of new music for years.

I also had a cousin who lived on our street who I looked up to because he had a great haircut, and he was always listening to The Kinks. One of the group had been arrested for shoplifting, and that made them very attractive round our way. My cousin then started listening to Bob Dylan, so I did too, trying to keep up with all those words, his voice making sense at a gut level.

He went to see him play the notorious electric 'Judas' show at the Manchester Free Trade Hall when Dylan was heckled for going electric and selling out his pure folk integrity. The best music in the world was following The Beatles into Manchester, which was becoming a significant music town. The local universities and colleges quickly started to promote concerts by original-sounding new British bands, the kind that stretched the blues into a prog rock that rarely made the charts, but for the next few years I was too young to go on my own and lose myself in their crazy worlds.

Soul music was my next big thing after The Beatles, particularly Tamla Motown, the UK wing of Berry Gordy's Motown label which had been a major influence on The Beatles. It had that joyfulness I'd heard when my mum's sister played Sam Cooke, and the sound of those records driving into north Manchester by Martha Reeves and the Vandellas, Smokey Robinson & the Miracles, and The Supremes, was irresistible. The Beatles led a British invasion into America, giving them something new, but this was an American invasion, and a foreign newness that pierced the Manchester grey.

It took me in a certain direction, towards dance music, and dressing a certain way, wearing my hair short as others started to grow theirs. There started to be two tribes, both emerging out of mod – those of us who continued the spirit of mod and dressed smart, short-haired and organised in blazers and Fred Perry shirts, caring about our appearance, dancing to Motown, Stax and the blue beat ska music coming from Jamaica, some taking mod style to spartan extremes as skinheads. Then there were those who branched out from a colourful, androgynous mod look into a hairy, hippie, scruffier student look, drawn to bands like Led Zeppelin, Jethro Tull and Black Sabbath.

The struggling, working-class kids tended to prefer the sound of soul and hard-edged rhythm and blues, identifying something subversive and encouraging in the rhythms and lyrics. Most of the more affluent middle-class, university types fell for what they felt was more grown-up and serious, condescending a little to the music they thought was more teenybop because it seemed exclusively single-based and for dancing to. It was albums versus singles, rambling conceptual adventures versus radiant, compressed energy.

In Manchester, coming alive with music lovers fancying a memorable night out hearing the very latest music, the direct, uplifting Black music led to clubs like the Twisted Wheel, and what became known as Northern Soul. I was too young to go to those clubs, and they were extremely strict on the door. I tried so many times to get into the Twisted Wheel, because I knew what was going on inside was my kind of music, and thought I might make it because I was quite tall. I'd have given anything to have experienced the Twisted Wheel.

No chance, the security was too tight, and I'd only get to know about the Twisted Wheel when it became part of Manchester music history, for almost single handedly creating a musical genre with an energy and determination that sounded northern as much as American, a music which eventually became more known at venues like Wigan Casino. Opening in 1971, the Casino took the baton from the Twisted Wheel, along with the Torch in Tunstall near Stoke, which had a brief, golden reign.

I got into Wigan Casino when I was about 17, and I was in such a state of shock at the sweat, the pounding beat and the movement, and the realisation that there was an etiquette to it all – which part of the floor you danced on, the no smoking, no drinking, which meant you had to be fired up according to needs and taste when you got there. Sometimes there was no DJ chat between records; it was just one after the other, which was really heady. I kept that idea at the back of my mind, and it became very useful later on.

You had to know what you were doing and hold on tight as time flew by. When I went back the next time, a little more prepared, I failed to get past the imposing gatekeeper Mrs Woods at the top of the stairs, checking membership cards and guarding the precious inside. She took one look at me, shook her head, and simply said 'No'. Then she looked past me and said 'Next'.

The Casino's competitor, Blackpool Mecca, with its Highland Room, was forty-five minutes away along the M6. The two shared fans, who made the trip between them to keep up the momentum and the hours of dancing. Following Northern Soul was a nomadic enterprise. I made it inside the Mecca a few times, mostly just watching from the balcony, in awe at the dancers and one great record after another. It was more intimate than the Casino, with a different musical vibe, maybe a little more progressive and eclectic. Afterwards, you'd crash out on the beach, a chill wind bringing you back down to earth.

I'd seen, briefly, the Casino, I'd sampled the magic of the Highland Room. The Wheel remained a mystery to me, a mirage always just out of reach. Any future Manchester club worth its salt would have to live up to the impact and influence of the Twisted Wheel and a different breed of Manchester dancers and characters discovering themselves through a shared love for music. Imagining what the hell happened inside the Twisted Wheel got inside me, and I'd wonder if there could be anything like it again, so I could experience a feeling I never knew.

3
A new thing

I started going to live shows again in my mid-teens to watch the Motown Revues that played in Manchester at the Gaumont and the Apollo. I'd be seeing The Four Tops, The Temptations, The Chairman of the Board, The Elgins, Gladys Knight, and most incredibly of all, Stevie Wonder, a non-stop one-man show in himself. He played loads of instruments, including drums, and charged around the stage with an inspiring, purposeful energy you never came across in Manchester. You wouldn't have realised he was blind if you didn't already know. They had a line-up of bouncers at the front of the stage in case he got too close to the edge and fell over.

After Motown, when I was 17, another inspiring musical revelation for me was at the New Century Hall, with its sprung dance floor, where I went to see a Motown-like revue showcasing Mojo, a great soul and funk label formed in 1971 as a subsidiary of Polydor. It was superbly A&R'd by John Abbey, the founder of *Blues & Soul* magazine, and offered a mix of reissued American classics and up-to-date funk catering for the nascent northern scene – sheer quality by Doris Troy, Tami Lynn, Lee Dorsey, Millie Jackson, The Three Degrees, The J.B.'s, The Delfonics, The O'Jays, and lesser-known songs and hidden gems by Little Johnny Taylor, Art Gentry, The Invitations. It was all guaranteed to turn you into a collector, on the hunt for the obscure and brand new before you even knew what being a collector meant.

On the show I saw, it was Rufus Thomas, Fontella Bass, Jimmy Ruffin, and Al Green. Green, who wasn't part of Mojo, was on his first visit to Britain. It was only a few weeks before his first hit single, 'Tired of Being Alone', which was so astonishing you both took it for granted and realised it was a miracle – one of those deceptively simple, deeply emotional soul songs that were underestimated at the time precisely because they were a hit.

When he appeared in front of us he was so delicate and composed, in a tight, brown suede suit with a small Afro haircut. He looked like no one else you'd ever seen and sounded like he knew exactly what teenage yearning was.

He was first on, and later I saw him leaning against a wall watching Rufus Thomas, with a bag casually slung over his shoulder, and I just had to go up to him and say something. He had the sort of cool that leaves traces wherever he went, so that it actually entered Manchester, and I couldn't think of anything to say other than 'I love your music Al'. It was true, but sounded a little corny. He replied, 'Hey, thanks, man', but he wasn't really there. He was from another planet. For a moment he was among us in Manchester, something inexplicable passing through on the road to greatness. Al Green – that voice, that grace and subtle power, that knowledge of what moves us – was something else that changed me.

Next it was David Bowie, thanks to my old neighbour Jean Sullivan, and her latest boyfriend, Phil Saxe, who had been a disc jockey at the Twisted Wheel and was absolutely mad for music of any sort. Together, they loosened my obsession with Black music and opened my mind to other music that was happening, that was rock, but that was also as strange and wonderful as soul seemed to be. There was so much music coming into Manchester venues, and I got into the habit in the early 1970s of going to see anything, just in case there was that thrill of the unusual I'd get from soul and funk.

You'd come across things you didn't even know how to label, like The Sensational Alex Harvey Band, whose rock was warped theatre. Then there was the glam outburst as the country itself seemed to go dark – especially Roxy Music and Bowie, whose music wasn't strictly pop or rock but contained elements of both, along with the intensity and intrigue of Black music. The *Hunky Dory* album was

David Bowie at the Free Trade Hall, Manchester 1973

the first white music I really listened to since The Kinks and The Stones and my brief flirtation with Bob Dylan.

Bowie played in Manchester a lot when I was 17, 18, when he was going through his Ziggy stage and becoming a star, and he sang Jacques Brel's 'My Death', which was so dramatic and enthralling whatever kind of music it was, and I completely changed course for a couple of years. I'd sit in my bedroom playing 'Jean Genie' and 'John, I'm Only Dancing' again and again, trying to crack a secret code, catching glimpses of some kind of amazing future.

Soul music had talked to me about what I was feeling as a teenager, this need to keep moving and discovering and deal with a confusing reality, and now Bowie was doing that, coming from another world. Like my soul heroes he brought such glamour and spontaneity into my life. When he made *Young Americans*, you could see and hear the elegant, endlessly curious sixties mod that had fallen in love with Black music – the mysterious provocation of records on Stax and Chess – as a way of making sense of life.

Most rock still sounded stale and ordinary to me, and not really about anything in particular. I went to see Steve Marriott, an idol when he was in the Small Faces, for the way he looked and sounded – urgent, off the street – who by this time had grown his hair long and was playing weak, meandering blues that was going through the motions. You would be going to venues, seeing terrible groups just for the sake of catching a gig, because there was always something on, and you never knew what you might get to see. But in that gap between glam and punk, as soul and funk were becoming disco, there existed a certain rock music limbo.

Bowie's verve and vitality led me to his New York idols, the Velvet Underground, and then to Lou Reed when he went solo – as somehow part of Bowie's new troupe of exotic outsiders, which included Iggy Pop, Dana Gillespie and Mott the Hoople. Reed was someone else who kept returning to Manchester, playing shows that had a crazed edge and a feeling of danger. He'd collapse on stage and get into fights with his roadies, and you got the feeling after a show he'd head out into town looking for a punch up. That was much more preferable to the fifteen- minute guitar solos of Rory Gallagher and the comical-seeming pomp rock of Genesis.

The Velvet Underground also led me to John Cale and his elaborate solo adventures. In his Manchester shows he came across as cool as Al Green, and as deviant as Bowie. When I heard his third solo album, *Paris 1919*, the words were less direct and much more bizarre than my favourite soul records, but he sang them full of emotion, like he was deep in every moment like Cooke, Green and Mayfield. There was an anxiety and restlessness about the music that made sense to me, and the songs were as sublime and atmospheric as Smokey Robinson's and Marvin Gaye's, if darker and more dangerous.

In 1974, I drove down to London with Jean Sullivan and Phil Saxe in his battered old van to see John Cale play with Nico of the Velvet Underground, Brian Eno of Roxy Music – who led me to the German electronics of Can, Cluster and Neu! – and another delightfully deranged singer with a Bowie-like knack for twisting reality, Kevin Ayers. The four of them were known as ACNE, a temporary surreal supergroup, all of them easily bored, always on the hunt for music that kept their interest and took them somewhere new.

It was the same with us, SPS (Sullivan Pickering Saxe), and here we were, the three of us sleeping overnight in the van after the gig at The Rainbow in Finsbury Park, parked at the side of the road in

Chiswick, West London, for some reason, miles out of our way, going on longer journeys and taking stranger diversions to find music you could lose yourself in, which made you feel alive. It wasn't dance music, but in our minds on the long drive home, we danced all the way.

Back home, there wasn't much local music that seemed to take on the world and make it new as much as Bowie, Reed, Eno, Nico and Cale. Nothing showed how quick Manchester music fans were to discover or even invent a trend, react to rhythm, and spread the news.

The smart hits of the Hollies and 10cc, the woozy English soul of Sweet Sensation and the wired, chaotic humour of Alberto y Los Trios Paranoias didn't amount to a Manchester scene, a Manchester sound. As soon as punk happened – for and by kids angry with the state of things who'd missed the sixties – a new Manchester music happened – and the kind of starting up, of starting again, that I was always looking for to stop me drifting into a permanent Manchester fog.

There were a few warnings around 1974 and 1975 that something was happening – groups mixing noise and art, or noise and trauma, playing in clubs in New York like Max's Kansas City and CBGB, kicking rock in the gutter – in the UK, groups like Dr. Feelgood and Eddie and the Hot Rods sounded impatient with British life in the early seventies and figured fast, stripped-down music was one way to flush out apathy.

The Beatles as an idea at the Apollo in 1963, the aura and consistency of those sixties Motown singles, the inspirational voice of Al Green, the changing styles of Bowie and Cale all had a huge impact on me. But if I was to choose a record that made the most difference to me as a music fan, Mancunian and also to my life and work, it would be *Spiral Scratch* by Buzzcocks.

The group had formed to support the Sex Pistols at their first Manchester show at the Lesser Free Trade Hall in May 1976, which they also promoted, feeling the need to have the Pistols give Manchester's stranded teenagers a tough talking to. The performance – with pale, skinny singer Johnny Rotten, mutant bastard offspring of Bowie and

Iggy, crouching down and clutching his can of lager, utterly indifferent to any audience reaction, vulnerable but completely in control, and highly amused by the effect he was having – has become enshrined as one of the all-time greatest rock gigs in history, which isn't just a boast with Manchester bias.

Buzzcocks weren't quite ready for the first show, but were when the Pistols came back six weeks later for another go. They recorded, pressed, designed and distributed *Spiral Scratch* themselves on their own New Hormones label, thinking it might be their only action as a group before they self-destructed – four fast, furious, uneasy songs about life, and lifelessness, set in a place that was definitely Manchester, but could be anywhere else, anywhere where you felt like a fish out of water.

It was so important because it came from inside Manchester, I bought it in Manchester, and it sounded like Manchester, in your face, and biding its own time. It looked so different, without appearing to try. On the plain black and white cover of the record, a blank polaroid photograph showed the group wearing ordinary clothes and unreadable expressions, putting as much distance as they could between themselves and the ageing, bloated long hair showbusiness of rock.

The songs had an abrasive simplicity that really made it seem music about starting again – and one of the songs, 'Boredom', an anti-anthem about feeling displaced and distraught, had a bonkers two-note guitar solo as if to rewrite rock history by burning down the tedious long guitar solo. Another song matter-of-factly celebrated orgasms. As simple as it was, there were real songs that packed in so much information and imagination without it tipping over into too much sorry detail.

Because it was from Manchester, of Manchester, it made you think, being from Manchester, that you could do something yourself, not rely on the outside world to supply you with music and action. You could make Manchester better by taking it out into the world. Manchester could make a difference. You just had to find a way to get started. You needed a purpose. Most of all, you needed a sound.

There were other important epiphanies. About ten years after *Spiral Scratch*, I came across another one of those sounds that herald change when I was working as a DJ at The Haçienda nightclub in Whitworth Street, which was making its own kind of impact and moving Manchester deeper into music history. My love for music – and everything that came with it – which had begun after the fogged-in Beatles show, meant I was beginning to make a living from it, including playing records in the club. I was seeing something special form around me because of those records and how they sounded, and how immediate and transfixed the response was.

After a few years of trial and error, I'd worked out what kind of records came out of the times we were living through and were getting the best response when I played them in the club. The best response meant that I could sense a shift in the mood of the dancers all around me, when they all came together at the same time, but were very much in their own world, a precious inner sanctuary, discovering something in the music that lifted them out of themselves.

Getting to know what these records sounded like meant needing more of them. At the time they were hard to find – and if they managed to make it to Manchester, and the kind of record shops that knew about them and stocked them, they tended to be coming out of Chicago and Detroit. They were electronic, insistent, a little twisted, laced with the remnants of a song or the beginning of a song, but they weren't songs – more a deliberately paced, emphatic jamming together of sound and rhythm.

Sometimes, something new would be slipped to me inside my DJ box – my control room – on records with white labels that had nothing written on them, or even on cassettes. I liked this way of sharing a fantastic new find; it was the essence of what I did. There was a generation among the community of music lovers when they found something no one else knew. You wanted to get the credit for discovering it, but you also wanted others to know what you had discovered. You were passing on valuable information, important messages, that sometimes were even life-changing messages. Sometimes you found the information first; other times the messages were passed on to you so that you could pass them on in turn.

If it sounded good, I'd play it straight away to get instant feedback from a dancefloor crowd who were on top of the world and didn't want to lose that feeling. Part of your job was maintaining and building momentum and moving from record to record so that the rhythm stayed the same but somehow kept changing. One false move, one bad record choice, one messy shift in rhythm, and the whole house of cards would come tumbling down.

One of the kids from Moss Side gave me vinyl copy of a new track he was raving about. He was in one of the dance crews that would show off their mad dance moves in The Haçienda, and someone whose taste I trusted. 'Adonis', he said, 'it's by Adonis' – which didn't mean anything to me, not that it mattered. There was something in his eyes that made me check it out immediately. I knew instantly I had to play it. The crowd wanted new action, and I had got some ready to go. I asked him if I could play it. 'Of course', he said. 'It's why I gave it you.' He wanted to see the reaction. So did I!

There was hardly anything there, but it had epic qualities. It was just a drum machine, the TR-808 at full precise pelt, with all the fills and stutters made in heaven, and an utterly infectious bass sequencer. There was no big keyboard riff; it was just a steady, driving, pulsating beat trapping you in time and simultaneously liberating you from time.

There was a voice singing 'too far gone ain't no way back, release my soul, I've lost control'. Combined with the groove and the sound, which for all its simplicity was like nothing I'd ever heard before, these words seemed like vital life-explaining philosophy, as if it was shining a light on the meaning of everything.

It had a similar urgency to the 'let's start again' energy that *Spiral Scratch* had – dead easy to play at home without needing a ton of expensive equipment. Same with Adonis. You could create that combination of tension and drive in ten minutes, if you knew what you were doing, knew the sound you wanted, knew what you didn't want to do, and had the timing, skill and drive. It was pure raw instinct matched with absolute belief that something new was about to happen. It was hunger really, and some combination of feeling and knowledge that had to be cut into what it's best to call wax.

I played it and everyone in the club lost their minds, everyone thinking the same things at the same time – basically, this is it, this is something starting right now that will make everything different. Everyone who heard it the night I played it heard the sound of a new music taking shape in real time. It's what I lived for, and here it was, coming to me out of nowhere. All I had to do was follow it with something as magnetic.

I found out the track was released on Trax Records from Chicago, which turned out to be one of the two great original Chicago house labels alongside D.J. International Records. I went to my main supplier, Spin Inn records, the local experts, as soon as I could, and they told me they were just starting to get some of this stuff through.

They said the vinyl was so cheap and basic it would wobble across the deck. This wasn't conventional commercial product. The guys who ran the label in Chicago used to run the electricity for their little pressing plant from the industrial unit next door. The state of the vinyl probably helped the sound – it was in all sorts of ways on the edge, with this 'here today gone tomorrow' vibe even as it hit like lightning. It was as though Adonis sent out shockwaves, which managed to make it to Manchester before they disintegrated, and then the rest of the world, our little neighbourhood version of it, caught up with it, and found the right drug and, would you believe it, the right dance floor, which was The Haçienda, and the right DJ, which just happened to be me.

I'd come alive hearing something like 'No Way Back' by Adonis, come alive playing it for the first time to a Manchester club crowd acting together to make something happen. It was like being born again.

4
A team for life

I was born on 21 February 1954 at Beach Mount Maternity Hospital on Rochdale Road in Harpurhey, very near the spot where, five years later, the compere, controversial comedian and one-time big band singer Bernard Manning transformed an old billiards hall into his self-styled World Famous Embassy Club. Part social club, part entertainment venue, part escape for locals from demoralising everyday grind, it became one of the most important clubs on the northern variety circuit.

Manning claimed he'd booked The Quarrymen, before they were known as The Beatles, a few weeks before they sailed to Hamburg in 1960 to become a resident band in various local venues. He reportedly said he didn't like them – too loud and no good – and he wouldn't be booking them again. He would book the acts my mum and dad liked – Tom Jones before he was Tom Jones, Cilla Black when she was known as Swinging Cilla, Frankie Vaughan in top hat and tails – and Manning himself liked to croon the popular ballads of the day, as if their sweetness could balance his scathing wit. In Manchester clubland history, in spite of or because of his vulgarity and bigoted nastiness, he became a local hero, an extreme version of challenging, no-nonsense Mancunian wit.

A little over twenty years after Manning opened his Embassy Club, The Haçienda opened alongside the Rochdale Canal, over the road from the viaduct taking trains out from Oxford Road into Lancashire.

Within a few years, the energy channelled by the Manchester of *Spiral Scratch* into the city of Manchester helped change the culture and reputation of the city, and Factory Records and their lofty Haçienda concept was one set of results. The Factory founders, a company of ambitious misfits formed around the unfocused, crusading disposition of local television presenter Tony Wilson, had a hunch they knew exactly what was missing from Manchester.

Factory's community-spirited love for the city's awkward, iconoclastic difference initially led to a punk club opening in 1978 on a lost, edge-of-inner-city corner of Hulme, which had the look of an unholy, abandoned part of town. This evolved into The Haçienda in 1982, with its own more distinguished, city-centred premises, and if not yet its own sound, certainly its own look and style, portraying Manchester as post-modernist as much as post-industrial.

It was another eccentric club opened by those committed to serving and lifting the community, taking the varied local club scene in vastly different directions, and it showed how far things had moved and the times had changed in the twenty years since the Embassy opened.

I was working at The Haçienda in various roles from its opening, part of its fanciful planning committee, booking DJs and bands as hard-edged disco, post-punk, hip-hop and electropop randomly fused into the insistent intensity of house. I was there to see Bernard Manning play his preposterous, feisty part in the opening night in 1982, cheerfully unsettling and needling most of the audience, who still couldn't help but laugh.

His improbable appearance helped demonstrate how The Haçienda's owners knew all about the city's distinctive club roots, music and otherwise, paying homage to them while determined to give Manchester a world-class venue. Not that it would be easy. There would be a few years of false starts, indecision and terrible – and wonderfully impractical – ideas. Mostly, it needed someone to help work out what the unique sound of the club, and the new Manchester it wanted to represent, would be.

Bernard Manning lived for most of his life in Blackley with his mum. My mum and dad, Bill and Margaret Pickering, moved there

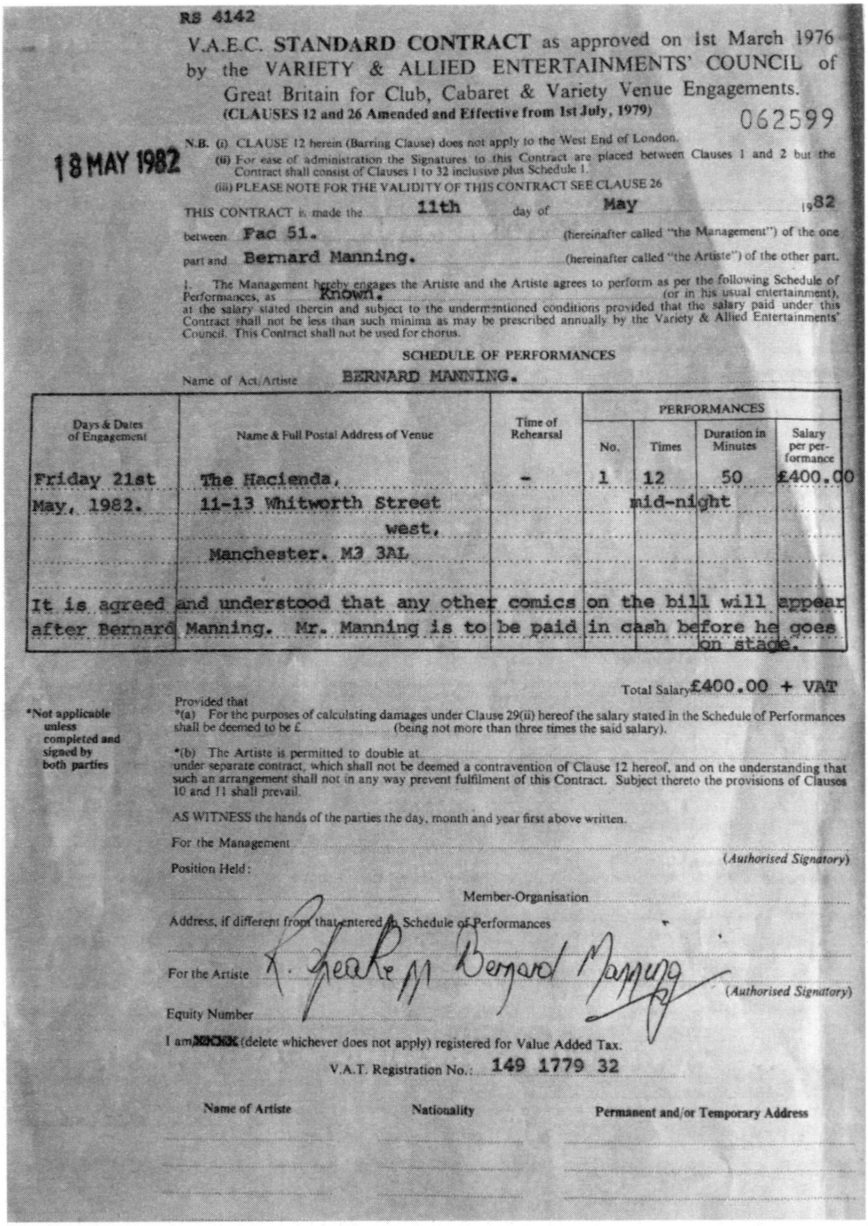

RS 4142

V.A.E.C. **STANDARD CONTRACT** as approved on 1st March 1976 by the VARIETY & ALLIED ENTERTAINMENTS' COUNCIL of Great Britain for Club, Cabaret & Variety Venue Engagements.
(CLAUSES 12 and 26 Amended and Effective from 1st July, 1979)

062599

18 MAY 1982

N.B. (i) CLAUSE 12 herein (Barring Clause) does not apply to the West End of London.
(ii) For ease of administration the Signatures to this Contract are placed between Clauses 1 and 2 but the Contract shall consist of Clauses 1 to 32 inclusive plus Schedule 1.
(iii) PLEASE NOTE FOR THE VALIDITY OF THIS CONTRACT SEE CLAUSE 26

THIS CONTRACT is made the 11th day of May 1982
between Fac 51. (hereinafter called "the Management") of the one
part and Bernard Manning. (hereinafter called "the Artiste") of the other part.

1. The Management hereby engages the Artiste and the Artiste agrees to perform as per the following Schedule of Performances, as Known. (or in his usual entertainment), at the salary stated therein and subject to the undermentioned conditions provided that the salary paid under this Contract shall not be less than such minima as may be prescribed annually by the Variety & Allied Entertainments' Council. This Contract shall not be used for chorus.

SCHEDULE OF PERFORMANCES

Name of Act/Artiste BERNARD MANNING.

Days & Dates of Engagement	Name & Full Postal Address of Venue	Time of Rehearsal	PERFORMANCES No.	Times	Duration in Minutes	Salary per performance
Friday 21st	The Hacienda,	-	1	12	50	£400.00
May, 1982.	11-13 Whitworth Street			mid-night		
	west,					
	Manchester. M3 3AL					

It is agreed and understood that any other comics on the bill will appear after Bernard Manning. Mr. Manning is to be paid in cash before he goes on stage.

Total Salary £400.00 + VAT

Provided that
*(a) For the purposes of calculating damages under Clause 29(ii) hereof the salary stated in the Schedule of Performances shall be deemed to be £ (being not more than three times the said salary).

*Not applicable unless completed and signed by both parties

*(b) The Artiste is permitted to double at under separate contract, which shall not be deemed a contravention of Clause 12 hereof, and on the understanding that such an arrangement shall not in any way prevent fulfilment of this Contract. Subject thereto the provisions of Clauses 10 and 11 shall prevail.

AS WITNESS the hands of the parties the day, month and year first above written.

For the Management (*Authorised Signatory*)
Position Held:
Member-Organisation
Address, if different from that entered in Schedule of Performances

For the Artiste R. Speake ... Bernard Manning (*Authorised Signatory*)
Equity Number
I am ~~XXXXX~~ (delete whichever does not apply) registered for Value Added Tax.
V.A.T. Registration No.: 149 1779 32

Name of Artiste	Nationality	Permanent and/or Temporary Address

Bernard Manning, Hacienda contract, 1982 (Factory Records)

from Broughton, Salford, when I was about five. You could see Manchester's taller buildings through the mist a few miles in the distance from the Rochdale Road, which ran through Blackley from the city centre towards Rochdale.

There were plenty of green spaces in and around Blackley, including Heaton Park, which could make it seem quite rural despite plenty of reminders of industrial blight and tightly packed working-class streets. There was a pig farm at the bottom of the hill near where we lived, and the farmer used to let the pigs roam around the street as if it was normal. You'd be walking along the pavements next to pigs.

We lived in a tiny, dingy flat with an outdoor toilet, reached by climbing some lethal-looking concrete stairs. I was always tripping on these stairs, once or twice avoiding a stray pig, so my knees were often freshly scraped or building a nice new crusty scab. There was a tin bath we filled with water in the kitchen, which was also our bathroom. My dad kept it all his life and used it to mix paint and stir concrete for his terrible do-it-yourself attempts. He had real difficulty getting rid of anything.

My dad wasn't Irish like my mum, and when they met he lived near Boggart Hole Clough, a large ancient woodland full of steep slopes bordering Blackley, Harpurhey and Moston, which was great to scamper around as a kid and got pretty creepy at night. Being Irish, when mum went round to meet him she had to wait at the end of the road, as the Irish were looked down on and mocked for their accent. This was despite the fact that the Irish had been coming over to Lancashire since the Industrial Revolution and the building of the railways and the mighty Manchester Ship Canal, which miraculously brought ocean liners into the centre of the city and turned Manchester and nearby Salford into an inland port.

The Irish came to find work and faced the typical complaints that they were taking jobs from locals. For all the time, energy and imagination they brought to Manchester, helping to build its modern miracles – however much they made it their home and put their mark on it – they would still be viewed as outsiders.

I inherited that feeling of not really belonging, of having to fight to survive and hold onto an identity – the result of a long history of famines, of being conquered, robbed, brutalised and demoralised. It made me a natural fit to fall for the more rebellious music and fashions that came along when I became a teenager. That eternal outsiderness also brought with it a community spirit, which the Irish fostered by sticking together in their new environment and taking care of each other.

I adored my mum's father, my Grandad Dan, originally from just outside Dublin, who came over after the First World War and worked as a navvy digging roads and then on the bins – typical jobs for the Irish, with their resilience and strength. He never said much, didn't like to make a show of himself, kept to himself, nursing his private grievances, and enjoyed simple pleasures. This made him down to earth but a little mysterious and seemingly incorruptible.

He was one of those old, solid blokes who seemed dead happy or perhaps dead depressed. You could never tell. Dead happy if he had a drink, his racing paper, his favourite armchair. Not so happy if he didn't. He liked to sit in front of a blazing fire checking the racing results, regularly wandering off to the local Catholic club for a soothing Guinness, and chain-smoking day in, day out, so his gnarled fingers were yellowy-brown.

Gambling was illegal at the time unless you were at a racecourse or had an account with a licensed bookmaker and placed bets by phone – mostly the well off, a glaring example of class inequality. However, there were always ways to bet to try and make a bit of extra money. Enterprising individuals worked from shops and houses, and there were street-corner bookies around the many pubs dotted around Blackley.

At the top of the village in Higher Blackley, on a street corner along Victoria Avenue, there was a huge pub called The Lion and Lamb, jutting out like the prow of a ship. A lot of pubs around there had 'Lion' in their name, apparently because an aristocratic local family had a lion in their coat of arms, and the pubs were named in their honour.

You'd place a bet down the side of the pub. There would be two blokes standing at each end of a cobbled ginnel running between two streets keeping watch for the police, and the betting would be done out of the boot of a car. My grandad would take me along sometimes and it was such a thrill watching him place a tanner each way on a horse, the sixpenny bit slipped to the bookie wrapped up in paper. Sometimes there was a shout that the cops were coming and everyone would scatter, although the cops seemed reluctant to grab anyone, going through the motions preferring to have a bet of their own rather than make an arrest.

The Betting and Gambling Act of 1960 legalised off-course betting, and by May 1961, licensed betting shops were conveniently placed on every high street. The illicit fun and games were over, and within months there were hundreds of betting shops – Hill, Coral, Ladbrokes and Mecca – all over the country.

At first my grandad missed the rough and tumble of illegal street betting – with all its adventure and strangely nicknamed characters, some of whom in my memory seemed one-legged and on crutches – and the regular punters had pseudonyms as well. He wasn't immediately at ease with the formality of the betting shops. A certain rough poetry went missing – but he very quickly adapted to the comfort and companionship, and to the idea that when you backed the right horse for once, you might actually get your money, which wasn't always how it worked on the streets.

It was still more about hope than expectation – but the betting shop soon became another smoke-filled home from home alongside the pubs. I now spent the time we were meant to be together waiting for him outside the shop, with its inside hidden from view, while he had a quick flutter. I was still hanging out on street corners.

Grandad Dan was also supremely influential because he insisted I become a Manchester City fan, which would have major consequences on my life. My dad was a City fan too, but we lived in a very Manchester United area, not least because several United players were born or lived in Blackley. The charismatic captain of the Manchester United squad, known as the Busby Babes at the time of the 1958 Munich air crash, Roger Byrne, was buried in Blackley Crematorium. They had become the first English team to play in the European Cup – against the wishes of the Football League – which added even more glamour.

My mum's brothers, my uncles Gerald and Denis, were City fans, and we were a family of City nuts in the middle of all the committed Reds. My grandad was an original hard-core City fan, devoted since the 1920s, bringing some defiant Irish toughness to the idea of being a football fan, which once or twice spilled over into what would later be called hooliganism. Sometimes that involved mugging a ticket tout to get a ticket for a match. For a fighter, football was something to take seriously. There was no segregation between opposition fans back then, and sometimes punch-ups would suddenly break out, just for the hell of it.

United had won the First Division championship – the Premier League of its day – three times in the fifties, in 1952, 1956 and 1958, under the tenacious management of Matt Busby. The Munich Air Disaster and the death of eight of its star players gave the team mythical, martyred status. My granddad had seen Busby in the 1930s when he played for City – when City were the main Manchester team – and he'd remained loyal even as Busby's United, with his faith in youth, overtook them and City started a slow decline. This was despite winning the FA Cup in 1956 – when goalkeeper Bert Trautmann, a former German paratrooper, broke his neck but carried on playing, an epic event soon overshadowed by the Munich crash.

I'm not sure if my dad would have been as bothered if I was tempted by United, but my grandad wouldn't have spoken to me ever again. We were dedicated Blues, though, me taking on my grandad's quiet pride at being different from everyone else. By 1963, I was starting to travel out of my immediate neighbourhood down to City's Maine Road ground in Moss Side and then to away matches in places around Lancashire and Yorkshire. I was beginning to see the world.

Sometimes I'd go with my dad, sometimes my grandad, often both. Before we got the Ford Anglia in City colours, dad would take me on the crossbar of his bike, which was a precarious seven-mile ride, and as we got closer to the ground we'd cycle past all these once-grand-looking houses from Manchester's heyday that were now beginning to decay into slums, and then rows and rows of tightly packed terraced houses with grey roofs that turned greasy in the incessant rain.

You'd start to see West Indians near the ground, and that was something you never saw in north Manchester. They were building – as best as they were allowed – new lives and new communities and bringing refreshing energy into the city, but at the time quite a novelty. When we got the van, we'd park a little away from the ground, trying to avoid the skinny, sly-looking Manc kids who'd ask for some money to mind your car, well versed in local hustling skills. You knew what was in store if you didn't want to pay them anything.

The first match that stands out for me, one of my earliest memories of going to City's battered but majestic Maine Road ground – the football equivalent of seeing The Beatles – was the Bert Trautmann testimonial in April 1964. It wasn't a competitive match but it was such an occasion it seemed like a Cup Final. It felt as if everyone wanted to get something out of their system and say farewell to this extraordinary player who had been through so much to end up playing for City. A German who proudly fought for his country against Britain, he decided to stay in Lancashire after internment in a prisoner of war camp and started to play professional English football, joining City only four years after the war.

Thousands protested when he started playing for City, shouting 'Nazi' outside the ground and threatening to stop watching City. City supporters soon forgot their fury, encouraged by a local rabbi – who had lost his parents in the Holocaust – writing to the local paper to propose that now the war was over, it was time to move on and forgive. Of course, Trautmann turned out to be a great goalkeeper, which helped, and likeable enough for City fans to warm to him, and then, after City's victory in the 1956 FA Cup and long frustrating months of recovery from his brutal neck injury, fall in love with him.

The dreaded Nazi became 'Our Bert', Mr Manchester City, a rare early symbol of renewed Anglo-German relations. He ended up playing for City for fifteen years and was now getting a farewell worthy of a hero.

It was a Wednesday night at 7.30 under the floodlights with the rain pouring down – still one of the great sights of my life – the bright green grass and the players in their luminous sky-blue shirts lit up in the dark by this intense light. A night match was particularly magical when you were only 10 years old, and there was something enigmatic about the blue that I was instinctively attracted to rather than the obvious unsubtle red of United.

There were officially 48,000 there, although some estimates suggested nearer 60,000 squeezed inside Maine Road at a time when City's average attendance was closer to 20,000. A combined City and United team played as a Manchester XI against an England side, which meant established United stars like Bobby Charlton made a rare appearance in a City shirt, bringing in some United fans, and the England side had Stanley Matthews and Tom Finney play for them, English legends with names that resonated then like Lennon and McCartney. Matthews was nearly 50, Finney over 40, and I swear seeing them play brought a tear to my grandad's eyes.

It might have been a friendly but the noise was immense and there were loads of goals, nine apparently, five to the Manchester team, but I wouldn't have been able to tell anyone the score at the time. It was a fantastic Manchester party, and there was a huge spotlight on Trautmann as he made his way onto the pitch through a guard of honour, and an invasion of fans after the game chanting Bert's name, taking ages to settle down so he could give a speech. At the end, grown men were swinging on the cross bars, breaking them in two. It definitely seemed like City were the right team to follow, even if United were the world-famous Manchester team, complete with star players including the magnetic George Best, and City were in the shadows, probably forever.

Somehow, listening to my grandad tell me stories of their heyday and the exceptional players who had played for them up to Trautmann, I liked that they were now in the shadows, and I liked that they were underdogs fighting for rights in a life that wasn't going to be easy or straightforward. It was like they were always having to start again and defy the odds – suffer trials and tribulations which sounded like real life from where I was living.

A few months after the Trautmann testimonial – this time at a game memorable for all the wrong reasons – it became obvious just how much City were in the shadows of the Reds. They played Swindon Town at home on 16 January 1965, and a barnstorming, apocalyptic rain hammered down for the whole match, which might have accounted for how empty the ground was.

It was the first season since the end of the 1940s that Bert Trautmann wasn't playing in goal, and they had been relegated to the Second Division, putting them even farther behind United. I was standing with my dad in the cheap scoreboard end, which had no roof, so we were absolutely soaked. Some fans were clambering over into the covered Kippax Stand, where the hard-core City fans usually stood and chanted, opposite the posh-seated Main Stand. The Kippax was filled with empty spaces.

With a few minutes to go before the match kicked off, we started to wonder where everyone was. We had never seen it so empty. It turned out it was the lowest match attendance in City's recent history – a handful over 8,000. Over time, as this low point grew in reputation, many times that would claim they were part of the brave faithful. I really was, and to make things even worse, we lost 2–1, both Swindon's goals scored by the best player on the pitch – a stylish, eye-catching winger called Mike Summerbee.

The match proved a turning point for City. It had to get better or it was only going to get worse. Within a few months, there were signs of change, and I was an early witness to it. I cycled down to the ground with a friend in the off-season during the school holidays, hanging out, looking for something to do, seeing if we could buy some old programmes in the souvenir shop, even spot a player or two. We once cycled all the way out to Prestwich when we were about 12, looking to clean some cars for some money, thinking as Prestwich was posh we'd get more money.

We knocked on one door of a large detached house with a shiny, expensive Jaguar parked in the long driveway. A well-dressed lady answered, and we nervously asked, 'Can we clean your car?' It looked clean enough on the outside, but we heard a voice behind her say, 'Aye, give them a go.' When she went off to get some water, we saw that it was Denis Law – the Scottish part of United's holy trinity of Best, Law and Charlton. Even a City fan couldn't help but be impressed by the sight of a revered footballer in the flesh.

When we cleaned the inside of the car, we saw that the ashtray was filled with cigarette butts and ash. We said, 'It can't be Denis Law, he's a First Division footballer, he wouldn't smoke. It must be his wife.' When we finished and shyly went to collect our shilling, it was Law himself who answered the door – golden-haired and larger than life with a lit cigarette hanging from his mouth. We couldn't believe it – that a footballer would smoke like a normal bloke.

At Maine Road, we managed to sneak our way into the ground, which looked completely empty. At 12 years old, getting carried away being a long way from home, you're always looking for a bit of mischief, to do something that you shouldn't, and we marvelled at seeing Maine Road completely empty, staring in amazement at a few dead pigeons. We sat in the Platt Lane end – usually something my dad and I couldn't afford to do – soaking it all in, feeling special and clever for getting into the ground.

Suddenly two ground staff popped up behind us, including the fearsome head groundsman Stan Gibson – a tough old stoker in the Navy during the war who would work for his beloved City for forty years after joining in 1959. He growled at us, 'What are you two doing?' and it looked like we might be in trouble. He took us around the pitch and down the tunnel, which was something of a treat, and we bumped into an old City player, Johnny Hart, who was then a member of the coaching staff.

He also pretended we were in trouble but then asked us if we came to any games. I told him I came regularly, and I muttered something about how I hoped things would get better when we got a new manager – the most recent City manager, George Poyser, had been sacked at Easter on the way to City finishing eleventh in the Second Division.

Hart said, 'Well, lads, your luck's in, we got a new manager today.' He said, 'We've got Joe Mercer.' I didn't know who he was, but Hart made it sound important, so I acted pleased. When I got home and told my dad, he wasn't so sure he'd be any good, that they might need someone younger – Mercer was 50 and had recently suffered from ill health. Mercer hired the 38-year-old Malcolm Allison to be his sidekick, and the Mercer–Allison era began. For a few years, the wise, shrewd Mercer and flamboyant, innovative Allison worked together brilliantly, and one of their first new signings in August 1965 was Swindon's Mike Summerbee, who had scored the goals in front of 8,000 downtrodden City fans at the beginning of the year.

Summerbee had a mod-type haircut and looked so cool in the classic late sixties blue and white kit with its pristine white collar, and also in the all-maroon second kit they wore in the first Mercer–Allison season with the striped socks. He would become my favourite player, part of City's own holy trinity of Colin Bell, Francis Lee and Mike Summerbee, as Mercer and Allison's stylish City won promotion back to the First Division in 1966, winning the league two years later, and the FA Cup the year after that.

Suddenly, supporting City lifted the spirits, and I spent my late City-following teenage years feeling pretty pleased with myself, a Kippax regular as the singing got lustier and the atmosphere livelier. I was so used to seeing them lose in the first few years I was a fan I couldn't believe they were winning most of their matches.

When they won the league in 1968, they had to win the last match of the season away at Newcastle, which they did, 4–3 – one of the great City matches. I was there with my dad in my duffel coat, travelling up on a coach which went from my dad's pub, and getting back home around midnight, in an absolute daze. When we won the FA Cup in 1969, I was so nervous before the game, I fainted. I don't think my dad had fed me on the long coach ride from the North, and people were running off to get me a sandwich. Years later I used that as a security question for the bank.

For a few years, during and a few years after the dream Mercer–Allison partnership broke up, City were trophy-winning rivals to United, building up enough memories, goals and great players like Rodney Marsh, Dennis Tueart and Trevor Francis to set us up for the leaner – and even leaner – years, and more time spent suffering torment as we trailed the United winning machine, possibly permanently.

City fans know all about patience, especially when things go from bad to worse, always hoping to be surprised one day. Supporting City, though, somehow always makes sense, regardless of how well they do.

5
A close call

Becoming a City fan meant making all sorts of connections with people who shared the faith which would lead to all sorts of consequences. I'd meet people along the way that I would know for decades, some of whom would become incredibly important in my life, outside of City and football.

I met Rob Gretton at a City game in 1974. I was 19 and he was a few months older. He became one of the great if totally idiosyncratic music managers and a significant part of the madcap unorthodoxy of Factory Records, but I first met him as a City fan with something about him that set him apart.

I'd seen him a couple of times on one of the crazy football specials that took football fans to away games. They were particularly big in the 1970s, not coincidentally alongside the rise of football hooliganism. A train packed with away fans pulling into the station of the home team became an obvious target for hard-nut home fans fancying a spot of carnage.

The firm running the special used older trains, usually without any heating, seats ripped with leaking dirty sponge, and because the carriages were crowded with football fans up for some argy-bargy, they would be filled with beer cans, little bottles of whisky, huge tins of cider, and the toilets would usually be out of service. Fans would be squashed everywhere, even in the luggage racks. It was all part of the service.

Rob stuck out because he always looked as cool as fuck, and he turned out to be as funny as fuck. I think he was so cool because he was so funny. He was a dead-smart Manc mod type with a great freshly clipped French crop haircut, a well-laundered, slightly bleached Levi jacket and jeans, polished brogues, and a brand-new City scarf immaculately tied around his neck.

He was in my carriage on the special taking City fans to the Nottingham Forest FA Cup match at the end of January 1974. We got off the train at the same time, and to get to the ground from the station you walked across the bridge over the River Trent near the Robin Hood pub. I was walking just behind Rob, who I had never met, and when we reached the bridge you could hear this awful guttural roar building up and the sounds of hundreds of boots stomping towards you coming at us from all angles. The Forest fans had set a trap for the visitors, and we'd walked right into it. There was naturally no sign of any police, who seemed quite happy to leave us to it.

Your first thought was fucking hell – here comes trouble. Suddenly, it was chaos, arms and elbows flying everywhere, and Rob grabbed my arm, and we shot off as fast as we could with this gang of mean-looking thugs in leather jackets and red scarves chasing us, looking for blood.

We ran into the pub, and they followed us all the way as we sprinted right through the pub, past the toilets at the back, into a backyard, avoiding a massive dog barking ferociously and wildly yanking its chain. We jumped on some metal kegs, climbed over a wall, across some back gardens, and we could feel them right behind us, shouting insults and starting to chuck bricks at us. We dived over a wall and cut through an industrial estate, desperately looking for somewhere to hide, and they were saying to each other, 'We're catching up, we'll get them.'

We sprinted past a few houses and spotted a garden surrounded by a wall with a tall hedge, and we dived under it. Rob and I still hadn't spoken, and he took the lead, whispering, 'Get on your stomach, get down, get down.' We held our breath, thinking we'd lost them. They were on the road the other side of the hedge, which was at a higher level than where we were, so you could see their lethal-looking steel-tipped boots. They were so close to us you could smell their boot polish.

We were looking at each other, and I was thinking, if they find us, we're done for. Their blood was up. After a couple of minutes, they gave up, and we heard them wander off, sounding a little aggrieved that they hadn't caught us and beaten us to a pulp.

We must have waited about five minutes, which seemed like an eternity, and then, still lying down under the hedge, he held out his hand and mock-formally grinned, 'Rob Gretton, Wythenshawe.' I replied, 'Mike Pickering, Stockport' – I didn't say Bramhall, the smarter part of town where I lived then, because that wasn't very cool. Even hiding under a hedge, having just got away without a damned clobbering by the skin of our teeth, Rob had maintained his cool. He revealed a unique, amused smile I was going to get very used to, full of sly charm, eyes sparkling with life-loving mockery. We were relieved to still be in one piece, and it was the beginning of a beautiful, ridiculous friendship.

It's easy to say in hindsight, but he did have a weird reliability and a real sense of empathy. He didn't have to grab me and help me get away. He could have let me be swallowed up by the mob, making sure he looked after himself. Later, in his usual dry way, he would say he'd always had his eye on me as being someone he'd like to know.

We started to go to matches together and were soon talking about the music we liked, and it was pretty much the same thing. We'd both passed the eleven-plus and found ourselves in a weird Catholic grammar school. Like me, he wanted to do things and he wasn't sure what yet, but we knew that it had to involve music. He was never going to leave Manchester, so he had to find or help make up a Manchester scene. He was a great mate to find in the middle of chaos, and we stuck together for years, one way or another – this first scrape preparing us for some of what was to come.

He was a happy-go-lucky tearaway growing up on the post-war satellite estate of Wythenshawe who, like me, had stumbled backwards into a Catholic grammar school and learnt enough to know he didn't want to go to university or become a solicitor or accountant like a lot of grammar school boys did. Good for them, but he fancied doing something else that didn't even have a name – something that might not even exist, although he turned out to make it up to suit his temperament. He would always say, as he got up to whatever he got up to in the music business, 'I'm doing this because the last thing I ever wanted was a proper job.' What he meant was never having a boss.

After we'd introduced ourselves for the first time, there was still the match to deal with, which turned out to be one of those calamities that over the years seemed unique to City.

It was a Cup match, and Forest were then in the Second Division, struggling as City had a decade earlier before they were rescued by Brian Clough and Peter Taylor just as we had been saved by Mercer and Allison. City played like they had recently been chased by a horde of skinheads and lost four nil. Duncan McKenzie got all four and we were nowhere to be seen. I can't remember much about the match, other than the pitch was a mud bath and the Forest fans kept flinging hard objects at the City fans. And the Forest fans really wanted to make it clear that our beloved Francis Lee was a fat so and so.

We went back home on the train, even though we might have been spotted again. There was talk about a lot of City fans ending up being thrown into the Trent – it could have been us – and having to be fished out by the police, and some of the city coaches had their windows smashed in.

Rob and I regularly met up on the football specials from Piccadilly Station, and went all over the country, often heading into mayhem for the sake of a football game. Sometimes we hitch-hiked, because those were the days when sticking a thumb out at the side of the road could take you a long way.

It was the time of the 1974 industrial action by the miners, which had recently turned into a full-blown strike that resulted in the three-day week. For a while, as part of a national energy conservation, clubs weren't allowed to use their floodlights, and you'd go to afternoon midweek matches, which was unusual – midweek was usually night-time. This was our first Sunday match because of the industrial disputes. And there were also bomb scares. You sometimes had to check if there was a suspicious package near you. There were a lot of hoaxes, so we just assumed we wouldn't find any bombs and didn't bother looking. God knows what we would have done if we had found a bomb.

That was the seventies for you. To be a football fan then was like entering a war zone. But you had to go. You were hooked. A few weeks later we lost the League Cup Final at Wembley. That was being a City fan for you: long-suffering and stuck with it, until it all changed, which for about thirty years, after the mid-seventies, rarely seemed like it would.

6
A blessed relief

If watching City could be a real pain, it could also be a pleasure, when now and then there was a special player, or an unexpected result, a surprise season. School was mostly just a nagging, annoying pain with few signs of relief. School as a Manchester Catholic lad meant that the pain could be both mental anguish and actual physical pain, as a cane, ruler or hand slapped your knuckles or legs or grabbed your ear. School taught me very little of later use as an adult, but it did teach me how to be an atheist. And very rarely ever do what you're told.

It left me with a lot of wounds to lick, which contributed to how faithfully I'd chase the sort of spirituality you'd encounter when you came across a great new song, or saw Mike Summerbee score a wonder goal.

My first school in Blackley didn't seem so brutal, but we spent more of our time learning how to walk than anything else. Learning how to walk as in practising for the annual Whit walks on Whit Friday in late spring or early summer, a procession where children held each other's hands, marched alongside banners containing religious texts, and expressed community spirit.

They were very big in Manchester in the fifties and sixties, and still going now if not as melodramatic. The walks were rooted in the Industrial Revolution, to try and distract the working class from their monotonous, menial working lives, to give them a sign of something that was positive that didn't involve drinking, betting or fighting in gangs.

It was meant to be as exciting as Christmas, but it had the opposite effect, at least for me and my friends. Our only reward after all the practising and the day itself was to get some buns and milk once it was all over, like it was still the nineteenth century.

My dad had no time for it. He'd be moaning to my mum, 'Why are they learning to walk all the time? Children can walk any time. Why do they have to learn at school?'

When I was about eight, we moved to Alkrington, in Middleton, a mile or two north of Blackley at the edge of Rochdale. Mum was a nurse, and dad had a steady office job, so they could afford a two-up two-down terraced house, nothing grand, but with a bath in a bathroom and a little more room. This meant moving to St Peter's Roman Catholic Primary School, where the nuns were at best surly and at their worst pure evil, at least to a kid. I swear one or two might have even been psychotic.

Going to church on a Sunday was also part of the deal, even if my mum and dad weren't particularly religious, which meant sitting on hard wooden pews for what seemed like hours, hoping those angels I was being told about were going to save me from all the eternal damnation coming my way.

During Holy Week, you were expected to go to Mass every day, which was brutal – the priest's sermons, the warnings about a God who was some crazy entity about to destroy you at any moment. I managed to avoid going for a couple of days when I was about ten, but I was found out. I was pulled out of the assembly, made to stand in front of everyone, and told to put out my hand so one of those terrifying nuns could whack it with a heavy metal spoon. It was definitely a torture instrument, and as it picked up speed towards my hand, I pulled it away at the last moment and ran like hell all the way home in a mad, teary panic. I just had to get away from this madness.

My mum was angry with me at first that I had run away from school, but when I told her why, she was furious with the school more than me. She rushed around to St Peter's dragging me with her and told the headmistress that she was the one who decided when her son went to church, not the school. And there's no belting him with a metal spoon.

I got away with that, although the dead-eyed nuns liked me even less afterwards, and I had nightmares about that medieval metal spoon. Very soon, my mum stopped us going to church on a Sunday, which suited me fine.

I wasn't in any way the brainiest of 11-year-olds, but miraculously I did pass the eleven-plus, which brutally separated kids into the promising and the more or less hopeless. This wasn't necessarily a good thing for me, as it sent me deeper into Catholic education. I went to Cardinal Langley school in Middleton, which took pupils from all over the north of Manchester and out towards Salford, Rochdale and Oldham. It was opened in 1959 by the De La Salle Brothers, a congregation of laymen Catholic educators keen to make their schools accessible to as many boys as possible. They were on a mission to transform the lives of young people, motivating them to, as they put it, create a better world filled with the love of Christ, and acquire a zest for learning.

I lost the zest very quickly. After a couple of days at big school I was totally out of my depth. I slipped down the ranks to the C stream in no time. I became one of those bored, restless kids who sat at the back of the classroom as far away as possible from the intimidating teachers, hoping I could hide my way through school, staying below the radar to avoid any potentially painful clashes with the Brothers and teachers – or tyrants and sadists – who controlled the hundreds of boys aged 11 to 18, mostly through fear. Here the metal spoon as instrument of torture was replaced with twelve smacks with a stiff leather slipper. If you were 'lucky' you might get the punishment delivered in instalments. You'd be slapped or smacked for the smallest misdemeanour – a bad mark in Latin, which didn't seem the end of the world to me, was treated as an act of rebellion and rewarded with a solid whack. This didn't exactly motivate you to learn Latin.

You were being trained to obey the law of God, which meant never questioning or challenging their approach to education. You were forced to look the same, think the same and believe the same things. That didn't suit me. I had this energy inside me that I wanted to let out, but not through lessons, rules or annual festivals. They seemed intent on training you to be priests – and if you didn't turn out that way, then you must be a Satanist.

The school made dark days even darker, and what made things worse – as with grammar schools generally at the time – was that they played rugby, not football. Rugby union, played in grammar schools, was middle class and associated with prestige and privilege, while football was considered working class and common. And since rugby had been invented at a grammar school, at Rugby in the early nineteenth century, the tradition had to be upheld. Unless you were built for hand-to-hand combat and had an aggressive streak, even sport was gruelling.

If Catholicism was fundamentally about seeking light and warmth – a religion based on lighting up dark times and endless wintry murk and cold – then rebel pupils like me could find alternative ways to discover the light.

We didn't go to the dark side, but we saw the light through music and our own individuality and creativity. Through our own language of dancing and culture. Most of us males who ended up working in and around Factory Records in the 1980s – and organising, or rather disorganising, The Haçienda – had all come through the Catholic system. Tony Wilson, with his own self-styled interpretation of a moral vision, stood loosely at the intellectual and pastoral head of operations, orbited by Rob Gretton, Martin Hannett, Peter Saville and me, each on our own missions – and certainly with our own minds. We had all emerged from Catholic grammar schools with this instinct drummed into us for ritual, discovery and, above all, some form of transcendence.

We found it around us through records and clubs, and through our own obsessions, passions and unity, our own intense emotions. We were a weird family, but weird in our own way, shaking off Catholic influence, though never entirely erasing its authority. We had a different calling, but we had been brought up to need a calling.

The strict, scrupulous Catholic schools tried to make you choose their way before you were ready to choose your own, but the fluid Factory cohort managed to escape the ruthless De La Salle grip. Something had gathered energy after Elvis and Little Richard, then

Dylan and The Beatles, Jimi Hendrix and Marvin Gaye – something that gave us clues as to how we could do it ourselves.

We piled up the world with different kinds of buildings, songs, images and compulsions that represented how we wanted to worship, and who and what we wanted to worship. We took something from being immersed in Catholicism from an early age – obviously doubt, anxiety and guilt, the usual clichés, but also a community spirit, a sense of social justice and various compulsions. We transformed Catholic doctrine into diverse ways of finding faith, truth and magic. We believed in something abstract. We developed a healthy suspicion of any form of authority.

My mum and dad's immediate mission as I became a teenager was to get on in the world – which, for many families living around Manchester, meant moving out of the more industrial, Lancastrian parts of the city and into the pleasant, historic, suburban village surroundings of Bramhall, south of Manchester, near Stockport. It was only twenty minutes by train into Manchester city centre, close enough to Maine Road to still feel connected, but it was a completely different world from north Manchester. It was like the difference between a black-and-white kitchen-sink film and a gentle coming-of-age film in full colour.

The good news was that I could say goodbye to the oppressive Cardinal Langley school and move to the co-educational Bramhall County Grammar School – a brand-new school that, in 1967, was part of an experiment to turn it from a grammar school into a comprehensive. Compared with the gothic aura of the Catholic school, it immediately felt more open, and the culture shock was heightened by the presence of girls. I had gone from hell to heaven, and it didn't take me long to go absolutely bananas with the freedom of it all. I still went to school regularly, more or less, but it was effectively the end of my schooling.

I couldn't concentrate at Cardinal Langley because of all the dogma, discrimination and suffering, and I couldn't concentrate at Bramhall Grammar because of the girls and what seemed to me a wonderful lack of structure. Now that I was liberated from the menacing metal spoons, I just wanted to mess around all the time.

The bad news was that Bramhall had its own quiet torments – compared with the rough edges of north Manchester, it might as well have been a neat and tidy village tucked away in the countryside, and I missed the liveliness of Middleton. Bramhall was mostly still and quiet, almost quaint, and there my appearance, which at sixteen had settled into the neat and tidy suedehead end of skinhead, was pretty unique. I always thought of suedehead as one of the more peaceful youth movements – skinhead without the menace, dedicated to music and dance.

I essentially had an austere mod look – the skinhead crop up top a little longer, maybe later getting a touch Rod Stewart feathery, Doc Marten boots or shiny brogues, a Crombie coat with a folded hanky in the breast pocket, a checked Ben Sherman or Brutus button-down, Fred Perry tops, jeans with precision turn-ups. It made me stand out in Bramhall, where the youth cults of the sixties were still to appear in any numbers. The point was not to look like a thug, but to dress to impress. In Bramhall, though, I seemed like an out-of-place skinhead. As it was important at that age to feel you were ahead of the game and in with the in crowd, I took the kudos.

Records and clothes needed money, so I started earning a bit of cash doing a paper round at fourteen, plus any odd jobs I could nab cycling around town, and as soon as I could, at sixteen, I left school. Oh, the blessed relief.

I was out of there, born again, hungry for work – not because I necessarily wanted to work, or liked the work I was getting, but so I could get hold of the records I wanted and the clothes that represented the records I wanted.

Hunting records took time and effort because most of what I was interested in never made the charts. I'd find out about which records to hear and buy – when I could afford them – by listening to the hour-long blues and soul programme on Radio 1 after the weekly chart show on a Sunday, reading *Blues & Soul*, and getting updates on what was happening inside the elusive Twisted Wheel from Phil Saxe.

I read a two-part piece in *Blues & Soul* in 1970 called the 'Up-North Soul Groove' by Dave Godin, the journalist credited with coming up with the name Northern Soul. He worked in a record shop in

London, and when football supporters from Manchester came in before a London match and asked for fast-paced Motown-type records – known then as rare soul – he wrote on the box eventually holding a collection of those singles 'Northern Soul'. The term began to be more widely used around 1973.

His piece made London out to be jaded and spoiled by its dying Swinging Sixties reputation, with its remaining soul scenes lagging behind what was happening in Manchester at the Twisted Wheel, and at the Blackpool Mecca. Trends were being set in the North, where, he said, soul music was booming.

Godin said that in Manchester, the kids were less concerned with creating an effect than with having a great time, and he was dead right. He was very much of his era, but back then it was an attitude I could identify with, especially when he said Manchester music fans 'equated soul music with good times, fabulous weekends, booze and irresistible chicks (who also incidentally dig these sounds)'. In London, he saw the end of something. Up North, there was optimism and hipness, and the best soul dance music was breaking out of the regions, reaching London only after making it big in Manchester and Blackpool.

It was exhilarating to read a piece that noticed how the North, especially Manchester, was at the centre of something special. The article was pure fanboy enthusiasm, but it was also full of inside knowledge about the songs and performers, old and new – cool and groovy, as Godin said – that The Wheel was the first to play, working hard to keep Manchester moving in troubled times.

The defiant energy and messages of desire and desperation, rooted in hardship, seemed to resonate with northerners – instant, unfussy blasts of desperately needed positivity. There was also a curt, subversive joyousness and down-to-earth realism in many of the songs that maybe London wasn't getting. The songs always got straight to the point. And the Manchester dancers had a lot of steam to blow off after a hard week's work – or a hard week looking for work or ducking and diving on little money.

In Part One, Godin's playlist of records – his 'discotheque specials' – included The Fascinations' 'Girls Are Out To Get You', a handful of tracks by some of the more obscure Motown artists: Earl Van Dyke, The Velvelettes and Barbara Randolph; Bobby Sheen's 'Dr. Love'; Dean Parrish's urgent, growling 'Determination'; Roscoe Robinson's 'That's Enough' from 1966; and Chubby Checker of 'The Twist' with 'At The Discotheque'. He didn't have room to mention all his favourites, so there was an impatient wait for Part Two: The Poets' 'She Blew A Good Thing', The Incredibles' 'There's Nothing Else To Say', The Ad Libs' 'Boy From New York City', The Flamingos' 'Boogaloo Party', Billy Butler's 'The Right Track', and Bettye Swan's 'Make Me Yours', which struck home for those of us looking for a way out of our surroundings – 'I know what I want and I know what I need.' There were also records which, when first released, didn't sell many copies, but when reissued became hits – like Jackie Wilson's '(Your Love Keeps Lifting Me) Higher and Higher'.

Records like these dropped into rainy, broken-down Manchester, into mundane Bramhall, with surreal force as if their sole purpose was to kickstart your life and light the way forward. Knowing they existed added a certain shine to your life and a swagger to how you walked down the street. They were calling you.

'Keep the faith', wrote Godin at the end of what seemed like a sermon – hallelujah to that.

I'd have a brilliant list of must-haves ready for Christmas and birthdays – not that many of the *Blues & Soul* list were easy to find; their rarity, and high cost, was part of the appeal. Sourcing rarities was an art form that would take years to learn.

I'd go into the local record shop in Bramhall – because even the quietest parts of town had a record shop – and order records I was after. They never had them in stock, but the ritual of waiting for some rare treasure and it finally arriving added to the experience of collecting records.

There were few other attractions in Bramhall outside the record shop – the newsagent could be a highlight of the week when I picked up the latest issue of *Blues & Soul*, and there was a large Meccano model of a Ferris wheel slowly spinning in the window of the toy-shop. One unexpectedly good thing at the time was the youth clubs in and around Bramhall – there was one on Jacksons Lane just up the road from our house, Cheadle Hulme's Parish a bus ride away, and one in Hazel Grove a couple of miles distant.

There was a definite youth club soul scene in the suburbs of Manchester around 1970, playing the sort of records that extended my soul education even further. These were usually put on mid-week in cold, dusty church halls, with orange squash and biscuits and absolutely no alcohol – but perfect for those who couldn't get into The Wheel and the all-nighters. The youth clubs were like a gateway drug, a safe passage into the more grown-up clubs and the Manchester club scenes to come. There was also the Bamboo in Hazel Grove, which would let you in on a Thursday night even if you were underage, turning a blind eye. It was down a back alley off the A6 – the London Road – at the end of the 92 bus route that ran the seven or eight miles into central Manchester.

It wasn't a straight soul club, it wasn't our crowd and you'd have to wait for records you liked, but it played a lot of Motown, which never let you down. The youth clubs, though, were well organised and safe, and even though they were thought of as chaste places where you went to play table tennis and board games, they turned out to be where you could hear great music before you were able to get into the real clubs.

You'd be hearing tracks that were being played in the Twisted Wheel, played by guys a little older than you who could get into the club and wanted to be DJs. They used the youth clubs for practice, and in these unassuming community halls played non-stop an amazing selection of music: 'Be Young Be Foolish Be Happy', 'Devil With A Blue Dress', 'Double Cookin'', Sam and Dave, Felice Taylor, Spencer Davis, endless Motown and the occasional blue beat and reggae on the Trojan label.

Youth clubs were set up so that local kids with nothing to do could meet up and find something to do, but somehow this micro-scene developed where you could discover the beauty of dancing to get the hell out of the dullness of where you found yourself. We all danced in lines, boys opposite girls looking at each other, trying our very best to do it with style, letting the rest of the disappointing world disappear. You felt that you were on the way, one step at a time, to love and, the songs made it clear, sex.

I met my first real girlfriend at the Jacksons Lane Youth Club Friday night dance, Irene Johnson, the daughter of the landlord at The Grapes in Hazel Grove. She wore a brilliant, shiny two-tone tonic jacket, which singled her out, and was a great dancer, which sealed the deal – as did her buying me, as a present, the 7-inch single of the Chairman of the Board's 'Give Me Just a Little More Time'. The beauty of those soul songs at the time, many of them masterpieces written by Dozier, Holland and Dozier – this one under a pseudonym, some of their others including 'Band of Gold', 'Baby Love', 'How Sweet It Is To Be Loved by You', 'Can I Get A Witness', 'Stop! In The Name of Love' and 'Reach Out I'll Be There' – was that they seemed written directly about the moment you fancied someone, chased them, lost them or stayed with them. 'Give Me Just A Little More Time' was an incredible song about young love, and hope for the future, and reflected the fever of first love. Those student types that dismissed these songs as teenybop schmaltz really didn't know what they were talking about.

Youth clubs helped induct a lucky few into a fantastic cult, and some of us started to think of music as something more than just a great night out and then back to normal, accepting the world as it is. It opened the mind and opened doors; you started to think about the mechanics of the music, where it came from, and who made it. Music made you hungry for more music – the sort that was your own secret.

7
A matter of life and death

I also fancied a scooter, to finish off my look and take me to youth clubs further out, even to the increasingly seductive attractions in Manchester city centre, where the record shops stocked the rarest of rare soul. It was for money alone that, as soon as I left school with a couple of barely passed O levels, I took a messy, smelly job at the Northenden branch of Mac Fisheries, a chain of fishmongers that sold fresh fish – soon to be in decline faced with seemingly more modern competition from frozen fish, especially fish fingers. I'd take early morning delivery of boxes of freshly caught wet fish, hundreds of dead eyes staring up at me, and have to gut them all and pack them in ice.

A few weeks of that gruelling routine, and I yielded to my dad's constant nagging that what I needed was to learn a trade. Faced with his insistence, and his unshakeable belief that somehow Manchester and its surroundings were still at the centre of the Industrial Revolution, I went to work at Mirrlees Blackstone on Bramhall Moor Lane in Hazel Grove, at the southern reaches of Stockport towards the Peak District. It was about three miles from our house, a massive engineering company with an international reputation, founded at the end of the nineteenth century.

These were the days when Britain still made world-class engines. Blackstone made diesel engines for ships and power stations which sold in numerous countries. There were thousands of employees; it was the size of a whole village. But, as with Cardinal Langley, it was obvious within a day or two that I didn't fit in. The whole place was a mystery to me.

I hung on the best I could because of my dad. There was an apprentice school within the vast plant, and you had to learn the ropes for a year or two attached to an experienced engineer. My mentor was an ancient, grizzled bloke from Poynton, down the road from Hazel Grove, who seemed permanently attached to his pipe. He was called Jack, but as far as I could see, a lot of the older guys working there were also called Jack, like they'd just become a faceless tribe of old Jacks. There were a couple of Spiders as well.

My Jack was about a year or two from retirement and looked like he'd been around since the firm opened. He was so pale it was as if he had been stuck inside for decades. We'd go days barely speaking, except when he needed to tell me something – how to do this, how not to do that. I spent a lot of time filing bits of metal, remembering the names of hundreds of tools and staring blankly at the pistons he handed to me.

One day, maybe just back from the nearby Dog and Duck, Jack suddenly looked at me a little more closely and angrily asked, 'What the fuck are you doing here?' I went, 'What do you mean?' He banged his pipe on his chair, sighed, and said, 'Look, I'm 64, you're 16, you work out the maths about how long you're going to have to stand here in this shithole wondering where your life's gone. I've been stood here in the same spot wearing the same greasy overalls for over forty years. If you have a soul now, you won't have one at the end.' I did the maths the other way and worked out he'd been there since the late 1920s.

It wasn't the greatest of pep talks, but on the other hand it taught me more about life than any teacher had. In his own way, he was doing me a favour, saving me from a life doing something that not only I didn't love or even quite like, but something I didn't understand. I would be a cog in a machine making cogs for a machine. No future, as a Johnny would sing in a couple of years' time, as if he had known a few Jacks in his life.

I stayed longer than I should have after Jack had mapped out my dead-end future and carried on pretending to teach me about electric pumps, cylinder heads and arc welders, when the main union at the company called everybody out on strike. We were protesting against the Industrial Relations Act, which set out to severely restrict the rights of workers and limit the strength of the working class.

It was conceived by the Conservative Party and Prime Minister Edward Heath in 1971, desperate to put a stop to the rank and file worker militancy that led to wildcat strikes and other spontaneous disruptions. Workers' wages had risen during the 1960s and there were few strikes, but this had led to inflation, and for their own reasons the Conservatives wanted to suppress pay rises and control the unions. It sparked a strong collective workers' response and a large 'Kill the Bill' demonstration in London, where 170,000 people marched from Hyde Park to Trafalgar Square.

The Labour Party opposed the Act, but it passed into law in March 1971. Unions fought back, leading to strikes over the next few months by dockers – five of whom were imprisoned – print workers, who shut down newspapers, transport workers and many others, including those of us at Mirrlees Blackstone. The Trades Union Congress threatened a general strike in July 1972, the first since 1926, and faced with a nation grinding to a halt, Heath's government were forced to back down.

The Act had passed, but the unions and their workers resisted the Tories' anti-worker policies. Within a few months the miners went on strike, using challenging new tactics that stopped work in the mines, leading to the shutting down of energy operations to conserve electricity and the introduction of the three-day week. TV broadcasts were cut off at 10.30 pm, and people used candles and boiled water to wash. It only lasted a couple of months, but it felt like living in the dark ages, seeming much longer. It was another reason why great pop songs bursting into life for a few weeks, reaching us via *Top of the Pops*, helped us feel the world wasn't always so dismal.

Heath's government called a snap election, forced to appeal to the electorate over who actually ran the country – the government or the unions. This led, in 1974, to a Labour government with Harold Wilson as Prime Minister, who repealed the Act.

Heath had underestimated the voters support for the unions, but by the end of the 1970s, Labour, with Jim Callaghan replacing an ailing Wilson as Prime Minister, suffered themselves from powerful unions, which would break them apart.

Strikes by binmen, nurses and train drivers led to the Winter of Discontent. In 1979, the Conservatives used the killer phrase 'Britain Isn't Working' to help put them back in power. Margaret Thatcher emerged as Prime Minister, ready to take control of the 1980s.

The strikes and demos and a general campaigning spirit of revolt at a time when workers were more politically organised – before Thatcher's legislative anti-strike revenge on the miners, and progressive culture, in the 1980s – got me excited, especially when we occupied the Mirrlees Blackstone factory.

A lot of the employees slept in the factory as part of our uprising, which was a horrible place at the best of times and became quite sinister in the dead of night, with rats running around everywhere. It was, though, more fun than working or pretending to work. There was some outrage because the union didn't look after the apprentices; they only looked after the qualified men. For some reason, us apprentices didn't count – we were like cannon fodder.

Once the occupation was over and the dispute settled down, things returned to normal, and I decided it was time to leave. The excitement was over, and I had to tell my dad that steady work was not for me. I didn't want to end up as a Jack, slowly giving away my life and wasting away.

I wasn't necessarily work shy. I was always looking for work, at a time when it was hard to find. The money as an apprentice hadn't been particularly good, so I found an evening job in a local Italian restaurant, washing dishes, folding napkins and running errands, mostly so I could buy records. If scrubbing filthy pots and pans for hours on end meant more records, I'd have done it for days.

The young Italian waiters in the restaurant were sharply dressed and drove cool-looking Alfa Romeos – you could see the Italian influence on UK mods – and after work they would often go into central Manchester to the clubs, where they started inviting me to go with them. Once, so that I could join them, I needed a sick note from Mirrlees Blackstone, and thinking I was being clever, I dropped a heavy iron bar on my foot. I stupidly thought I would just bruise it. A few years later, my big toe was still playing up, and I needed an operation to fix what had become a form of degenerative arthritis. I told the doctor I'd injured it playing football, not wanting him to know how thick I'd been.

At the time, it seemed logical and gave me a few hours to get ready to go into town. My Italian workmates' favourite Manchester club was Placemate 7, on Whitworth Street, where the Twisted Wheel had been. The times were always changing, and its day was over, leaving behind some poignant wagon wheel reminders on the walls.

Placemate had seven rooms, each with their own scene – soul, jazz-funk, chart pop, rock and roll, oldies, Bowie/Roxy, all very sophisticated. Sometimes we'd go to Fagins, Time and Space or Rotters, but the conceptual Placemate was the best one, where you could find your personal room or randomly switch from room to room.

It got to be risky business going to city centre clubs in the early seventies, or venturing into the suburbs where you didn't belong. You'd get sniffed out if you strayed beyond your postcode or turned up to a show wearing the wrong uniform. It could be very tribal if your face didn't fit. Walking through Piccadilly Gardens at night, there was a good chance someone would pick a fight if they took against you for how you dressed or cut your hair.

It would be like the Wild West, and even on a late-night bus ride you would be taking a risk of getting into some altercation. Throwing out time, when the pubs shut around eleven, was particularly turbulent – guys just spilling out onto the pavements giving each other a battering for the sake of it. There was definitely tension in the air.

Fights could happen without any notice. After the time we spotted Al Green in the audience at the Mojo revue in New Century Hall, my school friend Nick Chambers and I met a couple of girls there and had a dance with them. We arranged to meet them at the same place in a week.

We turned up, in our best soul boy finery, and found it was Mungo Jerry playing, who to us were a novelty pop group who'd had a bouncy big hit with a holiday song, 'In The Summertime'. They offended our hard-earned sense of decency. We felt we had the best musical taste, and that didn't include Mungo Jerry.

This was a time when music was a matter of life and death. Some might have called us snobs. We just loved music, it was such an important part of our lives, and we didn't have time for anything that wasn't up to our rigorous standards.

To cap it all, the girls didn't even turn up, and on the way out we got beaten up by a bunch of lads who didn't like the way we looked or where we came from. They wanted to know, and we said Wythenshawe – thinking that was street enough to pass their test, rather than admitting we were from soft Bramhall. It still wasn't the right answer, and we got walloped and robbed, left with black eyes and nasty bruises. I've still got the scars as a grim souvenir.

The things I loved the most – football and soul music – involved a level of danger that didn't suit my peace-loving temperament. I hated fighting and didn't understand violence, but it was part of the local environment.

By 1974, old enough to get into clubs without worrying about being underage, I had gravitated to the Pips Club – a basement under Fennel Street, behind the cathedral, as the posters said – a multipurpose nightclub refracting Mancunian contrariness, a kind of rehearsal for punk, post-punk and new wave, and later for The Haçienda a decade on. At the same time, it was a prototype for the Bowie-inspired New Romantics of London's Blitz Club, and for the more elusive goths with their still more secretive spaces.

There was a steamy warren of rooms blending subcultures a little more fashionably and eclectically than the Placemate 7. One was for the tribe I was closest to – the guileful, working-class Perry Boy football lads with their Motown and jazz-funk – known as the Commercial Room. But having swerved a little towards Bowie, I favoured the Roxy Room, a black-plaster cave with stalactites hanging from the ceiling that probably looked tacky in daylight but at night was electric. It was exotically, futuristically glam – more Bowie, Roxy, *Transformer* Lou Reed and *Raw Power* Iggy than Slade or Sweet.

The Perry Boys, with their fondness for a bit of the old ultraviolence, could make the Commercial Room troublesome at times, but no one went into the Roxy Room to cause trouble. They went to show off, and to be among those who weren't bothered that boys wore make-up, and where girls could wear what they liked – however revealing – without being leered at.

It used strobe lights, like Bowie did when he fake-fellated Mick Ronson on the Ziggy tour. The pulsing flashes made everyone appear to dance in slow motion, lending the room a distinctly 1970s sense of modernity – a world away from the sweaty, earnest Northern Soul clubs.

You were part of a stage show, everyone dressed theatrically, creating a space inside Manchester that somehow stood outside it – a place where, even before punk, the idea began to take hold that Manchester could make music of its own, music that belonged in that room rather than coming from elsewhere.

Some Roxy Room regulars would go on to form groups like Joy Division, Simply Red and The Smiths – on the other side of punk, when the penny dropped that you could do it yourself and live inside your own creation. The room had really been waiting for music to arrive – music then unknown, partly because the machines that would help make it didn't yet exist, or were only just being used by experimental German bands, with Kraftwerk still finding their groove. There was only so much Bowie and Roxy to go around, though Sparks and Cockney Rebel helped, and sometimes that meant records by pop groups like Sailor, if only because they dressed up in costumes. Even Leo Sayer might get a look-in with his clown suit.

For the Roxy Room I needed a fresh look – something that would blend in and stand out. There were plenty of Bowie clones, and now and then someone so flawlessly Bowie you'd swear it was him, until they opened their mouth and spoke like their day job was as a bus conductor from Urmston. Bowie seemed an impossible dream, so I copped out and went full on Bryan Ferry, 'These Foolish Things', with the white tuxedo, dickie bow and black patent-leather shoes – we all used to hit the charity shops, and a lot of it was home-made. Other times it was 'Love is the Drug' GI Joe Ferry, with the eye patch and pressed army uniform.

At Pips you could live a fantasy, belong to a community of like-minded, music-loving souls – but real life was political turmoil:

strikes, regular factory closures, rising unemployment, especially among the young, and the haphazard transformation of inner Manchester into ugly housing projects with built-in expiry dates and numerous no-go zones. At the edges of it all, the frustration and anger at the state of things, a spreading sense of futility, was turning into routine violence.

I was relatively insulated from it all in leafy, affluent Bramhall, yet infected by that pervasive feeling of futility. Music, clothes and football, and playing records with Irene, could only go so far towards counteracting an inner emptiness – a sense of vague uncertainty about the future.

I was still searching for satisfying work, something that gave me a purpose. I'd known for a long time I was never going to be a professional footballer – the dream of a 10-year-old – and making a living out of music seemed a ridiculous thought, living in the North. You'd get to play your favourite records now and then in the youth clubs when there was no outside DJ, but it never seemed a plausible way of earning a living. Getting into music professionally in any capacity felt like an impossible dream – about as likely as suddenly appearing on television and becoming a celebrity with no immediately obvious talent.

One day I strode into the large Ladybrook pub, with its classic Bramhall mock-Tudor front, round the corner from my house, and asked if they had any jobs. My luck was in, and I started serving in the tap room, which was basically where the draught beer was just mild or bitter, and you'd have to go into the main bar for lager, which was Skol, which no one who knew what they were doing drank.

The landlady, Irene Harrop, was a classic northern character – pink hair piled high like Lucille Ball, mouth plastered with bright red lipstick, ruling the roost and always putting on a kind of show. The wages were rubbish, but it was cash in hand, and I picked up a lot of tips – the usual order was 'Pint please, and one for yourself, mate' – so you'd add twenty or thirty pence for yourself.

Naturally, it was Boddingtons bitter – Boddies – brewed in central Manchester and one of the city's best-known brand names. Back then it was only sold in the Greater Manchester area, and it was dry, mouth-puckeringly bitter, straw-coloured and much stronger than its 3.5 per cent gravity suggested. It cost twenty-two and a half pence, which the old money regulars still thought of as four and six. The regulars tended to bring in the exact change for two pints.

The beer was easy to pour. Pull down the lever, and boom, half a pint into the glass, and boom, another half pint filled up the pint glass, with a nice creamy top – a live white lather that made the first sip quite a ritual. It was a rare bit of luxury in a humdrum world. The same blokes would come in most nights, more or less the same time, often including my dad with his dog, for their two pints of bitter, a game of darts and a smoke – because it was what you did, and maybe moan about the same stuff you'd moaned about the day before.

Locals couldn't do without what was like a liquid-gold drug to them. I remember one night the brewery was on strike and we didn't have any Boddies, which completely ruined the regulars' precious anchoring routine. At first they wouldn't believe me when I said there was no bitter. The look on their faces was utter disbelief, then absolute anguish.

One man looked at me with suspicion and snapped, 'What do you mean, no fucking bitter?' I tried to explain about the strike. He simply asked again, 'Pint of Boddies please.' I explained about the strike: it means we've got no bitter. He slammed his fist on the bar, told me to fuck off, and stormed out. Without his bitter, his world was turned upside down – he'd have to face up to reality.

It got very repetitive watching it unfold: pint, darts, boring chat, home, repeat. I felt myself slowly becoming one of them. I saw my future in the smoke-filled bar, with the right amount of change in my pocket for two nightly pints. It might have suited them, but I wanted something more. I was getting stuck in a hole.

There were some who came into my pub who were around my age, and I made friends with others who wanted more than just passing the time in their local. Nick Chambers, from the Mojo revue at the New Century Hall, and I began going round the posher houses in Bramhall with ladders and buckets, offering to clean windows. They were owned by the kind of people who liked to say they lived in Cheshire, which sounded swanky, rather than Stockport, which sounded common.

We didn't have a car, so we walked the streets carrying ladders on our shoulders. We were pretty enterprising and had some slick introductory patter worked out, giving the owners a sob story – 'We've graduated from university, but there's no work for us. The queues at the dole office are massive. Any chance of doing your windows?' We did quite well, and it gave us a bit of extra cash in hand. We also did some labouring for Nick's dad, who was a builder, helping to dig out the foundations for extensions he was working on. Even in tough times some people have money, and big houses to make even bigger as Bramhall increasingly became one of the most desirable places to live in Greater Manchester.

Another friend I made was called Martin, who went to the same school as me but was a few years younger, so I hadn't come across him before. He seemed a couple of feet taller than me and was perhaps even more music-mad. Like me, he was fascinated by the minutes before a show – admiring the stage set, the size of the PA system, the roadies moving around the stage getting everything ready, and then the lights going down ...

I didn't know his surname at first, or perhaps he'd made up a punk one, but one day I found out my new friend was called Martin Fry. He was obsessed with David Bowie and felt that dressing in a calf-length patent leather coat placed him somewhere in the glam vicinity, which was probably true. It certainly made him stand out in staid Bramhall – and even in Manchester city centre – often dangerously so.

We shared the same rituals – *Top of the Pops*, the music papers, soul music, the trip to Manchester from dead Bramhall on the bus so we could find the newest pop-culture treasure on record and in magazines and books. We both had this drive to make our own entertainment. His sometimes insanely romantic drive led him to become the lead singer of a Sheffield group called ABC, although he showed no sign of any interest in singing when I first met him.

His love of the music papers led him to start a fanzine, *Modern Drugs*, which I also wrote for. But somewhere along the way he joined a group, began singing for them, came up with a million concepts, and within a few years was actually appearing on *Top of the Pops* – which, when we'd talked about it in Bramhall, had seemed like a fairy tale.

My memory is that we first met in the Ladybrook because Martin would come in for a spot of underage drinking, and I wouldn't be too bothered about enforcing the rules. He'd come in a lot, probably because, once we knew each other, I'd slip him free drinks. Martin might remember it differently.

8
A contribution from Martin Fry

We went to the same school in Bramhall, but Mike was a few years above me – and at that age, that's huge. I used to walk a lot around Bramhall, which I found suffocating; it was so quiet and still. It might have been adolescent paranoia, but when I walked down a street of big houses in one of the quieter neighbourhoods – they were all quiet, but some quieter than others – it could feel as though the curtains twitched as you passed. It was as if you were intruding on everyone, even where you lived.

The only thing it had going for it was that it was twenty minutes by train to Manchester – but when you got there it felt so different from Bramhall, as if you'd been on a twenty-hour flight. Another point in its favour was that George Best of Manchester United – the so-called fifth Beatle – had built a modernist house in Bramhall, a white brutalist cube like something out of the TV series *The Prisoner*. It was just round the corner from my house, and as a youngster I used to fantasise about knocking on his door. A butler would answer. I'd ask if George could come out and play, and we'd kick a ball against a wall for hours.

One day I actually did ring his bell, and he came out with a pile of pre-signed George Best photographs and gave me one. The fact that someone so famous lived so close had a profound effect on me. There was this sense of glamour right on my doorstep. He used to get the local police to fetch his drink from the off-licence so he wouldn't get caught drink-driving.

I'd walk everywhere in Bramhall, but the best walks were those that took me to catch the bus to Stockport town centre or the train to Manchester – to see amazing bands, visit the newsagent to buy the *NME* (a portal to other worlds), and to the pub where, underage, you could still get served a pint of Boddingtons.

I knew from a very early age that I wasn't going to stay in Bramhall. I had that restless spirit – what Bruce Springsteen was calling being born to run. I was ready to run, and as a young teenager I had it planned out that I wouldn't do anything that tied me to Bramhall or made it difficult to leave. I decided I would never have a steady girlfriend there. I wouldn't learn to drive there, which would force me out. I just wanted to get out. Some people might have visited Bramhall and wondered why you wanted to get out because it was so nice. Well, you wanted to get out *because* it was so nice. It wasn't what you were looking for as a seventies teenager.

The first time I met Mike was on one of my Bramhall walks in 1976, a few months before I actually did leave Bramhall to go to university. I was going one way and Mike the other, and there was, naturally, no one else in sight. Mike was carrying a set of ladders and had this great smile that, for some reason, made me think, well, there's someone else who also wants to get out of Bramhall. Maybe he was going to use the ladders to climb out.

It helped that he was dressed a bit punky – not London punky, with the mohawks and chains, but suburban punky, Manchester punky. You wore clothes that didn't really belong to any of the obvious tribes, things you found in charity shops, clothes that weren't branded – maybe a Fred Perry top might be okay. We were a bit more creative about the look in the North: splatter t-shirts with paint, sewing badges on V-neck sweaters, trying to find shoes that no one else was wearing. Nothing from a shop that claimed to be selling punk clothes. Certain groups would dress the same way, like Wire, The Prefects, Subway Sect, Gang of Four. They'd formed because of punk, but dressed like surrealist academics.

Punk only really lasted for about five months as a radical break with rock clichés. After a few months of the Pistols, and around Manchester the Buzzcocks, it was Generation X and Billy Idol on

Top of the Pops, and it was over. If you were truly punk, you moved beyond punk. Mike and his ladders made me think – he agrees with me.

I'd been very picky choosing friends in Bramhall. I'd tried the Cubs, the Scouts, tried playing football with schoolfriends – all the things you try to do to fit in when you realise you're finding it hard to fit, and it worries you that you don't. But I didn't really have friends; I was a classic loner, spending a lot of time in my head. Then suddenly I met this bloke on the street, jauntily carrying some ladders as if it was the most normal thing in the world, and we started chatting.

For some reason, Mike and I had an instant connection. Maybe it was because when the Buzzcocks came up – and because we both dressed like we knew who they were – we actually did know who they were. We bonded over the Buzzcocks. I'd never met anyone in Bramhall who was interested in the same things, and we stood there talking for ages. I remember thinking, this guy is on a journey somewhere. It's easy to say in hindsight, but we instantly talked for hours about music, and I thought: music is going to take him somewhere.

We were inseparable for a while, and over the years – even when we were doing other things, and not seeing each other for a year or two, or even more – we were still close. The t-shirts changed, the rhythms changed, the haircuts changed – well, Mike's more than mine – the drink we had in our hands changed, the person having the hits changed, the drugs we took changed, the families we had grew, but we were still close. We were always still chatting away about music, making plans, setting ourselves up for the rest of our lives, getting ready for a time fifty years later when we would remember the time we were about to make our escape from Bramhall. There was a light at the end of the tunnel.

9
A European

Some Scottish City fans who'd come into the pub one night mentioned they were going to Greece for a few weeks, and it made me think I should join them – to see what was out there. I started to save up my tips. I was no longer a teenager, and it was time to move out of my parents' house. Maybe some independence was what I needed, and the Greek idea started to sound increasingly attractive.

There was one last regular job – at the urging of my dad, who'd worked at the same firm for over twenty years and was worried I was beginning to drift aimlessly from odd job to odd job. He kept telling me I needed security.

I made the tedious daily trip from Bramhall to Eccles to work in a factory that made raincoats – one of the last lingering signs of when Manchester's garment trade was famous around the world. It was a dreary job, working with depressed-looking people who seemed to know the firm's days were numbered.

No one there seemed bothered trying to make the place a good place to work, and when after a few weeks I mentioned to my friendly boss I was thinking of heading out to Greece for a few weeks, he made no effort to stop me going. Instead, I got an emotional speech that reminded me of old Jack's at Mirrlees Blackstone.

'You're mad if you don't go', he said. 'Look at me. I've been here for thirty years. I've been nowhere and seen nothing. When you're my age, do you want to look back at the same boring job? Get out of here. Get some stamps in your passport. Have an adventure. What have you got to lose? Go to Greece.'

So I did.

My Manchester-grumpy dad, with his stubborn learn-a-trade mantra, thought I was simply being lazy and avoiding responsibilities. He was not at all happy about me going and told me I would never amount to anything if I just fucked off on holiday when times were tough. For him, it wasn't how the world worked. My mum, coming from the Irish side, slipped me a £20 note and told me to have a great time.

At the end of May, I set off with these two Scottish lads. We got a bus from King's Cross, which took over three days to get us to Athens. It was a punishing journey, and didn't seem like the holiday my dad thought it was. Going through Yugoslavia along these terrible roads was particularly hairy, passing wrecked buses and crashed cars heading deeper into what seemed a war zone. I began to think maybe I'd made the wrong decision.

From Athens, I headed out on my own, picking up information about where to go from other travellers I met. I had a little rucksack and a sleeping bag, and I was on the road. I didn't know what I was doing; I was just looking for good times, for something different from what I'd known.

I jumped from island to island, slept on beaches, and picked up odd jobs waiting on tables and pot washing. In Crete, I worked in the banana fields under the mountains. Who knew they had banana fields in Crete? The water they used to grow the bananas came down from the mountains, and you had to clear the rocks out from the water in blistering heat, which was back-breaking work. But you got fed, and you met other people from around the world, who'd give you advice about where to go next.

It was like a dream. Greece was very basic at the time, much simpler than now, and hadn't been affected by mass tourism. You'd bump into a few hippies, lots of Australians strung out on opium who'd been through Thailand, India and Vietnam, then made it to Istanbul and on to Greece.

I met some great characters and adventurers from all over the world, all needing a change of scenery for their own reasons. I'd never meet the like in Manchester, where many adults you encountered seemed ground down by time and lack of money. The entire trip was an education. It changed my whole approach to life, gave me a new kind of confidence, and made me understand Rob Gretton's determination never to settle for what he called a proper job, with a boss ruling over you. He'd been outside Manchester and experienced a wider, different world when he left his office job to work on a kibbutz in Israel with his girlfriend and later his partner, and his confidant and counsellor, Lesley.

You'd land on an island recommended by some stray backpacker you'd met, and it was like a small paradise – a soft sand beach where you'd sleep among a small community of travellers, an isolated tavern, lots of whitewashed houses, and dramatic sunsets. Breakfast was coffee and a smoke. You'd get a great meal and a tin of pineapple juice for not more than a few pennies.

I made it to Santorini, which is now an expensive, fashionable destination, but it hadn't been commercialised then. To get from the port into the picturesque village, you had to make your way up a steep, winding and inhospitable path, with the impossibly blue Mediterranean opening around you. You'd put your bags on a donkey and walk alongside the long-suffering animal. Those same paths will now be filled with people – a traffic jam of tourists getting in each other's way – but then there was hardly anyone there.

The Greeks were friendly, helpful people, most of them going out of their way to make you feel at home. I was living on less than a pound a day, with an ultimate destination in mind – aiming to see my Aunt Brenda in Rome at the end of September. She'd lived with us in Blackley, a convent girl a lot younger than my mum, and she'd turned out to be a brilliant linguist. She'd moved to Italy in the early seventies, and I planned to visit her after a few months in the Greek islands.

My ticket allowed me to stop off in Corfu, and on the ferry there I met a lively French guy from Nîmes in southern France and paired up with him for a while. It was how things happened – like a metaphor for life, where your path could change because of someone you met, who gave you an idea or a bit of new knowledge that set you off somewhere you hadn't imagined before. It was all very impulsive, which suited how I was feeling at the time. I didn't mind getting out of my depth or feeling a little lost. I was in the mood for new experiences, game for anything, which meant sometimes I could be quite reckless. Making friends was all very innocent. There was no sense it might be dangerous to wander off with a stranger into the beyond, with limited means of communicating back home.

My new French friend expertly sneaked us into a campsite so we could use their communal facilities. He'd done it before and knew how to get things for free or next to no money. I met a couple of girls from Venice I got on with, and they invited me to stay with them. There was no worry about what was going to happen next, like there was in Manchester. It all took care of itself.

After a few days of bliss with the girls, swapping addresses and phone numbers, promising to meet up in the future, I got the seven-hour ferry from Corfu to Brindisi in southern Italy, thinking I'd catch a train to Rome, where Brenda was. By that time, I'd run out of money, sold everything I could, including my sleeping bag and rucksack, and it was pretty much me and the clothes I was standing in.

On the ferry, I met some rugby-playing university students from Coventry who were also heading to Rome. I was learning the gift of the gab, or maybe had something northern that was likeable. There were always people to talk to on journeys like these, doing the same thing as you, and within hours it was like you'd known them for years. I persuaded them to lend me the money for a ticket to Rome. I showed them the address where my aunt lived, honest to God, and they believed me when I said I'd meet up with them and give them the money back.

Making it to Rome after a five-hour journey with my new Coventry pals, whom I would never have met under any other circumstances, I made my way to my aunt's apartment in the centre of Rome. It looked impressive compared to our little house in Blackley, surrounded by restaurants and cafes. I rang the bell, but there was no answer. I waited outside for hours, and there was no sign of her. There was no way of getting hold of people in those days, and I began to think that after travelling around Greece I'd lost track of time and arrived on the wrong day.

A neighbour who lived in the same block eventually spotted me slumped outside looking helpless and told me that Brenda was in England. My heart sank. She was marrying her boyfriend Enzo, a happy occasion I somehow knew nothing about. Her neighbour smiled and shook some keys, which were for Brenda's apartment.

They knew I was coming, and they had predicted the state I'd be in after a few months crisscrossing the Greek islands. They didn't think I'd have anything left but a torn t-shirt, cut-off shorts and worn-out sandals on the verge of disintegrating.

Inside the flat, there was an envelope with some welcome cash, and there were even some clothes laid out for me. Enzo worked for a company that supplied clothes for prisoners about to be released, and though the clothes were pretty basic, they did the job. Any signs of my self-conscious suedehead affinities had long disintegrated, and my careful crop had grown out into an unruly mop. My white Manchester skin had been blasted by the sun, and I was verging on the beach bum, even hippy.

I hadn't had a bath for months, relying on the sea, rudimentary cold showers at the campsite in Corfu, and occasional waterfalls. There was one quiet bay on Syros, under a sky so blue it seemed an hallucination, where a waterfall cascaded at the edge of the beach, with pure, clean water coming down from the mountains. That kept me clean for a couple of days. It was the kind of beach where you'd fall asleep after midnight, after drinking and smoking with some new friends, and wake up the next morning surrounded by local families setting up their picnics, politely ignoring the rough-looking foreigner yawning and scratching himself.

A quick hot bath at Brenda's, the first for months, and I got myself ready to pay back the loan to the Coventry lads. We'd arranged to meet at a cafe near the Colosseum at seven in the evening. At four, there was a knock at the door, and it was a serious-looking Italian in a uniform with a peaked cap. He didn't speak much English, but my immediate thought was that I was in trouble.

My heart skipped a beat, and after the next door neighbour came to translate, it turned out this was a chauffeur friend of Brenda and Enzo, Franco, and he was going to show me the sights.

I'd gone from sleeping rough on beaches to driving around Rome in the back seat of a brand new Mercedes. He haltingly explained he was taking me to a restaurant near the Villa Borghese Gardens, Rome's Central Park. In turn, I managed to write down the address of the bar where I was due to meet the Coventry group.

As we pulled up at the cafe, I could see them all outside drinking, and I rolled down the window, waving the cash, saying, 'Yes, this is how I usually roll.' They couldn't believe their eyes, and a couple of them piled into the car. I paid them back, and we drove off to the restaurant. It was a classic old-school Italian restaurant, with photographs of Burton and Taylor and Frank Sinatra on the wall, and we ate and drank in style as though it would never happen again.

My new driver took me for a pedicure and manicure, obviously taken aback by the gnarled, filthy state of my poor English nails which almost needed sawing off. After a couple of days riding around Rome in what was temporarily my limo, having the time of my life, I was in the mood to phone the girls I'd met in Corfu and arrange to go and meet them. They lived in Venice, but specifically the more industrial mainland suburb of Mestre, and there was a week more living the life, as one of the girls' fathers was a famous doctor.

It was all becoming a bit Talented Mr Ripley, and I felt myself drifting. I could hear my father grumbling at what I was becoming, floating through life. It wasn't exactly a trade, but I travelled to the south of France in time for the grape-picking season, the *vendange*, which was exhausting seven days a week, sunup to sundown work my dad would have approved of. You'd get a room in primitive living quarters, a few francs a day, bread, cheese, chocolate during the day, plus naturally great meals at night, and all the wine you could drink. From mid-September to October thousands of pickers were needed, and there was absolutely no red tape. All you needed was your passport, and you were in.

There were students and school-age travellers from across Europe, along with a few older people, and although the work was hard – effectively labouring in the fields, backbreaking, cold, wet and repetitive – it was as much a social affair as anything. Being an English northerner with my own lusty, carefree appetites made me something of a welcome anomaly to the French locals, whose image of England was mostly shaped by uptight southerners and tired English clichés.

After a few days I was picking grapes in my sleep. My mind began to drift back to Manchester – the clubs, my friends, gigs, the start of the new '74/75 City season, with their dependable captain under Mercer and Allison, Tony Book, now managing the team. After more than five months away, I started to wonder if I was missing out on anything back home. What was Martin up to? And Rob?

I made my way back to Manchester.

10
A change in the air

I was welcomed back into the Ladybrook like a returning hero, though my dad, in his usual seat with his usual pint, wasn't too impressed when he first saw me – the longer, wilder hair and the ruddy tan I'd picked up from hours outdoors in France. He shook his head, looked me up and down and groaned, 'What the hell's just walked in?'

The cash I showed him that I'd earned in the fields of France only made him more suspicious. It was great to be home though, and it was the best night I'd ever had in the pub, but now I had a different worldview because I'd seen beyond the little world of Bramhall. Pubs were great, if there was more to life than pubs.

I tried to repeat my Greek odyssey the following year, this time with my Bramhall friend Nick Chambers, eager to sample the easygoing otherworld I'd told him about. The Greek part was fine and clearly seduced Nick, but nothing went as smoothly as the first time. Nick, to my surprise, fell for the lifestyle so completely that he ended up staying and never came back.

I should have known he was getting comfortable in Greece when we found the neatly folded clothes and passport of a Swedish traveller on a particularly lovely beach on one of the islands. Perhaps he'd gone for a swim and got into trouble – or, he was Swedish after all – taken his own life.

They were still there a few hours later, and, fearing the worst, we reported it to the local police – not before helping ourselves to a t-shirt and shorts, while Nick grabbed a pair of clog-like sandals.

We never heard what became of the missing Swede, but Nick loved his clogs and took to wearing them all the time. Dead man's shoes, I called them. Nick didn't care. They fitted, and they were perfect for Greek beaches.

Nick lives in Italy now, and I sometimes think that could have been me. At times I was drawn so deeply into an alternative life, an alluring new reality, that Manchester became a distant, almost dreamlike place – a past life.

On this European trip there were no happy accidents, no chance meetings, no unexpected discoveries, no mysterious chauffeurs in fancy cars taking me for manicures, or cash-in-hand jobs. To cap it all, the Venice girls didn't answer the phone. Everything had fallen into place the first time. I'd had my moment of revelation – the first cut was the deepest – and the second time felt a little bit of a let-down.

Another chance encounter during my first trip was meeting two guys whose family lived in Rome, conveniently close to my aunt. They had just started art college in Manchester, and their dad had bought them a house in Didsbury. Not long after getting back, I moved out of my parents' house and in with them. Even leaving home was connected to those first few months in Europe. It taught me the art of making things happen.

By the time of my third summer visit to Greece in 1976, my second with Nick, there was something beginning to happen in Manchester that would lead to *Spiral Scratch*. There was something changing, you could sense it, feel it in the atmosphere at Pips and other clubs, how the response to David Bowie and the concerts he'd played in Manchester was going to lead to something creative.

There were other signs as well that seemed to continue Bowie's flamboyant bohemianism, much of it coming from New York. But it took the two gigs at Manchester's Lesser Free Trade Hall in the summer of 1976 by the Sex Pistols – with a more English directness bouncing off the grim state of the nation – to activate it.

There was something distinctively Manchester about the attitude that had been building in the clubs since the Twisted Wheel, and developing further in the Roxy Room at Pips. It needed the Sex Pistols, but there were people in Manchester ready to act the moment Johnny Rotten and his gang of reprobates made their sneering protest. Even though they used guitars and amps, they stripped everything back, sped it up, and spoke directly to the mess and misery of street life and the reactionary retreat of British culture.

The Pistols' shows were attended by a few Pips regulars and other music fanatics who were reading the signs in the music papers, but their impact on the city grew when the maverick broadcaster Tony Wilson of Granada Television – to the alarm of some of his colleagues – booked the group to appear on his avant-garde rock show *So It Goes*.

It turned the Lesser Free Trade Hall shows into a kind of trilogy; and for this third act, looking like uncontrollable English ruffians – bordering on political terrorists and making a mockery of rock music and even television itself – they played 'Anarchy in the UK', weeks before it was released as a single. The scandalous, confrontational theatre of the Sex Pistols was a few steps on from the costumes and self-creative artistry of Roxy and Bowie, but it made perfect sense to us Pips-goers. The aim was to sound as mixed up, made up and messed up as you looked and felt.

The Pistols, as a pop group, also had clear links with the riotous early mod days of The Who and the Small Faces. It felt like the next step on from mod music stirred by pumped-up R&B and the shirty, indignant Detroit rock of Iggy and the Stooges, Alice Cooper and MC5. It was a new kind of energy, shooting out in all directions, and Manchester music fans had always been quick to respond to energy – to turn it into a scene and shape it with their own style and wit. We were ready for them.

I was only going to stay in Greece for a month, but after a couple of weeks I told Nick I was going back home. Something was happening, and I didn't want to be idling in the sun while it was. In that sense, my dad was right. What good was loafing and lounging when there was some kind of revolution in the air at home? I'd been searching for something, and it was coming, although it wouldn't necessarily help me get a mortgage or put me on a pension scheme.

My City mate Rob was already joining in, running a lively xeroxed fanzine for Slaughter and the Dogs – a group of driven Wythenshawe teenagers brought together by Bowie's hyped-up glam, who made an expedient switch to punk as it began to make its presence felt. They had performed at the first Sex Pistols Manchester shows – plucky, but a little puny next to the sheer nerve of the Pistols.

Rob declared himself president of their fan club, which for a while may have had only him as a member, and co-financed their debut football chant single, 'Cranked Up Really High'. Alongside Vini Faal, he soon began bringing the first wave of punks up from London – The Slits, Siouxsie and the Banshees, The Vibrators and The Adverts – to play at The Oaks on Barlow Moor Road in Chorlton, opposite the cemetery. Astonishingly, Johnny Thunders (straight out of the New York Dolls) and the Heartbreakers appeared on the little stage upstairs, which had previously been a cabaret lounge. That was one of the great punk gigs, probably helped by the bottles of brandy and Baileys Johnny liked to drink before a show, bringing with it the style – and stench – of New York. I went every night and got closer to Rob, who was in his element, introducing this energy into south Manchester. For me, it was a crash course in the sheer difference of punk.

The Oaks had been a great soul pub in the first half of the 1970s, and DJ Dave Faversham would end every night with the plaintive 'Long After Tonight is All Over' by Lorraine Silver, a teenage sixties UK soul singer who had become a Northern Soul favourite. Rob, the soul fan, made the necessary post-Pistols adjustments to the venue and was putting on these punk nights in Chorlton in early 1977 – nights that were already helping to seal Manchester's bona fide qualities as a pioneering punk city.

I made it back to Manchester in time to see, with Martin, the Sex Pistols play a third Manchester show in 1976 at The Electric Circus – a former cinema, ex-bingo hall and once the Top Hat Club run by Bernard Manning, stranded on a scrap of wasteland in Collyhurst. It was only a mile or so up Rochdale Road from the city centre, but seemed to exist in a different time zone. Manchester, with its slow recovery from blight, was within touching distance, yet Collyhurst never seemed to benefit from the regular slum clearances – or the construction of housing estates and high-rise flats.

The Electric Circus made its own nimble switch to the new punk sensation after hosting rock shows by 1970s album bands who rarely made the album charts – let alone the singles charts. Within a few months, it went from showcasing Van Der Graaf Generator, Blodwyn Pig, The Groundhogs and – because the wider world would eventually get to know some of those weird underground bands – AC/DC, to mostly featuring punk.

The location and surroundings – the sense of danger and dereliction lurking around dark corners and down crumbling roads and alleyways that appeared to lead nowhere but patches of rubble – made it the perfect place to move from one unsettling world into another, more urgent, reality. Its walls, painted black to cover up the horror show interior, also perversely helped to heighten the degenerate atmosphere.

In December, inside the stinking, run-down venue that once seemed closer to a prog rock version of a working men's variety club than the legendary New York punk venue Max's Kansas City, I saw the Sex Pistols play alongside the increasingly and wonderfully derailed Johnny Thunders and the Heartbreakers, Buzzcocks and the Clash. More unbelievable signs of what was happening in New York – a different punk in a different kitchen – came with the one-two-three-four of the stupidly quick Ramones, and the twisty, twitching, exotically clean-cut Talking Heads, who were as much funk as punk. Their music came from Al Green and James Brown as much as Television and the Ramones, which made total sense to me.

The core fans who'd side-stepped from Pips via the Lesser Free Trade Hall to the Electric Circus slashed and despoiled their glam costumes, chopped into their Ferry hairstyles or rinsed out their red Ziggy dye – or, if they'd come to punk from other places, crudely cut their long hair – and a new scene formed around them. This time, one of our own, Buzzcocks, was gaining national recognition and offering more direction than the Pistols to the Manchester punk groups that followed, with their more experimental, eclectic outlook. Manchester was becoming post-punk in parallel with the emergence of punk itself.

Us early adopters used a tucked-away gay nightclub, The Ranch, as our unofficial social club. It lay beyond a door that gave nothing away, down some unpromising stairs in the cramped basement beneath the more full-frontal Foo Foo's Palace. It was anything but a palace.

A lively cabaret club along cobbled Dale Street off Piccadilly Gardens, it was owned by local treasure and drag queen Foo Foo Lamar – aka hard-as-nails Frank Pearson – who fancied himself living a grand Las Vegas show-biz life with his gold Rolls-Royce, and would belt out his theme song, 'I Am What I Am'.

Foo Foo Frank generously welcomed all manner of misfits and hedonists, including the new punks, and while upstairs hosted the obligatory hen and stag parties, in the murk downstairs the few punk records so far released were played, alongside the Bowie, Roxy, Iggy, Velvets/Reed and Ronson axis at full volume. The final-song ritual for the hardy 2 am all-sorts reluctant to head into the night was Liverpool's bright-minded pre-punk Deaf School's 'What a Way to End It All'.

The early 1977 release of Buzzcocks' *Spiral Scratch* added four much-needed tracks to the playlist, and guitarists Pete Shelley and Steve Diggle regularly held court, inspiring and encouraging bands like The Fall, The Worst and The Distractions, all of whom played one of their first shows at The Ranch. If you were watching The Fall perform, standing a few feet in front of ragged, fired-up singer Mark E. Smith, you'd be showered in his mucky spit as he expelled his fractured thoughts, ending most words with a sublimely bitter snarl.

They'd usually be followed by a kind of rampaging punk choral – Boddingtons-fuelled John the Postman's sweaty, deranged a cappella delivery of the sloppy rock and roll sea shanty 'Louie Louie' – which would usually collapse into a mass frenzy as others jumped on stage and joined in the transcendent celebration of amateurism.

The noisy, chaotic room was a kind of laboratory for the Manchester scene forming around Buzzcocks, complete with its own in-house fanzine, *Shy Talk*, put together by one of the barmen, Steve Shy. Bernard 'Albrecht' Sumner and Peter 'Hooky' Hook were there too, transforming from moustachioed Pips poseurs, via the Lesser Free

Trade Hall Pistols epiphany, into local punks planning their own band – which, a few months later at the end of May 1977, would emerge as Warsaw, playing their first gig at the Electric Circus. By January 1978 they were known as Joy Division, playing a first gig under their new name at Pips itself, which inauspiciously featured an audience fight that Hooky tried to defuse – inheriting, in his own way, the Foo Foo mantle.

The Ranch was filled with incongruous cowboy props and, although bands played, there was no stage – the musicians performed on the same level as the audience. In a way, it was an offshoot of the Roxy Room at Pips, tucked away from prying eyes, and those who were seeing punks immediately standing out from the crowd, and standing up for something, became targets of disaffection and even hatred.

It was tribal – not only the Perry Boys resenting this effete-seeming new mutant tribe, but also an incongruous revival of bullying Teddy Boys, who loathed the punks' unashamed divergence, along with non-aligned hooligans intent on giving someone a good kicking. People were reluctant to leave in the early hours not only because it was a safe place – if there was any trouble downstairs, no-nonsense Foo Foo would quickly sort it out, apologising for the kerfuffle with, 'In every bed of roses there's at least one prick' – but also because, outside, there might be monsters in the dark waiting to pounce.

Frank lived in Bramhall, and I saw him once walking down the street when I'd gone to visit my mum and dad. I went up to him, introduced myself, and told him how fantastic and life-changing The Ranch had been, and how brilliant it was of him to help make it happen. I said, 'You gave us space to breathe when we were outcasts.' He replied, 'Well, dear, aren't we all?' He knew that, as far apart as we might have seemed, we shared a similar spirit.

11
A record label

I was in touch with Rob Gretton via City and landline – often from a phone box – as he found his own way into the emerging scene, at first a little on the edges but soon managing, in his unflappable way, to be in the right place at the right time and move closer to the centre. He was working by day at Manchester Ringway Airport as a baggage handler, and by night he'd begun DJing at the Rafters Club on Oxford Street, another place reached by heading downstairs where special things were happening, and which, during 1977, had become one of the key city-centre punk venues.

Things were moving fast – though in the middle of it all Rob was as laconic as ever – and Howard Devoto, Buzzcocks' highbrow, firebrand lead singer, had already left the group by spring 1977, feeling limited by punk and what was fast becoming a visual and sonic formula. On 27 October that year, his stranger, more scenic new group, Magazine, pushing into post-punk territory, played their first proper show. It came a few weeks after a brief appearance at the final event permitted at the Electric Circus, before it was closed down following objections from the local fire service and Manchester City Council. The building may have been a firetrap – and it was certainly falling down – but the main concern was that what was happening there seemed seditious.

The two final shows at the Circus were, fittingly, complete carnage – as if the performances by Devoto's new group Magazine, The Fall, John Cooper Clarke, Buzzcocks, The Negatives, The Drones, Steel Pulse, The Panik and Warsaw were all conspiring to help demolish the building from within.

The Panik were a more or less second-generation punk band from Prestwich that Rob had helped to form and was managing. He also produced, in just a few swift hours, their first EP, *It Won't Sell* – a very Rob title – featuring 'Modern Politics', 'Urban Damnation' and 'Murder'. He released it on his first attempt at a record label, Rainy City Records, with the slogan, 'We're so bored with London'.

Rob had found a photograph of some rent boys parading on a New York pavement in the late 1960s; they looked so much like Manchester punks on their way to The Ranch that he used it for the cover. Rob then nicked Warsaw's drummer for The Panik, forcing Warsaw to post an ad on the noticeboard in the then more community-minded Manchester Virgin Records shop on Lever Street. That noticeboard had led Howard Devoto to discover his remarkable Magazine guitarist John McGeoch – and it helped Warsaw find their new drummer Stephen Morris, who remained with the group as they became Joy Division and later New Order. Rob was, indirectly, helping to organise Joy Division before there even was a Joy Division.

Every few weeks, Rob would be up to something, keeping me up to speed at a City match. At one point, he told me how he'd tried to poach Warsaw's singer, Ian Curtis, for The Panik – but Warsaw was on its way to becoming Joy Division, and their new drummer had made enough of a positive difference to the overall sound and power for Ian to sense something was happening and decide to stay where he was.

Rob was on DJ duty at Rafters, mixing some reggae and soul in with the punk, on the night of a talent contest on 14 April 1978, when seventeen local groups competed for the chance of a record contract with Stiff or Chiswick Records. The London labels had been quick to race up North, hunting for the next Buzzcocks. It was Joy Division's second or third appearance under their new name, and while Warsaw had been closer to the angry, well-intentioned punk of The Panik, Joy Division were something else altogether – as though they'd travelled through some subspace warp field since the end of 1977.

A wide-eyed, bowled-over Rob couldn't believe it when Joy Division – who hadn't impressed him much as Warsaw – took to the stage at two in the morning, the last of the groups trying to catch the attention of the London record labels and whoever the judges were. The run-of-the-mill Warsaw had become the best band he'd ever seen. Also there was TV presenter Tony Wilson, whom Rob met for the first time – an encounter that would prove as significant for the future of Manchester music as his 'discovery' of Joy Division.

Rob was soon managing Joy Division, having met them in a pub a day or two later. With his low-key, winning ways and a few laughs, he convinced them of his worth. His first order of business was clear: even if Stiff or Chiswick offered them a deal, they were not to accept. 'This will all be done from Manchester.'

He also mentioned to the group that he knew Tony Wilson – which was just about true, at least since the day before – and that Wilson had been impressed as well. At the time, this was very encouraging to those who saw Wilson on television just about every night and who knew he had his own TV show, which he could put you on. At Rafters, singer Ian had hurled abuse at Wilson for not putting his group on TV, but overnight they slipped into an inside track. Who knew there was such a thing in Manchester?

With Tony Wilson – TV famous locally but also a mythologising spokesman for Manchester's revolutionary originality and extreme music enthusiast – Rob was soon pursuing one of his basic tenets: that you didn't need to go to London to make a record.

Rob told me about a record – two singles in one package – that was to be released on a label Tony Wilson was financing called Factory Records. There was a whole new set of similarly bloody-minded local characters Rob was now working with, and because they were all making it up as they went along, Rob could be the manager of a group as well as part of the record label that would release the group's records. There seemed to be a plan, but part of the plan was that there was absolutely no plan. At times it just seemed an excuse for a lot of amorphous, far-fetched playing around.

Each personality with their own particular skills in Tony's orbit that had somehow fallen into place at Factory had their own plan. The graphic designer Tony had found, Peter Saville, and the experienced local producer Martin Hannett, who'd made the Buzzcocks and Slaughter and the Dogs records, were two uncompromising perfectionists whose roles were clear enough – and you kind of understood what Tony did, even if he was a complete one-off. He was part Manchester entrepreneur, part Manchester radical, part Manchester show-off, part Manchester romantic, and when it came to running a business, part enlightened amateur stubbornly doing things his own way. It was strange to hear Rob talk about his new friendship with Wilson – the man off the telly – which seemed to place him in a world you'd never get near. Sometimes it all seemed so vague I thought, well, this will go nowhere; other times he sounded – for Rob – so excited and determined I thought they knew exactly what they were doing.

Other Factory personnel – and enlightened amateurs – like Tony's mercurial actor friend and ad hoc guru of sorts, Alan Erasmus, brought a nameless energy into the process. It was hard to define, but without it there would have been no Factory.

As things turned out, Joy Division would not have been Joy Division without Rob. Without making much of a show of it, and making everything seem like fun, he guided them in the right direction. Without seeming to be a professional music-business manager, he professionalised them. They wanted to work outside the usual system, but he knew there were certain factors they could not avoid.

It was his cheerleading belief that they really were the best band in the world, which hadn't rung true when he was devoting his time to Slaughter and the Dogs and The Panik, but did now – and it rubbed off on the group. He took the organising pressure off them, motivated and protected them, and gave them space to become something special. Even when struggling financially he bought them clothes to give them a coherent look and spent his own money on backdrops for the television shows Wilson was now booking them on to. He loved them, and they loved him, but from the outside it was hard to see how it worked – the gnomic and comically elusive Rob, and the shy, hardworking band discovering an intensity and resonance at odds with their everyday goofiness.

Rob draped a certain anonymity and mystery around Joy Division because he thought they were too shy and awkward to come across in interviews as strongly as their music. They had things to say, and were courteous, even gentle – at least when sober – and had a clear sense of their own aesthetic, but they tended to retreat into their shells during interviews. He let Saville's enigmatic artwork and Kevin Cummins's brooding black-and-white photographs in distinctive local settings answer certain questions about who the group were.

I was struggling with money too, even as being in Manchester through 1978 and 1979 was as exciting as I'd always hoped it would be. The city was producing important, original and widely acclaimed music – music that was being covered in the national weekly papers, shifting attention North – not just danced to in clubs. The first Factory record, 'A Factory Sample', was like an avant-garde variety show. It featured a Hannett-produced Joy Division, the hard-edged Sheffield electronic trio Cabaret Voltaire, Tony's beloved Vini Reilly's guitar project, The Durutti Column, and the mischievous comic John Dowie. In its minimal silver sleeve, it looked more like a work of art than a record.

It was like a manifesto – visually, conceptually and musically – for whatever the label might become. It might have gone nowhere, but the record stood as a memento of those shadowy Manchester moments that emerged in the wake of the Sex Pistols, when a few stoners and musical upstarts began to have visions – and who knew where that could lead.

There were new venues where the local and the national were beginning to mix, and gigs to go to every night. The first albums by Buzzcocks, The Fall, Magazine, John Cooper Clarke and especially Joy Division were genuine shape-shifting classics, and Buzzcocks and Magazine were already appearing on *Top of the Pops*. Meanwhile, having Wilson – a hippyish, Cambridge-educated television personality happily mixing with the hoi polloi – able to feature Factory music on his avant-garde variety shows was a classic piece of Manchester grifting. Manchester was on the move.

In May 1978, Factory, together with local music promoter Alan Wise, began their eclectic nights at the Russell Club – a West Indian club in Hulme near the notorious Crescents estate. The Russell was where Alan Erasmus's dad used to take him, and he thought it the perfect spot when Factory wanted to stage their showcases: out of the way, hard to reach, and challenging an audience rather than making it easy for them.

After the early label shows by Joy Division, The Durutti Column and other acts associated with Factory, the Russell was, by 1979, settling into its own rhythm as a venue. TV's Tony Wilson – increasingly the Warholesque impresario of Manchester's Factory – now added 'club owner' to his list of pursuits, a fine traditional local occupation.

Wilson was now someone Johnny Rotten could ask whether he still had his club – a question that led to Rotten's new experimental post-punk group, Public Image Ltd, playing a low-key show there, with Tony's latest pet project, the gloomy dance act A Certain Ratio, supporting.

The Russell Club put on some great gigs, but it was drifting away from being a central part of a fast-changing Manchester scene – part of the city's creative pulse – and becoming simply another venue bringing in new music. Compared with Factory's artwork designed by Peter Saville, beginning with the incongruously elegant posters for the Factory nights, and the club posters by Howard Devoto's artist girlfriend Linder Sterling, the Russell itself felt very much old, back-street, working men's club Manchester. For a while, the contrast between the music and the setting was part of the experience, but that soon made less sense.

I went to as many Joy Division shows as I could and wrote about them playing the Russell Club for Martin Fry's fanzine, *Modern Drugs*. It was snowing outside, and I wrote that the stage was a block of ice – which seemed to suit the music. Rob rang me up, and said I was the first person to write a live review about them as Joy Division. I didn't know if it was true or not, but he seemed pleased with what I'd written. I felt I belonged to whatever it was.

Usually, a manager of a band at that stage of their career – a few shows in, sometimes playing to a couple of dozen people – would have said, 'Do you want to interview them for the fanzine?' But not Rob. Rob had his own way of doing things. It rubbed off on me a little, but making money from music still seemed a remote possibility.

I was in my mid-twenties, as restless as ever, still on the dole, muddling through, and the work problem was beginning to get me down. While Factory was in its early days – more a club than a record label – and the initial punk and post-punk excitement had settled a little, with local bands like Buzzcocks, Magazine, and even John Cooper Clarke signing for major labels, as if something sensationally local had already come to an end, I decided to try an employment scheme that had been set up by the Tories and expanded by Labour – to deal with what was called 'increasing industrial change' and skill shortages.

The government-funded Training Opportunities Scheme (TOPS) was intended to help adults in their twenties not only find work, but also, if they were already employed but unqualified, train them and provide valuable early experience in various trades or the service industry. It was a popular scheme, with a waiting list to join.

It was attractive to me because it provided a fairly generous allowance of about £25 a week – more than you received on the dole – plus a free bus pass. The courses lasted between six months and a year, and you were likely to secure a more stable job afterwards than window cleaning or working behind a bar. I got onto a catering course at Salford Technical College, where I was given a chef's uniform – including a pair of trousers I really liked – and a full set of knives. I found myself enjoying learning something new, having some structure, and I completed the course with an actual diploma.

I got a job straight away in the canteen inside the twenty-eight-storey CIS Tower office block in Manchester city centre. The CIS Tower was Manchester's first skyscraper, inspired by Chicago buildings, and built in 1962 to house the Co-operative Insurance Society. For years it was the only skyscraper in the city, standing four hundred feet high – Manchester's first building taller than the nineteenth-century Town Hall tower. An anomalous brutalist landmark, its corporate logo on top gave it a very futuristic appearance. It remained the tallest building in the city until overtaken by the Beetham Hilton Tower in 2006, which helped balance the then skimpy city skyline before Manchester's twenty-first-century building boom began.

The food wasn't very adventurous, but it was a great place to work. I started in the downstairs kitchen and was soon moved up to the executive restaurant on the twenty-fourth floor, almost at the top of the building. From there, the view stretched for miles across the Pennines to the north and east, Cheshire to the south, and even Wales to the southwest.

I was working on the executive floor on 8 May 1979 when the six-storey Woolworths on the other side of Piccadilly Gardens caught fire – the kind of shop fire that hadn't happened since the Second World War – leading to the deaths of ten people.

It was during the lunch service at about 2 o'clock when we saw thick black smoke billowing out of the building and licks of lethal-looking flames – the burning of cheap furniture making what started as a small fire many times worse. A damaged electric cable ignited the foam fillings. All of us in the restaurant could see what was happening, watching the fire brigade frantically getting their ladders open. There were hundreds of people trapped inside, and you could see some pouring out of the front doors, climbing out of windows and even running across the roof. There were bars on the windows of the upper floor, and firemen were hacking away, trying to break them open. It was horrible, and it was stated later in an official report that Woolworths was a 'death trap', with the flammable furniture releasing toxic smoke and the number of obstructions that were in the way of people being able to get out. After considerable campaigning, the fire led to the banning, a few years later, of flammable foam in furniture.

A few weeks after the fire, as if to confirm subconsciously that the eruptive Manchester of *Spiral Scratch*, the Electric Circus, The Ranch and Rafters had passed and the new scene had burnt out, I had an attack of wanderlust – the same impulse that had first sent me off to Greece. Nick had stayed there, Rob was busy with Factory and Joy Division, having fun witnessing at close range the madness generated by Tony Wilson's energy, and Martin had gone to university in Sheffield, taking *Modern Drugs* with him.

I'd go and see him occasionally, and he'd found himself in a small but active Sheffield scene, surrounded by The Human League, Cabaret Voltaire and Clock DVA – all with their own lovingly warped sense of the electronic future of music. I felt a little on my own, so I went off looking to see what was out there.

A friend at work was going out with a girl who was half-Dutch, and they mentioned that they were going away for the summer to work in the Western Frisian Islands – a wild, remote archipelago stretching across the northern coast of the Netherlands. She had distant relatives there and said you could get a job serving in cafes and washing up, while sleeping in a large campsite.

It sounded good to me. My Greek trip had shaken things up, and I'd fallen for the idea of Europe – how, when I was there, things just seemed to happen. It felt like I needed some more of that: something unexpected that hadn't happened to me for a while in Manchester.

12
A girl with dyed red hair

When I arrived, it was much more remote than I had imagined. Even on the main island where I stayed, Terschelling, there were next to no cars – most people travelled around on bicycles. You arrived at a small pier on a ferry from Den Helder in the far north of the Netherlands, and the landscape seemed to be nothing but sand dunes, farmland and a few houses.

The town was tiny, with a few bars and restaurants, and it was clearly a well-kept secret even among the Dutch. Walking around, there seemed to be more sheep than people. I exaggerated how much of a chef I was and got a job in a bistro, lived in a big tent on the campsite – mostly filled with hippy types – and stayed there for a few months, a colder reprise of my Greek days.

A girl with dyed red hair visited a couple of times, somewhere in a Dutch hinterland between hippy and punk. She seemed really interesting – much more knowing and mysterious than many girls I met in Manchester. I got to know her; she was called Gonnie Rietveld and was from Rotterdam. We bonded over music, and she was curious about the stories I was telling her about what was happening in Manchester – how music and the fashion that came with it were remaking and rebuilding the city, perhaps even more than orthodox cultural influences.

In September, at the end of the season, she said, 'Why don't you come back to Rotterdam with me?' It sounded like Manchester the way she talked about it – always fighting to get out of the shadow of Amsterdam just as Manchester was constantly defying the unedifying dominance of London. It had been bombarded during the war like Manchester, and was needing rebuilding and revamping, and the locals were as tough talking and suspicious of bullshit. In the winter of 1979, I moved in with her and her mum and brother, Reinier, in Rotterdam.

You had to have some sort of stamp in your passport to stay in Europe in those days. I got a reference from the bistro on Terschelling, added even more exaggeration about how much catering and professional cooking I'd done in Manchester – as a head chef! – and found a job in the kitchen at the Rotterdam Hilton. After working there for a month I could go to the local police station, get myself a stamp, and stay in the country for a certain amount of time.

It was hard work, so I left once I'd got my stamp and was back to thinking about work. I was enjoying it in Rotterdam, seeing loads of gigs with Gonnie because, like Manchester, it was one of those cities regularly on the touring itinerary of international acts. As always, I needed money, but decided to stay in Rotterdam. There was an atmosphere there that I liked – the way the Dutch lived their lives seemed so much more logical than back home. They had a more focused view of how the city's regeneration first developed with its art, music and culture, and I talked with Gonnie about actually making music and forming a group.

I found out that if you worked somewhere for six months, when you left they'd pay you unemployment benefit equal to what you'd been earning. I found work in the canteen at a shipping and transport college on the River Meuse, where they taught students who were going to run the barges that ran throughout Europe from where the Rhine–Meuse–Scheldt delta enters the North Sea.

From where I worked, I could see the famous post-war Trans Europe Express line that Kraftwerk mythologised, watching the trains on their journey through Europe from the Netherlands to Switzerland. The sight completely captivated me. I felt part of Europe – an internationalist – whereas being in Bramhall, despite all the Manchester life nearby, had often made me feel provincial and small. To see the train that travelled across the continent, this icon of connection, filled me with a powerful sense of possibility.

After six months in the college canteen I quit, and the Dutch government, as promised, effectively paid my wages for the next few months. I wasn't sponging – I had plenty of plans for what I wanted to do, inspired by the projects Rob Gretton had been involved with back in Manchester, by the electronic society Martin belonged to in Sheffield, and by how what was happening in Rotterdam reminded me of Manchester two or three years earlier. Scenes were vital then – a form of political activism and resistance – created by a few people wanting to belong to something, which in Manchester and Sheffield became movements. Having money coming in meant I didn't need to worry about earning while I tried to make things happen and become part of a scene.

Rotterdam was its own happening: an open-minded place, a big city yet, like Manchester, strangely intimate, with an underdog attitude where people said exactly what was on their minds. It was becoming an ever-shifting meeting place for all kinds of music and musicians, poets and nomadic aesthetes. Many had come over from New York because of the easy access to drugs of all kinds, including heroin. So, alongside the grungy, shamanic early electropunk coming in from Germany and Belgium, there was the crazed variety of New York no wave acts, many of them on the wild and smart Ze label.

James White and the Blacks used to play there all the time, hyperactively cramming punk, free jazz, demented disco and zonked funk into one dark, infectious groove. Joseph Bowie's Defunkt were Rotterdam regulars and mixed extremist intensity with deadly, danceable rhythms – without which the Red Hot Chili Peppers would have been clueless. Tuxedomoon saw nothing wrong with mixing synths and saxophones, already pushing experimental electronic music beyond post-punk.

With the almost philanthropic support of the Dutch government and the local council, who looked after their people almost to a fault, I did something I never would have done at home and learnt to play the saxophone. I loved the way it careered through the post-punk funk of Defunkt and Tuxedomoon. As part of an unemployment scheme in Rotterdam, you could get saxophone lessons for about a pound a session. I had a brilliant teacher who taught me the basics and how to circular breathe, and within weeks I could make some noise to go with the rhythms Gonnie and I were hearing in our heads.

This combination of downtown New York insubordination and European bohemianism was all in front of us in Rotterdam, mixed up in our heads with the British electronica we liked – much of it on Daniel Miller's Mute label – and the disco and soul we enjoyed. Influences had gone wild; you might play something electronically beguiling on Mute by Thomas Leer, Fad Gadget or Robert Rental, then follow it with something from Motown by Marvin Gaye or Stevie Wonder. Through the haze of some heavenly local weed, the two things mysteriously merged in your mind. It helped us find the sound for the group we formed, Quando Quango, which seemed to have a Ze ring to it, and you couldn't quite work out where it came from.

The 'quando' was very European – it could be Italian, Spanish or French – while the 'quango' came with me from England, where in the seventies the idea of the 'quango' was endlessly debated as fringe policy bodies associated with the government, but independent. It was a nonsense word that had become the centre of serious political debate. Our use probably arose from a late-night, stoned conversation, jamming together a couple of words as if we were jamming punk and funk. It was dance music, but coming from this raw mix of New York, Manchester, Rotterdam and somewhere as yet unspecified, we were drawn to the dissonant.

We started playing to friends and friends of friends at parties in a squat that had taken over a disused waterworks along the river. Gonnie's brother Reinier was on drums, Gonnie triggered synths and sequencers, while I blew sax and shouted. It wasn't great – which made it kind of great. We'd find a rhythm, throw a load of noise on top and give it a title. It made us happy, which was a good start.

There was no thought of making money, or even, early on, making records; it was simply being in the moment and seeing where you went next. If you had the space – and we had this perfect post-industrial building to experiment with, run as a creative commune with no grown-up outside influence – you felt you could do anything.

We played a handful of early gigs in front of a few paying customers, and I noticed it helped that I was from Manchester and was English. The Rotterdam audience for these kinds of new hybrids loved music coming from outside and looked down on local versions, hoodwinked into believing it was only authentic if it was from New York or England. If Gonnie introduced the songs, the audience would drift to the bar. When I introduced us and spoke before the songs, even if the song was in Dutch, it was like, 'Oooh, English. Manchester! That's where it's happening.'

To an extent, there was truth in it. I'd come over as a kind of innocent expert, witnessing and contributing to the emergence of a scene, having experienced punk arrive in Manchester. It inspired locals to form bands, manage them, print fanzines, design posters, find venues, become DJs and even release records. Fans turned into creators without initially realising it was happening.

I started DJing, just playing records as I had at parties and youth clubs back home, and now in Rotterdam, where I thought I could play better music than whoever was DJing. The sound systems were always great, so it felt like the next step on from playing in someone's house or a draughty church hall.

There was a cafe where the DJ would get too stoned to carry on, and I'd take over for a little while. I didn't speak or anything, never said what I was playing – it was just one record after another that I reckoned suited the mood at the time, something I sensed in how people stood around a room, how they responded to a certain record. I taught myself to DJ using two Technics decks and a mixer, following my own instincts.

There was a hall, Hal 4, attached to the waterworks where I started putting on events called Rotterdam Must Dance. We cleared it out, brought in a generator, built a temporary stage and called it Utopia. I began to learn how playing records could itself be a musical performance. There'd be a particular change in the air, in the eyes of those present, when you moved from, say, 'Jingo' by Candido to The Normal's 'T.V.O.D.'. Two different sound worlds and timelines collided and coalesced, and in the middle of an ordinary night in the middle of nowhere, for just a handful of people, there'd be a minor revelation. You could go from Chic's 'Good Times' to The Cure's 'A Forest' and there was a kind of freedom to it that seemed somehow important. Playing Chic confused the locals, because they saw it as a pop record, so it became a subversive act. In a way, to the Dutch, playing Chic was weirder than playing Suicide. Crown Heights Affair seemed stranger than Throbbing Gristle.

The Dutch weren't really dancers, they were listeners, even to the New York music with its combination of avant-garde noise and dance rhythms, so the night was a radical idea, even to simply use the word 'dance'. To locals with more of a reflective, rock counter-culture sensibility, suspicious of trends and fads, dance music meant disco, which at the time was becoming so commercialised it seemed to be the devil's music.

I made it obvious this was no disco by the way we presented the night and designed its flyers, using collages of cryptic information, and through the bands I started booking from scenes I knew back home. I would put on Rotterdam versions of the Factory nights at the Russell Club, one featuring Tony's boys, The Durutti Column and A Certain Ratio, plus new Factory group Section 25, who had taken the electronics lurking in Joy Division a step further.

I brought over The Human League for one of their first shows with their new lineup after one half of the group had become Heaven 17. They had added a couple of teenage female backing singers they'd found on a night out in a Sheffield nightclub. Initially, this seemed a desperate act, as though the cleverness had left the group with Heaven 17, but it was soon seen as a conceptual masterstroke. At the time, it still didn't give much clue that one of Sheffield's oblique, if playful, futuristic electronic units would soon be topping the charts as a household name. Sheffield was about to go pop.

I also put on Captain Beefheart, with his Dutch roots and influence on bands like Pere Ubu, and emerging mysterious European electro-art acts like Allez Allez and Liaisons Dangereuses. This made it clear there could be a connection between the underground and dance, between seriousness and pleasure. A Movement could, and should, include movement. It was outside the bounds of corporate and political control. Dancing was a form of liberation.

Anything to do with music was attractive to me, especially if it also involved travel. I started working for the largest concert promoters in Holland, MOJO, who began small in the late 1960s as hippy fans of the Doors and Jefferson Airplane, taking their name from the old Muddy Waters song.

Dutch crews had a good reputation working on big tours by international acts. American groups would often pick up the Dutch crew and use them throughout Europe. Initially, I was only humping equipment and doing a lot of dogsbody work, but if you got on one of the larger European tours, it was well paid – one hundred guilders a day when a month's rent in Rotterdam wasn't much more than fifty.

The bonus was the kind of acts I was working backstage for: Stevie Wonder, Abba, The Rolling Stones, Boomtown Rats, Robert Palmer, Randy Newman – and even watching Julio Iglesias was an education. He played the Rotterdam Ahoy, which had very steep sides, and his fans would throw flowers and all sorts of clothing at him. I had to wear a hard hat because something might hit your head and rip it open. He used this line every night – 'Why do you love me? I'm so skinny.' His band would be in hysterics. By the time Bruce Springsteen was going on his River Tour in 1981, I was doing the lights, following him with the main spotlight.

The highlight for me was working some of the shows on the Kraftwerk Man-Machine tour, right in the middle of that astonishing run of albums: *Autobahn*, *The Man-Machine* and *Computer World*. Before the show, they would be quietly sat backstage, and I would be sent out to find the macrobiotic food they wanted to eat.

The crew and band would all eat it together, barely a word being said, like Kraftwerk were monks who'd taken a vow of silence, and then they'd do the show, sometimes leaving it to their robot replacements. We'd be backstage with Kraftwerk joining in with one of their rituals while the audience were watching Kraftwerk on stage. They'd slip away from the backstage area and take their position on stage, then materialise backstage a little later for a few more mouthfuls of rice while their robots took over. Once or twice, I swore I saw one or two of them smile ever so gently, which was a shock to the system.

Their sound system was just astonishing, so the music was all space and power. They'd taken on board Giorgio Moroder's electronic disco for Donna Summer and arranged it as the most dreamlike technofunk. One of the things they'd taken from the modern discotheque was how in the disco the spotlight was on the audience, whereas in a rock show it was only on the performers, and often, only the singer. To Kraftwerk, this awed attention on the individual seemed fascistic. They were finding ways to shift that emphasis, and their shows, with their exquisite disco flow and very deliberate theatrical setting, already dabbling with virtual reality, were unlike anything else, before or since.

Feeding Kraftwerk and sitting quietly with them – while they were apparently performing – seemed the height of glamour. At that point, it seemed I would never have to leave Rotterdam to get what I wanted. I was close to the absolute centre of everything I loved musically, feeling as European as Kraftwerk in a country that seemed socially better organised than England. I was performing music, playing music, working with the best musicians in the world, and still mixing with my friends and favourites from Britain who I could invite to play in Rotterdam.

With his natural charm and ability to talk his way through life, Martin Fry from Bramhall had insinuated himself into the electronic music scene in Sheffield, which had been sparked by Kraftwerk's performance at Sheffield University in October 1976 in much the same way the Manchester punk scene had been triggered by the Sex Pistols' Lesser Free Trade Hall gigs a few months earlier.

We'd kept in touch the way you did then, with occasional phone calls that could seem as though you were talking to another planet, and he told me about a Sheffield trio called Vice Versa he'd interviewed for his *Modern Drugs* fanzine. They had their own label, Neutron, and they released a few singles that were well received in the music press. They loved playing around with the paraphernalia of being in a group – the merchandise, badges, press releases, posters, and even a video.

They were inspired by the energy and social commentary of punk but, being from Sheffield, they wanted to use tape machines, a Korg

Minipops drum machine they'd bought cheap off a club singer, and various effects – with a serious intention to bring avant-garde ideas into the mainstream. There was something in the water in Sheffield that generated all these electronic musicians, but also, because of the effects of deindustrialisation, there were plenty of spaces that once produced steel goods that were now empty where groups could rehearse and make a lot of loud noise, much of which didn't sound like songs.

Like Martin, Vice Versa were Bowie and Bolan fans who also liked the sleek organisation of Chic, John Foxx-era Ultravox, the electronic post-punk of The Normal, and the conceptual mystique of Throbbing Gristle. After a few minutes of the interview, finding out they shared similar ideas about the future of music, Mark White and Stephen Singleton asked him to join the group, replacing the third member, David Sydenham.

I got them a short tour with Young Marble Giants and some small gigs in Rotterdam and further out in Holland and Belgium, for about £150 or so. It was easy for them to tour, using backing tracks and their portable Wasp synthesisers. They'd drive over in a car with all the equipment they needed. Their shows, despite the primitive quality of their equipment, were noisy, energetic, and a little deranged. Mark was the intense singer, Stephen chanted along, with Martin as sidekick throwing shapes, looking severe and dropping in some random noises on his synth.

Vice Versa were over once when I was having trouble with the Dutch authorities, and my playing the immigration system was getting a little edgy. I was due to drive them to Belgium to play Plan K in Brussels, an old sugar refinery that had been turned into an arts centre on Rue de Manchester, where Michel Duval and Annik Honore had started putting on events. Their opening concert on 16 October 1979, brought together Joy Division, playing abroad for the first time, and Cabaret Voltaire with William Burroughs, which is exactly where the serious European fans of Factory-based music felt it belonged. The married Ian Curtis of Joy Division had met Annik a couple of months before, when she interviewed the group after a show at the Nashville, and then spent the night at an ad hoc after show party with Curtis and the group listening to David Bowie's *Low*, until everyone but her fell asleep.

She became actively involved with Joy Division through the formation of the Factory-associated Factory Benelux label, and the avant-deluxe post-Factory imprint Les Disques Du Crepuscule that released Joy Division's unbelievably stately 'Atmosphere'. I liked her, and loved the projects she worked on, but she was a bit too intense for me – probably intense like some fans thought Joy Division were, when in fact, off stage, outside their songs, they just wanted to have a laugh and enjoy their freedom. I think Ian was drawn to Annik's intensity – the books she read, the films she watched. She was a European intellectual, which was where his mind secretly belonged, I suppose, if not obviously so in Manchester. Even among the most cerebral of Manchester bands, it was still Boddies and football. It was still strangely risky to appear too arty in Manchester.

Annik was involved in the arts scene, up on all the new post-punk groups – or cold wave, as the Belgians called it – and, to put it bluntly, Ian's wife Debbie wasn't. When Joy Division played Plan K, they played the song that would be considered the ballad of Ian and Annik's romance, 'Love Will Tear Us Apart'. They'd only met a few times, but the song made their brief alliance seem intimately epic, and his suicide a few months later feel inevitable. The song was a kind of premonition – both of a heightened romance with a mystery woman so unlike his wife, and of the confession of one.

Vice Versa were playing Plan K a few weeks after Ian Curtis had died by suicide, caught between domestic life with Debbie and their new child, and his feelings for Annik and the Europe that came with her. Communication was sketchy at the time, and the news of his death wasn't likely to appear in the mainstream press. In our little world, Joy Division were hugely important, but their debut album *Unknown Pleasures*, for all the strong reviews and music-paper coverage, had sold only a few thousand copies.

I heard about Ian's death a few days after it happened. Someone told me in Rotterdam, once the weekly music papers had come out, and I rang Rob in a state of confusion – 'What the fuck is going on? Ian's dead?'

'Sorry, yeah, a lot going on', he mumbled. He sounded the same as usual – dead matter-of-fact – but at the same time he sounded exhausted. He was being to the point, yet missing it by a mile. He didn't know what to say. Neither did I. He asked where I was. 'I'm in Holland.' 'Oh, you're still there. What's it like out there? Anything happening?'

He briefly told me what had happened with Ian – yeah, he'd killed himself. They'd had to cancel the upcoming Joy Division American tour; it was a bit of a mess. I asked what they were going to do. He said, almost as though thinking it for the first time but it was bloody obvious, 'Well, I'd like them to carry on. They'll have to use a different name. Joy Division is finished. Anyway, speak soon.'

I remember thinking a bit later, well, I've heard Bernard sing – so if he's the new lead singer, good luck with that.

I'd been with them only a few months before. Joy Division had come over in January 1980 to play Rotterdam, at the council-run Lantaren, which was promoting a lot of post-punk groups like Gang of Four and The Cure. My final memory of them with Ian is of me, Gonnie and the group racing around Rotterdam on the little bikes we'd hired – laughing our heads off, getting stoned, playing jokes on people, and listening to the maddest dance music we could find.

Ian had his problems – we knew about his illness, his epilepsy – but he seemed so alive in Rotterdam, enjoying the city, these first trips abroad. For all the depth and insight of his lyrics, he was still a provincial lad, just beginning to see the world.

The gig itself was chaotic and spectacular – the kind of thing I'd got used to with Rob's enterprises. For some reason, when they performed, the usual elevated stage had been taken out. The band were on the same level as the audience, who stood right next to them at eye level as they played this incredibly dramatic music, with Ian flying around, pushing himself to the limit as he did more and more right in front of everyone – like it was someone's front room. It felt like the gigs inside The Ranch, so the group took it in their stride. I said to Rob, 'Why is there no stage?' 'I don't know.' 'Well, was it there when you did the soundcheck?' 'No.'

He said he'd assumed the stage would rise up for the show. No one had checked. He shrugged his shoulders and gave one of his dopey smiles. He enjoyed the mistakes, the slip-ups, as much as the triumphs and successes. It kept everyone on their toes; it was part of the adventure. Maybe he was thinking, this is nothing – wait until we encounter a real tragedy.

After the show, the promoter and a few others who spoke to me were absolutely furious that this group they associated with William Burroughs, Pere Ubu and Throbbing Gristle were so immature – larking around and having little to say about their 'art'. They thought they behaved like yobbos. One guy was ranting – probably thinking of the beautiful, dark and cosmic Saville sleeve for their debut album *Unknown Pleasures*, and Hannett's moody production – 'I was expecting an artistic group, but you're a bunch of thugs!' 'Yeah, we're from Manchester', I said. If Tony had been around, he would have added, 'We do things differently there.' There was a lot of confusion, and laconic Rob being their manager only added to it.

Looking back, it feels like ages after Ian had died that I was driving Vice Versa to Brussels for the Plan K show. In reality, it was only a few days. I couldn't get back to Manchester for the funeral because I didn't have the money, and I was also dealing with visa and work problems. It wasn't really talked about, and life went on.

On the way to Brussels, leaving Vice Versa in the car outside, I had to stop off for a job interview at a prison in Rotterdam, where I'd been sent after reaching the limit of my dole payments. I needed another six-month job to extend my stay.

The prison seemed more like a holiday camp compared with British ones, but as I didn't want the job, the moment the doors slammed behind me and I was inside the building, I pretended I had claustrophobia. The official interviewing me quickly realised I had no interest in the position and was there only because I'd been told to attend. 'You don't want this job, do you?' I admitted I didn't. I said the idea of being in contact with prisoners made me nervous – and anyway, I couldn't speak Dutch, so I wouldn't be much use.

'Ah', he said. 'I'll put it in my report that you don't speak Dutch well enough to work here.' That meant I had to go to night school and learn to speak Dutch. I'd sit in this dreary room with a bunch of Moroccan and Turkish kids, but I did learn – and it bought me a few more months in Rotterdam. Technically, though, things were getting trickier and trickier as an immigrant.

I raced out of the prison back to the hire car and managed to get a nonplussed Vice Versa to Brussels and Plan K on time. They played a great show of fanatical electro – Martin moving like a maniac, none of them smiling once – which satisfied the locals, all dressed in black.

To save money, they would sleep on the floor of my flat, and they started to talk about making their music a little funkier, even changing their name. There was a pop group hiding inside these experimental noise makers.

We'd go to this Rotterdam record shop I loved called Backstreet Records, run by Peter Graute. He was known as Peter Backstreet and played a significant role in bringing those New York no wave acts to Rotterdam. He was a specialist in music that could be filed under 'danceable weird shit'.

Peter's record shop had this lounge – the pop corner – where you could take records you were interested in and play them, smoke some weed, and they had great punk, post-punk and electro records. We noticed there that what Vice Versa were doing was becoming a crowded little niche market. They felt they'd done all they could as this warped, whimsical synth trio and were looking to expand their concept, becoming more of a self-consciously stylish performance art pop group in the tradition of Roxy Music and Sparks.

Peter also ran a record label attached to the shop, called Backstreet Backlash, and had access to a small recording studio nearby, operated by his friend, the recording engineer Martin Van der Leer. On a day off from the mini Netherlands tour I had organised, we all went down to the studio to mess about, with Vice Versa using the instruments and synths lying around. They came up with a couple of electro-primitive pop songs that became their final single, a grand, obscure 'farewell' released on Backstreet Backlash, titled 'Stilyagi' and 'Eyes of Christ'. It was the first time I had been in a recording studio, and the first time I was credited on a record sleeve.

As the session was coming to an end, more people started arriving, and it turned into a party. Martin began making up lyrics and singing them over a simple groove – something about Samuel Beckett: 'Do do do the funky Beckett' – and some nonsense about Rotterdam, with Mark playing a scratchy, punky Chic guitar sound. Getting carried away, rhyming 'Rotterdam' with 'pots of jam' and 'leg of lamb', lanky northern Martin started going all James Brown on us. We were in hysterics, but the funny thing was, he had a strong singing voice, which no one knew about, including himself.

Vice Versa drove home, and a few days later Martin rang me – they were now called ABC, and he was their singer. An avant-garde electronic band on their own independent label with a limited budget, sleeping on my floor, were on their way to signing with a major label, making charts around the world, travelling first class and staying in five-star hotels. And I'd witnessed the moment when one thing began to become the other – which made me think: the recording studio is an amazing place. I wanted more of it.

13
A new order

Hooky, Bernard and Stephen of the shattered Joy Division – with Rob – carried on as a new group, the same but different, with a new name, each of them taking turns singing. Rob was right: what else could they do but carry on. On 30 July 1980 they played at the Beach Club, opened by Richard Boon and Tony's wife Lindsay Reade, as the No-Names, replacing the ethereal cold wave of the Names from Belgium, who couldn't make it.

From the very beginning, the three remaining members had no wish to play anything by Joy Division, and their early shows were as much rehearsals and works in progress as settled performances. They were feeling their way through a fog.

The Beach was inside a small pub on Newgate Street, round the back of the Arndale Centre, and while knowledge of Joy Division grew on the back of a rock and roll suicide that sent 'Love Will Tear Us Apart' into the charts, they were beginning again in one of the venues of a shadowy new Manchester scene. They were doing it the hard way, as if Joy Division had nothing to do with them, even while they remained under its shadow.

In September, for a couple of shows in the north and then on the east coast of America, where they had been due to go as Joy Division, they were slowly taking shape, introducing electronics and backing tapes, driven by sheer perseverance, and hearing a new sound in the clubs of New York they visited while they were there.

They tried one of Tony's left-field ideas for a new singer – Factory's psych-folk troubadour Kevin Hewick from Leicester, whom he was fond of at the time – but that didn't work out, and it was decided that Bernard's voice was the least shaky. For the fourth member they clearly needed, Rob felt they should find someone nobody would expect, yet someone who had to come from within the group, which was now more than ever a family.

He suggested Stephen's girlfriend, Gillian, who was then studying graphic design at Stockport College, and suddenly, with barely any musical experience, she was thrown into a uniquely complicated situation. They called her their apprentice. It was a classic Rob idea, fulfilling his role as an extra member of the group – outside yet inside – and it solved many problems they hadn't even realised they'd face. They had been hanging by a thread, and now they were complete, Gillian understanding better than anyone the group's strange dynamic – a mix of nonchalance and complete commitment.

Rob told me about the first show with Gillian at The Squat in Manchester at the end of October, and in his own low-key way he seemed excited that this New Order was going to work. For a group whose previous name had been taken from those given to brothels in Nazi concentration camps, Rob's initial idea – to call the new line-up the New Order of the Kampuchean Front – was a little too political for the rest of them, who wanted something more neutral this time. They were happy to settle on simply New Order. Gillian, innocently enough, thought it referred only to the group's 'new order', while Rob would smirk knowingly when I said it still seemed to carry ideological overtones. He also mentioned, almost in passing, that he, Tony and Alan were looking for new premises for what Factory had been doing at the Russell Club in Hulme. There should be a bit of money coming in from Joy Division, and they wanted to find somewhere nearer the city centre.

We decided between us that New Order should come over to Rotterdam to play Hal 4 for my Rotterdam Must Dance night. They performed on 18 December 1980 – their first European show. They were unmistakably a new group, and some of what they were doing had begun to flicker with sharp, danceable rhythms, as a rock line-up evolved into something more fluid with electronics and drum machine. You could hear the influence of Kraftwerk, Ian's great favourite; there was a hint of Sheffield that reminded me of Vice Versa, and a touch of the weird, danceable stuff that felt just right in that big hall in an industrial city by the water, surrounded by wasteland.

Rob, fast becoming an authority on all sorts of arcane areas, was impressed by what we'd managed with the venue and its atmosphere, built up from scratch in a derelict, squatted part of town. He enthused – as much as he ever did – about the idea of opening a new club in Manchester, something like the underground nightclubs that had sprung up in New York to play post-punk-influenced dance music now that disco had been ruined. They were more than just dance floors. Those clubs tended to be located in edgy districts and no-go zones; it seemed part of the experience – leave behind the damaged, abandoned outside, and head into dazzling signs of transformation where rhythm transmitted possibility.

'Things are picking up in Manchester', he said to me, 'you should come back and have a look'. He said it would be great if I could help him with this new Factory club. It seemed more his dream than Tony's – maybe Alan also fancied it; Peter and Martin not so much – and he planted a nagging feeling inside me that maybe I was missing out on something.

I was happy in Rotterdam, feeling European, meeting Kraftwerk, making things happen, seeing scenes form, but Gonnie was thinking of going to university in England. I wanted to stay, but part of me wanted to go back and join Rob. Bureaucracy forced my hand. The local authorities were losing patience with me and beginning to realise how I was playing the system. I attended a routine appointment with the police department responsible for immigrant stays, thinking I was just going to get the stamp I needed in my passport to stay a few more months. Instead, they kept hold of my passport, told me I had overstayed my welcome, your time's up. They were pretty horrible to me, which I wasn't used to in Holland, and I snapped – well, I don't care, I'm going home anyway. When can I have my passport? They said when you've got a ticket home. Right, I'll let you know when I'm ready to leave and you can send my passport round to me flat. Oh, no, they said. You'll have to come and collect it. I almost felt a big Dutch door slam behind me. It was definitely time to go home. I half thought, I bet Rob has set this up.

I'd always loved waiting by a quayside for ferries on my trips around Europe. Life was still for a moment, and you were about to head into the unknown. But as I was waiting for the North Sea ferry to take me to Hull and then home, I felt a bit uneasy. I loved Europe. I would be going back to a very different lifestyle than I had in Rotterdam. But I loved Rob and New Order and what was happening with Factory. I loved British music. I missed the football; I missed City.

The ferry trip sailed overnight, and there was a disco on board, usually filled with sad blokes getting really drunk on their own as the boat rocked and the music pounded before they went back to life, work, family. Yeah, I thought as I headed back to Bramhall, a couple of people almost miserably dancing to Abba in the disco, Rob's words ringing in my ears that he thought would bring me home – we'll have a laugh.

Yeah, I thought …

Manchester must dance.

Part II

Playing

14
A caper

I was back in Manchester in March 1982, and with nowhere to stay and not wanting to go back into my parents' house in Bramhall, I moved into Rob and Lesley's big, detached house in Chorlton Village, which they were doing up. I thought it would only be for a short while, but I ended up living there for the next four years, rent free, which was really the time it took to get The Haçienda up and running. There was no time for me to sort out my life while we were trying to sort out what to do with the club – how to make it work, how to take the premise of a Black, gay New York club and merge that with what had become in Hulme, a left-of-centre indie/new wave rock club.

Rob was also running New Order, which could be described as the second most complicated job in town after running The Haçienda, with his Factory work the most complicated part-time job. I was immediately part of this complication, doing a job that was never specifically defined or titled, but which essentially meant sticking close to him as he drifted between managing an eccentric group, an eccentric club and an eccentric record label. His ambition to never have a proper job meant he ended up juggling a series of roles that were always in motion, yet he acted as if none of it was work.

Ostensibly, based on what he saw I had been doing in Rotterdam, Rob asked me to book acts and sort out the DJs. Inevitably, it was never as clean or as clear as that. I became his sidekick, working alongside Rob in the way Alan worked alongside Tony. No one worked for anyone else at Factory – it was as equal as possible – and everyone did what they could to muck in and make it work. Everyone helped each other out, even if it meant getting in each other's way. It was all based on Tony's northern socialist belief that people should not live and exist in isolation but work in co-operation – which looked good on paper but was difficult to apply to running a nightclub, at least the sort not built to utopian principles.

In Alan's case, helping out meant making a virtue out of splendid vagueness – and contributing the common sense of a realist who spent most of his time dreaming, and partnering Tony in the established local ritual of smoking draw, at times to a Rastafarian degree.

Probably because Rob slyly timed it well, I was introduced into the Factory inner circle when Tony and Alan were comfortably high – disappearing into the smoke filling Alan's sprawling flat on Palatine Road in Didsbury where, astonishingly, early Factory was conceived and planned. Tony never turned a hair when Rob brought me into the fold, trusting Rob knew what he was doing, although he could never quite work me out – sometimes, like Rob, I was a yob from Wythenshawe, other times I hailed from a leafy suburb of Stockport, both of which were delivered as healthy insults and signs of respect. I was just Rob's mate for a while, even as I went to Factory board meetings, made records for the label and booked acts for the club. I could have put it as my occupation in a passport: Rob's mate. Moving from watching Tony on television to working alongside him happened very naturally, because he acted the same off screen as he did on it – except off screen there were more obviously drugs. Everything about life and living was a performance to him, and everyone around him was there to help the performance.

Rob and I were inseparable for the next few years, not least because one of my designated tasks was being his driver – I'd drive him everywhere, including City matches. He could drive, had just passed his driving test and had recently bought one of the earliest Audi Quattros in the country, which had only started production in 1980. It was a real fuck off high performance car, but a bit too high performance for Rob. He was ready to become a driver of this flash car, but when he took delivery he couldn't drive it. Or, he didn't want to drive it. He didn't like it, or he didn't like the roads he would have to drive it on.

Maybe he preferred to stay in the passenger seat to keep up with Alan and Tony's weed-smoking numbers. I had to learn the certified Wilson technique of being able to roll joints on my knees while driving. I'd soon learn an everyday greeting of Rob's: 'What are you doing?' 'Nothing, Rob.' 'What should you be doing?' That was the cue for me to get out a packet of Rizlas.

He was particularly perturbed by motorways, which we needed for our trips to watch City play away. He said to me, 'The bends are too long.' I would tell him there were no bends on a motorway, they're straight. 'No', he insisted, 'a motorway must curve. It has to.' He was right; there were slow curves built into motorways to ensure drivers subconsciously concentrated and didn't crash. He felt the curves, there but not there, would ruin his concentration and cause him to crash. This summed up Rob's beautifully disjointed thinking about things – break through the outside pig-headedness to find unassailable logic.

Driving to football would usually be futile, as Rob's timekeeping was abysmal. He was always slow switching between one task and another, with the kind of optimism that thought if he needed to be somewhere at three, then you left the house at three – as though he could magically transport himself wherever he was meant to be. He felt that people who were always on time were uptight and not to be trusted. This often meant we'd arrive at a match at half time, then decide to drive straight back home, because City never scored in the second half.

Rob's home office was the centre of New Order operations, and with Lesley as Factory office manager striving to give inner rigour to the label's precarious business practises, we would get early test pressings of their records.

A few days after I got back from Rotterdam, I heard the test pressing of New Order's fourth single 'Temptation' 12-inch, which they had produced themselves. More fractured than the shapely 7-inch, where New Order proved whatever else they might be they were always a fantastic pop group, it hit me that it was more a New York dance record than an indie post-punk rock record – the kind of thing I would have played during one of my Rotterdam sets. In hindsight, it was as though they were composing a soundtrack to the hoped-for transition from the straight indie and proto-gothic nature of the Russell Club to The Haçienda, intended to be a Manchester extension of the underground nightclubs that played the best, hardest, most danceable music in New York. I would tell Rob, 'This isn't a rock record, it's a club record.' It would break through the clubs, while Rob and I would plug the 7-inch ourselves, driving down to London and blagging our way into the Radio 1 offices – two stoned Mancs grinning inanely, telling these Radio 1 producers they should be playing the New Order single.

It would have been sad and pathetic if it wasn't for the fact it was a fantastic record. Even those producers who couldn't play it had to admit that. Or they just wanted to get rid of us.

When we were together all the time, when it never occurred to us there was anything beyond the time we were living in, let alone beyond the eighties, it led to some great moments as City fans and work colleagues.

I came over from Rotterdam for the FA Cup Final at the old Wembley Stadium against the Tottenham of the Argentines Ossie Ardiles and Ricky Villa in 1981. City were unexpectedly in with a chance of a cup after a few years of comings and goings. Since October, they'd been managed by John Bond, who had replaced the sadly declining Malcolm Allison earlier in the season and lifted us from the bottom of the First Division by the scruff of our necks. I'd got a ticket, Rob hadn't, but we headed there together, for some reason thinking we could swap my ticket for two lesser-priced ones.

We got off the tube and we spotted Andy Peebles, the Radio I disc jockey who had once worked for Piccadilly Radio. The year before, he'd done the last interview with John Lennon before he was shot in New York.

Rob, being in a Rob mood, thought that maybe he had a spare ticket, and he sort of joined in with Peebles' stride and introduced himself: 'Rob Gretton, manager of New Order. Have you got a spare ticket for the match?'

Peebles and the friend he was with, thinking they were being accosted by some random Manc ruffian – which in many ways they were – ran off as fast as they could, Rob chasing them down the stairs toward Wembley Way. 'I'm from Factory Records! Help me out!' I said, 'You've scared them off, Rob.'

Rob got into the match, slipping in through the turnstile before me and saying to the ticket collector, 'I don't suppose you're up for a bribe, are you?' Which he was! We were in. It was an old Rob trick. Hand over a note or two, push up his glasses, another match for free.

We lost the final after a replay to one of the greatest goals ever scored at Wembley by the Argentine Villa. Sometimes, though, the match was not necessarily what the day was about. It was something to wrap an adventure around.

My greatest Rob match day event was the same year, in the semi-final against Bobby Robson's First Division champions Ipswich on 11 April, who we beat one–nil despite being underdogs, so we could have our hearts broken by Spurs in the final. The night before, New Order, supported by Dutch post-punk band Minny Pops, were fortuitously playing a gig at the Cedar Club in Birmingham, which was something like their twenty-fifth performance.

Rob and I usually never planned anything until the last minute, and we decided instead of driving back up to Manchester and coming back down the next day, we'd get roadie Terry Mason to drive the car back up, and we'd stay over and get the train back after the match. We didn't have tickets, but we knew the touts, and they'd sort us out.

We were backstage after the show. Rob had his trusty maroon briefcase, and as usual, all he ever had in it was the contract for the gig, a pack of Benson & Hedges fags, a disposable lighter, a bit of weed, and after the show when he'd been paid, a tidy wad of cash. After this show, he had something like a grand, and he said to Bernard, 'Be a pal and take the briefcase with the cash in back with you, and put it away safely.' He then got his cigs, lighter and weed out.

Bernard, being Bernard, thought it would be funny to leave us with the cash knowing we were going to the match the next day. The band made a quick getaway, leaving us with the case and the cash. The caper was on.

We left a club that was obviously in one of those desolate areas, mostly concrete and broken lampposts, surrounded by dual carriageways. We had to walk through dark, grim underpasses, past kids in Fred Perry shirts lurking with menace, carrying this stupid briefcase with a grand inside. I said to Rob, 'If we get mugged', which seemed quite likely, 'someone's getting a nice gift.'

We got to a Holiday Inn and stayed the night, Rob probably sleeping with the briefcase. When we made it to the ground, we managed to get a couple of tickets. We still had the briefcase, and Rob was saying, 'Well, we'll work it out, something will occur.' Going in, we got searched of course – it was the hooligan years, and the police were out in force. Naturally, they looked into the case. There was a half-full pack of Benson & Hedges, a Bic lighter and a thousand pounds in cash – Rob had used up his little stash of weed the night before.

We were taken to a cabin to explain ourselves. Rob decided it was best to call the promoter, and luckily we managed to get through. A bemused promoter confirmed, 'Yes, that's right, I paid them a grand in cash.' They kicked us out, and Rob asked if we could store our briefcase there while we watched the match.

'Fuck off!'

We're in the Holte Stand, packed with raucous standing City fans, because this was before seats-only stadiums. Rob's got the bag jammed between his legs. After ninety battling minutes, there's no score and the match goes to extra time. So far, nothing dramatic enough has happened to make Rob think the briefcase was threatened. After one hundred minutes, City get a free kick in front of us, and Steve McKenzie stroked the ball to our heroic captain Paul Power, who curled it into the net.

Crowds are often said to go crazy, but the City crowd really did go crazy – about as crazy as I have ever seen in sixty years of going to City matches. The celebrations seemed to go on for five or six minutes as everyone banged into each other.

All of us in the City section seemed to be lifted off the ground as we were thrown about, seeing the goal that was surely going to take us to the Wembley final right in front of us. I ended up carried right onto the edge of the pitch by a joyous mob of fans gone mad. Rob wasn't with me.

I looked back and saw Rob standing on his own in the middle of the circle of emptiness that had opened up around him as the crowd exploded with excitement. They had separated as they celebrated, leaving Rob exposed, his glasses askew, and he'd been moved from his original place too, because there was no briefcase between his legs anymore. I spotted the case a few yards to his left as the crowd started to surge back into its original shape.

There's panic in Rob's eyes as he tries to force his way through the madly swaying crowd to grab it. I jump back into the stand and run towards the case, making a dive for it. For a second or two, I seem to be hanging in slow motion as I slice through the crowd and grab hold of it just as everyone's back where they were. I pull it to my chest, and Rob and I look at each other in horror before bursting out laughing. What the fuck! What a goal!

We'd scored and kept the money. It was one of my favourite City matches, made even more memorable because we'd held on to the bloody maroon briefcase under the most challenging of circumstances. Rob, the manager, at his very best.

On the noisy train back to Manchester, some very merry City fans started cheerfully mocking Rob as he clung tightly to his case. 'What've you got in there? Money?' 'Yeah', Rob drawled, 'a thousand quid in cash.' 'No need to be sarcastic', they said. Mmm, I thought, they don't know Rob.

They didn't know what he was capable of.

15
A pale, elusive metallic blue colour

Our odd little family unit lived on the upper floors of Rob and Lesley's house, where Rob had his office with his trusty avocado-coloured telephone, from which he did most of his business. He wrote all his notes and things to do in these little green books, because somewhere in the middle of his scattiness, he was incredibly organised. He'd get up in the morning and hang around for a while in his short Japanese kimono, his bollocks hanging out, with a cup of tea on his knees and a sweet smile on his lips. He'd been very fit when he was younger, a black belt in karate, but that was all slipping, and he started smoking weed non-stop in the early eighties. When Lesley and I wanted to go to bed, he would always say, 'One more, let's have one more.' 'Oh, Rob, we want some sleep!' He was insatiable. He was also very thoughtful, and quite a deep thinker, but he didn't want you to know that.

Premises had been found for Rob, New Order and Factory's dream club – Tony had been infected by Rob's passion, grafting onto the project all kinds of highfalutin utopian wishes. They were from different extremes of loving to tease and wind up people – Tony would be the one saying about The Haçienda, 'Structures are shadows, cast into the future.' Rob would answer anyone asking who he thought was going to come to such a club perhaps out of place in grimy run-down Manchester with, 'Anyone with two arms and two legs.'

They had settled on an old yacht showroom in a warehouse stranded amid boarded-up warehouses and scars left by old industrial development. There were few signs of life apart from some car repair shops under the viaduct which occasionally opened, up to something or other. The location resembled the rusting, slumming New York areas Rob and New Order were nostalgic for after sampling Paradise Garage, Hurrah, the mysterious, funny punk Mudd Club – with its doorman and sarcastic mirror ball – and Danceteria on their gig-playing trips there. Coming in off isolated, menacing scaffold-encased sidewalks into a vast room filled with flashing lights, pounding bass, laughing faces and crashing waves of joy, it seemed the whole place was constantly changing shape and changing the shape of your mind.

'Ruins and labour shouldn't be left idle', Tony would say in a Haçienda planning meeting, to bemused looks from me and Rob and blissed-out murmurs of contented agreement from Alan. He had come up with a name for the club inside the books he liked to read – and give to others as gifts – about the unruly 1960s French Situationist artistic movement, committed to disrupting the monotony and superficiality of everyday life. At one point, the favourite name among everyone but Tony, especially with Peter and the designers, was simply to use the number it was randomly allocated in the rapidly growing Factory catalogue, defining the label as both business and artwork – Fac 51. That had some sense of Factory intrigue, but not enough for language-loving Tony.

Calling it The Haçienda didn't seem very Manchester when Tony told Rob and me his idea – the bemused brothers once more – but on the other hand, there had been successful clubs in Manchester with unlikely names like Rotters, Fagin's, Takis, Jigsaw. Tony explained that it would become itself and it would become Manchester, and after all, it was a group called Joy Division who then became New Order who were paying for it, with a little help from outside investment. At what point did they start to sound like they came from Manchester? Everything could become Manchester once enough people believed.

Also, Tony worked for Granada TV. That was a weird name glowing in striking red lights since the early 1960s on the side of their studios off Deansgate, and that became inextricably linked with Manchester. Besides, it said in one of his books: *The Haçienda must be built*. We could feel ourselves falling for it, and Tony would not be moved. Essentially, Tony wore us down with his insistence on the name. When he was in full flow, you had no chance of making him change his mind.

He never mentioned it to me, and no one else ever mentioned that he had to them, but as a Cambridge-educated book lover who'd learnt Latin at school, Tony no doubt knew that 'haçienda' derived from the Spanish for 'making things', itself from the Latin *facienda*, meaning 'things to be done'. He probably knew that 'haçienda' referred to ranches, estates and buildings – including self-sufficient factory-type workshops – popular during the Spanish colonisation of the Americas in the seventeenth and eighteenth centuries. He usually had a look on his face that suggested he knew these things and couldn't believe no one else did.

When I joined up with Rob and Factory, they were in the process of turning the large disused warehouse they'd found backing onto a slimy part of the Rochdale Canal into a functioning club – as if they knew what they were doing.

House designer and Factory visual mastermind Peter Saville didn't think interior design was his area. He recommended Ben Kelly, who mixed art and interior design, to work on the inside after they had collaborated on the 1980 debut album sleeve for a Liverpool electro group, Orchestral Manoeuvres in the Dark. They had released their first single, 'Electricity', on Factory – a perky perversion of a Kraftwerk melody – and, in the rush to sign northern indie/new wave/electro bands, had signed for a Factory-inspired subsidiary of major label Virgin, Din Disc.

Rob, Tony and Alan showed Ben around this huge, filthy space filled with rubble. At that point, they were more or less the only people in the world who believed this space could change people's lives, but Ben could see it too, or at least he took on the challenge of turning these ruined premises into a heightened northern version of the ultimate New York nightspots they'd fallen in love with.

One thing he gathered from the conversation, and having worked with Peter, respecting the aesthetic he had established, was that it was a rare chance to do something completely original. It was classic Factory – stumble across the best possible person to do something, someone no formal business would have considered, and then let them do what they wanted, checking in occasionally to make sure it was going in the right direction. What was the right direction? You knew it when you saw it.

It was a blank canvas that needed filling. Traditional approaches to such a refurbishment would have merely created another ordinary building, erasing its history as if embarrassed by it. Tony, Rob and Alan imagined he'd smartly do it up with some splashes of colour – Rob's first impression, and probably his second and third, maybe affectionate, maybe not, was that Kelly was a 'poncy southern git', even though he was born in Yorkshire – but Ben wanted to create a kind of illusion, a grand stage-set. (To give Rob some credit, Ben had moved to London in 1971.)

Kelly had some ideas about what to do with all the walls – he eventually found the pale, elusive metallic-blue colour he was looking for on the cover of a Bryan Ferry album, *The Bride Stripped Bare*. With his colleague Sandra Douglas, one of his ex-students, he found ways to retain the metal skeleton of the warehouse to reflect the interiors of Manchester factories and workshops, and devised a practical solution to the problem of the building's fixed columns ending up on the dance floor.

He painted them in hazard stripes, especially red and black, and yellow and black, so that they wouldn't get in the way of the dancers, and created a line of bollards and cats' eyes to map out the dance floor, making a connection with the flickering strobe lights that lit the long, dimly lit runway that took you into the Paradise Garage. The frail, empty space was repurposed, reused, reforged into something else, retaining its bones, shedding the dirt and destitution.

He sampled post-industrial landscapes and industrial machinery left to rot, with warning stripes slapped on them. It was like the music that would (eventually) get played inside – filled with references to other things, material that was reused and reimagined. Even though for a while the connection wasn't properly made, when it was, it made so much sense.

He'd sampled Manchester's past and turned it into the future, which one way or another was exactly what Rob, Tony, Alan and

Ben discussed at that first meeting, before A Certain Ratio, giving a sullen, locally accented twist to New York art-funk, turned up and asked Kelly to design their album cover.

After a few years, Kelly's designs for The Haçienda took on a life of their own, and the stripes and The Haçienda colours spiralled off into pop culture, becoming part of Manchester's identity well into the twenty-first century. Tony kept saying 'The Haçienda must be built'; it was written in the Situationist Manifesto like it was written in the stars. It's one reason he was so stubborn about the name – he'd received a secret message transmitted through culture and felt a certain responsibility to history, specifically Manchester history. To have something better, we must build it. Forty years later, you can read Ben Kelly talking about how, because of its influence, The Haçienda never dies.

Before it could become a Manchester legend, and enter wider culture, there was a lot of dust to deal with, and music to find.

16
A sound effect

The Haçienda was just about finished – a bit wet behind the ears, part of the floor not yet laid – more or less ready for a 21 May 1982 opening. There was nothing outside the new premises announcing its existence apart from a small granite name plaque set inside the wall. No big showbiz lights, no obvious sense of theatre. If Tony wanted intrigue and secrets, then here it was – easy to miss. Outside, it wasn't really there, just another Manchester street corner you'd usually pass by quickly.

Inside, you passed through various entrances, doors and arches – there was a cloakroom, originally meant to be a video games room – and suddenly this huge space rose above you to distant skylights, with a balcony overlooking the bollards and columns marking out the dance floor, bar and stage. There were loads of staircases, alcoves, bars and hidden corners which were like abstract echoes of the rooms at Placemate 7 and Pips where you could hide yourself from the main area, creating your own atmosphere and organising your own territory.

If you didn't know your New York, it didn't look like a night-club, or even some contrary version of a discotheque. Those used to Factory's playful, wayward and sometimes deadly serious ways took it for granted that it didn't immediately make sense, but looked like what a club involving Tony Wilson, Rob Gretton, Factory, New Order and Peter Saville would look like.

If you also happened to be a student of architecture, your mind would be blown. It was as though a spaceship had landed in the desolate middle of Manchester, and the controls had been handed over to a few quixotic, devil-may-care Mancunians who didn't have a clue how to operate it.

Ideas about what the club was were further muddied – or maybe completely clarified – by having the growling, nonplussed trouble-maker Bernard Manning, chosen to represent gritty, grotty northern royalty, declare the venue open. 'I've played some shitholes in my life, but this is something else', he began, which led to him returning his fee. The night also featured an appearance by the Latin-influenced punk-funk South Bronx ESG Scroggins sisters Renee, Valerie and Marie. The result of the club not being quite ready was all the sawdust making them sneeze during their soundcheck.

A group formed by their mother to get them away from the dangerous local street life, ESG's instinctive, magically unselfconscious late-seventies mix of disco, punk, pop, minimalism and proto-hip-hop rhythms accidentally hit the New York no wave post-punk sweet spot as defined by the records on the Ze label.

Not part of the hipster scenes and struggling to get noticed, in 1980 ESG supported A Certain Ratio in New York, and suddenly were folded into the anarchic Factory world when Tony Wilson took a fancy to their punk presence and askew vivacity. Like the pop impresario he had become, he immediately asked if they wanted to make a record. The good news was that Martin Hannett, who had demonstrated visionary ingenuity with *Spiral Scratch* and Joy Division, would produce it. The bad news was that, because this was Factory – used to making records among friends or for the hell of it – there was no contract. Classic impractical Factory – throwing people together quite arbitrarily to do work, and if it worked, it was genius; if it didn't, it was one of those things. Having them collaborate with Martin Hannett was inspired, with him applying what he had learnt producing Buzzcocks, Joy Division and the guitar of Vini Reilly's The Durutti Column to the swirling, nascent hybridisation of ESG – an insidious clash of sonic intensity and primal spontaneity.

The three-track single recorded in New Jersey included an instrumental recorded in the last few minutes of the quick-fire session, where everything was done in one take. This featured a spacey, siren-laden track called 'UFO' – their one-off style and strange, sparse fury dressed in full-on Factory force. It would become one of the most sampled sounds and effects in music history, its otherworldly sirens a foundational part of hip-hop consciousness, tracked by the likes of Beastie Boys, Wu-Tang Clan, J Dilla, Public Enemy (many times), 2Pac, Nas, TLC, Miles Davis, Burial, De La Soul and NWA.

A song inspired by science fiction films foresaw the future and kept appearing in different forms and places over the years. It also came from the freewheeling wild west period before sampling was monetised, so while it changed the musical world, it did little to help the group financially or make much difference to their own world.

The EP didn't sell but was loved by influential critics and got noticed by the New York cognoscenti. It helped ESG become New York underground icons, appearing at all the clubs that had inspired the Factory idealists to build The Haçienda. They were, in effect, New York Black royalty and part of the opening ceremony.

To many on the disorientating Haçienda opening night, those coming in as Factory fans – white indie kids transferring from the Russell Club – their cracked dynamics, early rap chants and buckled funk rhythms, often just voices, synth blips and derelict drumming, were as incongruous as Manning's nasty jokes.

For me, it was a sign of the kind of music The Haçienda was built for – even if no one knew it at the time. Tony, who had an increasingly old-fashioned loyalty to the 'seriousness' of albums, was never keen on putting out dance music – 'It will never sell, darling' – but we happened to have put out a great dance record and had the group on for The Haçienda opening night, as if it was part of the well-oiled plan. It was an answer to a problem we didn't even know we had at the very beginning. There was no plan, though – it just seemed like a good idea.

At the time, there wasn't much of this kind of music about. We'd have to wait for the right sounds to fill the place, and in the meantime work out what to do with the club's sound. Forty thousand pounds had been spent on installing the best sound in town, which was money well wasted.

The design wing of Factory – Tony getting more excited as the interiors made the fantasy a reality – had dictated where the small speakers should go, and the studio wing chose the sound system, thinking what was needed was the sound of an expensive London recording studio.

The technicians setting it up were from a major London recording studio, and they were the best people to do the sound if you were kitting out a recording studio. A club was a completely different world – you need to understand the space you are in and the purpose of dance music to send you off the planet and elevate your soul – but Tony refused point-blank to change direction. I think if he heard the words dance music, he turned off. Whereas if he heard that Pink Floyd used this particular studio, he was convinced.

We argued for hours, and I kept talking about Paradise Garage in New York, our holy grail, which had these six almost circular stacks dominating the space. This long, beautiful room inside a concrete parking garage was where Larry Levan – the pilot, the priest, the resident DJ – would throw the sound from one to the other, using the system as a mixing desk, highlighting and moving the sounds around. The sound ran around the room.

It was mind-blowing, and I tried to convince bloody-minded Tony that this wasn't disco, it wasn't mindless and moronic, it was an experimental, spiritual, artistic structuring of music that needed the absolute best sound system. The sound system was the DJ's instrument. What we had was an acoustic guitar – we needed an orchestra. It was futuristic in some ways, but as an instrument for the DJ to play, it was somehow pre-war.

Ask ESG, Tony! They knew how important the Garage sound was in helping it create the sanctuary, the temple, the paradise. It elevated and propelled the electronic instruments being increasingly used on new dance records, and completed a kind of circuit. It was a pure, intimate sound on a vast scale.

It seemed obvious you built a club around the sound – it was the centre of the whole experience, taking you to another place again and again. Tony didn't see it – or rather, he didn't hear it. He made it clear he knew what he was doing. He'd thought of the name, hadn't he? Look, it even had a fancy restaurant! And we're going to give away free badges.

What the opening night proved to those of us on the club wing was that we'd built something in the image of a New York dance club but we had nothing like a New York dance club sound system. And if it had been built as a live venue, it didn't even have a live venue sound. Maybe that's what Manning meant when he called it a shithole. We'd got the garage. We hadn't yet got the paradise.

17
A love tempo

Rob had a soft spot for Quando Quango, and Gonnie soon came over to join me so we could continue with the group – our relationship turned into a marriage before we left Rotterdam. Rob and Lesley came over for the wedding, which shows just how much we had become like family.

As well as my duties at The Haçienda, and as roving aide-de-camp for Rob, I also became an artist on Factory with Gonnie. We would have put a record out in Rotterdam; we felt we were ready but were never quite organised enough, so it made sense that we made one for Factory.

Gonnie and I had been excited witnessing Vice Versa and their synths in the studio in Rotterdam, and invested in some basic electronic equipment. Within weeks of Gonnie arriving, we made a double-sided 12-inch single, 'Go Exciting'/'Tingle' — Fac 67, released in October 1982. It was even more un-Factory, conga mad and ungloomy sounding than ESG, although we were in the Factory spirit of enlightened amateurs and brave weirdos.

We wanted 'Go Exciting' to sound like the post-punk disco warm-up for a Brazilian street party made by no-waver enthusiasts, and 'Tingle' is a slapdash sign of how thrilled we were to be in the studio. Revolution Studios on Church Road in Cheadle Hulme, next door to an off-licence, had been opened in 1975 by local musical force of nature Andy Macpherson, who'd mixed The Who's legendary *Live at Leeds* album and engineered Buzzcocks' *Spiral Scratch*. His studio was an early Factory favourite – another reason Manchester became such a music city was that there were good, relatively inexpensive, well-run and well-equipped studios like Revolution, often in unlikely looking Stockport streets, and A Certain Ratio had become regulars there.

We were working after-hours to cut costs, our budget not up to peak time, which usually turned into through-the-night sessions, which suited the Rio De Stockport mood we were after. The Revolution tracks sounded like we were having a great time at three in the morning, and there might have been a kitchen sink in there.

In hindsight, they sound like I am sifting everything I'd learnt playing records, making music and watching experimental electronica in Rotterdam, in the process of searching for a Haçienda sound. The record didn't catch fire, reviews were indifferent to hostile, although it made more sense in Latino New York, which thrilled us, as we must have got something right and not sounded too inauthentic.

Donald Johnson, the drummer who'd helped A Certain Ratio achieve their streetwise funk groove, also helped produce it, ensuring the rhythm was spot on. Reinier was still drumming for us. As much as a warm-up for a party, it was also a warm-up for our next Factory single, 'Love Tempo', Fac 79, where the influence of A Certain Ratio and New Order – fusing Factory funk and Factory electro – was more apparent, alongside the freakish QQ no wave theatre and slivers of avant-garde jazz. The Factory links were becoming clearer.

This was inevitable, as it was produced by Bernard Sumner from New Order with Donald, which was typical Factory – your records maybe didn't sell, if you weren't New Order, but they were in the greatest sleeves – where Tony liked to spend the money – and you would get Factory's best, most adventurous musicians to work with you.

Bernard was round at Rob's house a lot, and we often talked about electronic music, which was increasingly becoming his main fascination. Both he and Stephen were buying synthesisers, samplers, emulators and drum machines; Hooky not so much, as he wasn't as interested. Kraftwerk at the Free Trade Hall in 1975 was as much an influence on Bernard and Stephen as that year's Sheffield show had been on Sheffield electronic musicians.

We played each other records we liked, and he was listening to European electronic music his friend Mark Reeder was sending him from Berlin, including electro-dominant Italo disco, and records where disco was becoming Hi NRG and where disco was going underground. Underground music was becoming a tangle of hybrids and sounds in progress, especially as DJs started to actually make music as well as play it, approaching a song not so much as a musician but as an artist thinking of a bigger structure – the overall sound of a whole night's music. They were creating music that fitted into their sets.

He played me 'Dirty Talk' by Klein and MBO, which used the recently released Roland TR-808 drum machine Bernard was obsessed with. He told us we should buy one. It was too wonky, too rinky-dink for mainstream musicians, but gave away some of Kraftwerk's secrets, and some of Italo guru and Donna Summer producer Giorgio Moroder's magic with a single live kick drumbeat. Enlightened amateurs, non-musicians and DJs could now make music and create rhythms without the complications of a human drummer who got tired, turning their record collections into low-cost, do-it-yourself sound where rhythms could run wild.

'Dirty Talk' was the kind of sparse, sweetly melodic Italian electro-disco that was a relief to New York DJs needing to replace the mainstream disco clogging the charts with something fresh and uncorrupted by commercial demands. The European Connection Instrumental mix was as light as air but with an insistent, deadpan 4/4 swing, sometimes just a bass line and percussion with minimal synthesiser loops. The drum machine seemed to have a mind of its own, and there were little glitchy stutters and off-kilter pauses.

The sound stripped away all the clutter and commotion of mainstream pop disco and pointed forwards. In 1983, New Order's 'Blue Monday' would emerge out of it, with added force and tautness and a tender, nervy vocal. Italo's easily edited, remixed, extended and technologically altered flow structured the beginning of house music, with its infinite possibilities.

The mix of disco, European electro and experiments with new drum machines and synth special effects started being played in parties in house basements, and then, as the word spread, at the Warehouse in Chicago, an afterhours private party, mainly drawing in gay, Latino and Black communities craving the unity and togetherness of early disco when it was connected with marginalised freedom struggles.

Disco was reincarnated, the same but different, still dance but with added deviance, in the city where it had been murdered. It was in Chicago on 12 July 1979 that a threatened, white, heterosexual, mostly male 'rock and roller' hatred for disco as a genre and subculture culminated in what became known as Disco Demolition Night. Piles of disco records were blown up at a Chicago White Sox baseball game, accompanied by the chant 'Disco sucks'. A riot ensued. It would be called the day that disco died, but ultimately disco – not the overcommercialised major-label version but its raw DNA – went underground and found a new name. Disco was reborn, intensifying its original radical spirit.

The Warehouse meant that what was being played there was called house, and one of the very first official house tracks on vinyl, 'On and On', in early 1984, was put together when Jesse Saunders had a rare white-label Italo disco megamix stolen and decided to recreate it, stringing together a looped bass, weightless Kraftwerk-like chords, Fad Gadget/Mute Records influenced effects, synth strings and random voices. A year later, the owner of the pressing plant they used formed Trax Records, which sent Adonis and his rough-and-ready mutation of Italo basics into Manchester. The tempo and momentum of 'Blue Monday' was the link between the white indie post-punk music the early Haçienda adopters came from and the house that was heading into the city.

It was only released as a 12-inch, but became the biggest selling 12-inch single of the 1980s, and made New Order – ex-punks, ex-Joy Division, on the ultra-arty Factory Records – the kings and queens of a format invented for dance music. It was a hit, and when they played *Top of the Pops*, New Order, in their infinite opposite of wisdom, decided to play live a song carefully built in the studio from blocks, loops and layers of electronics.

Most groups mimed, but New Order had their integrity, which in the early 1980s for certain groups was a prized asset. The BBC *Top of the Pops* sound of this superbly produced electronic masterpiece sounded like it was coming out of a transistor running out of power, which might have been their tribute to the sound of The Haçienda. Bono of U2 was on the same show, and he said to the group, 'You know, it's amazing you did it live. Wish we'd have done it like that.' Rob took one look at him and said, 'Why didn't you then?'

Bernard was fascinated with how this pre-house electronic music was being made, with sounds and rhythms criss-crossing the Atlantic, picking up new variations and subtle shifts in direction as they passed back and forth. He wanted to try producing other people's records to extend his learning outside New Order. He loved the new machinery and electronics, and there was a definite punky, DIY ethos in how the music could be put together. It meant he could leave Joy Division where it was and start from scratch.

He could be a bit moody and introspective, but he loved technology. It ran in his family – a passion for machinery and inventing things – and after a lull following Ian's death, looking for a direction and fighting negative emotions, he started tinkering with machines. He preferred electronic music for its intricacy and how it energised and occupied him, channelling his thoughts. It was amazing in the studio watching him work on 'Love Tempo', with Donald in control of the rhythm, bringing in his brother Barry from Sweet Sensation on bass, and Bernard diving into the machines and structure. Simon Topping from A Certain Ratio added percussion, becoming more than a part-time member, so Quando Quango were like an annex of A Certain Ratio.

The 'Love Tempo' session taught me so much about the building of a song's dynamics and also made me realise the importance of surrounding yourself with the best possible people when you were making music, something I've done ever since.

The original version didn't do so well in Britain but was one of Factory's best-selling singles in America. It didn't fit into where the white music press fashion then was – that eclectic, post-punk, often electronic new pop that included ABC, Teardrop Explodes, OMD, Flying Lizards, the Associates, Orange Juice, Culture Club, The Human League, Heaven 17 and Yazoo. It didn't fit because it was dance music. There was still an attitude, that Tony shared, that dance meant the perceived frivolities of disco, which completely discredited it. New Order, being New Order, somehow got away with it and could still be a pop group with punk integrity while experimenting with new dance rhythms.

Kevin Cummins took some great photographs of Quando Quango in the back alleys of Manchester's Chinatown around 1983. We were in these wild-looking tracksuits like they wore in New York, we were holding a beatbox, Gonnie had the big hair and ESG attitude.

Were we female, were we Black, were we dance, were we pop, were we jazz? We were all of that – and most of all, we were Manchester – you could see it in our eyes. No one could keep up with it. This caused another disconnect with the British music press, because no one looked like that then – and they didn't know where to place us.

Ironically, in New York, 'Love Tempo' was embraced by the more progressive DJs, whose open-mindedness meant they included British electro-pop and even punk and post-punk among the no wave, electro, hi NRG and proto-house. For them, Quando Quango were part of where no wave was becoming proto-house – and Bernard's evolving experience in the studio definitely helped make the links.

Even the messiah Larry Levan at The Garage cottoned on to it, helped by the fact that Factory Records had developed a reputation in New York clubs as an exotic label to check out for surprising records and useful oblique beats. In Britain, Factory was seen as a label for intense young men who wore long coats and would never think of dancing. Larry was important because he would give anything a fair hearing, and didn't have that music paper snobbery – he'd play The Clash, and then cut right into expectation by following with Level 42, which in Britain were seen as more pop-funk.

'Love Tempo' also caught the ear of Mark Kamins, who had lived with Madonna for a few months in 1982 when she was having a hard time getting noticed. He produced her first record that year after introducing her to ace record company man Seymour Stein at his Sire label in New York. Stein signed her when few were interested, many put off by her scary-seeming determination. A big, loveable, crazy bear of a man, Mark would become very much a mentor to me, encouraging me to think of the role of the DJ in a completely new way.

After DJing at Trax in the late seventies, he started playing records at the original Danceteria in 1980 – at the beginning of that anti-Studio 54 time, when the clubs needed to be something other than celebrity hangouts for the rich and famous where the music was less and less important. He worked alongside a mysterious punk DJ from Leeds called Sean Cassette, who had been at Hurrah on West 62nd Street – a pre-Studio 54, insider nightspot and creative community that lasted from 1976 to 1981, playing punk, new wave and industrial. It was known as a rock disco.

It was made successful by gay liberationist, actor and ultimate New York scenester Jim Fouratt, who became friendly with Tony Wilson – who loved Fouratt's enthusiasm, trickiness and taste, and his way of hiring people he believed in. When Fouratt moved on to open the first Danceteria on West 37th Street in 1980 with visionary nightclub man Rudolf Piper, he took Sean with him.

Sean would be playing Wire, Public Image, Cabaret Voltaire, and when at the second Danceteria on 21st Street he and Mark played together, they found that they could move from Sean's early Human League to Black New Yorker Mark's James Brown, from the English Clash to the American B52's – and it worked. Even going from Factory's Section 25 to the kitsch of Boney M could be magical, and it was such a different way of playing records from what was happening in Britain, where you'd have clubs serving a particular genre. Clubs like Placemate 7 and Pips in Manchester had tried to puncture that, but their rooms were still segregated. In New York especially, the 'rooms' were all in one room.

It was weirdly rooted in the British class system – a kind of snobbery that meant you stayed in your own lane, your own neighbourhood, your own musical world – whereas in New York, Chicago and Miami, it was more of an anything-goes culture, as long as it worked and the dancing kept going. Everything was mixed up, and it had a creative impact that you could see in the early 1980s as music changed so quickly – the Black music was getting punkier, and the punk and post-punk was getting Blacker. It was a response to the 'death of disco' – Disco Demolition in Chicago in 1979 – driven by an anxiety that disco was replacing rock as the sound of America. If disco was despised, obliterating its original innovations and idealism, a whole new group of creative minds were reactivating its original eclectic energy.

There were different floors and rooms at the 21st Street Danceteria, but by the time Mark took over the second floor – with all his records with him in his booth – he had absorbed the lessons learnt working with Sean, and he didn't stick to one genre or musical style. He didn't want to be pinned down, and spontaneity was the key. He served up all sorts of mixes and would go from Mantronix to Anne Clarke on Rough Trade to 'Hip-hop Don't Stop' by Man Parish, and the records that were emerging in quick response to the eclectic spirit encouraged by the clubs – like Arthur Baker's production of Afrika Bambaataa's 'Planet Rock'.

Factory were very good at developing international connections – Tony loving driven New Yorkers like Jim Fouratt – and they had an informal headquarters in New York which the film and video producer Michael Shamberg looked after. It was one of the reasons why A Certain Ratio would be in New York, being supported by locals such as ESG – and an early Madonna. For a while, the underdog Manchester hipness of Factory outtrumped the fixated New York energy of Madonna.

18
A New York anglophile

Factory also had a committed supporter in the young New York promoter, booker and dedicated anglophile Ruth Polsky – a rock journalist who had become one of the world's leading experts in British post-punk music. She'd gone to NYU and lived on the corner of Houston and the university. She was one of Jim Fouratt's most successful hirings, originally as his assistant at Hurrah – not least because of her musical taste.

Even though there was no obvious money-making potential in it, just for the sake of getting them over to America for the interested few to experience, she would bring over most of the new British post-punk bands – The Mekons, Gang of Four, The Smiths, Echo & the Bunnymen, The Slits, Delta 5, The Au Pairs, Josef K. For a lot of that scene, Ruth was pivotal in introducing them to America. She'd help Fouratt book Joy Division for a short tour in May 1980 that had to be cancelled because of Ian's death – which happened the night before they were due to leave for America.

Her taste in music makes so much sense now, but at the time it was a risk. Few outside a small niche knew who any of these bands were, and they often had to announce themselves at the start of their show. There'd be blank faces at first. She brought Cabaret Voltaire over, and she helped make a few insiders see the link between the New York club scene and the electric sounds developing in Sheffield – and on the Mute label.

At first, no one knew where to place them – it wasn't rock, and they certainly didn't dress rock, and it wasn't dance, as any funk was totally distressed and burnt out. For Ruth, it was obvious something like Cabaret Voltaire should be in New York as the clubs were breaking up genres, playing electronic music and extending the range of dance. She promoted music as a creative act as much as anything – and was a major part of what was an insular scene but, to those inside, was very important. She was also instrumental in bringing ESG over to Manchester for The Haçienda opening night – after they supported ACR on one of the shows she arranged.

Rob and Tony loved her, and New Order loved her because she had such an impact on their early success in America and had this knack of bringing miserable Mancunian buggers out of their shells.

She adored Factory. I think she would have loved to have lived in Manchester – but she made it her job to look after this new British music, much of it from Manchester – and make sure it had a stage. She'd put some of us up, sleeping on her lounge floor – just to save paying hotel bills. If we didn't stay with her, we stayed at a place round the corner, the Earle Hotel – which became the Washington Square Hotel in 1986 – the one Joan Baez sings about in her 'Diamonds and Rust' song – the crummy hotel on Washington Square. It was even crummier when I would stay there – in one of the cheap rooms below ground level – where you'd just see a sliver of the ground from your window.

I remember waking up there once with this weird, strangled squeaking sound – and it turned out this massive rat had been caught by a glue trap under a radiator. I ran up to the lobby to get it sorted, and they just thought it was a very natural thing, and I should deal with it myself. It was better to stay at Ruth's. New York was a dirty, dangerous place in the early eighties – which in some ways made it more interesting than it is now, but in other ways, a lot less easy-going. It helped to have a great local guide like Ruth to ease us in.

She took Quando Quango over to America in early 1983 to do some small shows along the east coast – Boston, Philadelphia, Washington – finishing with a couple of shows in New York. She arranged it all, came with us on tour and looked after us beyond the call of duty. She was fan, friend and collaborator – and she also connected with writers and photographers, joining everything together.

We played in New Jersey at the Abraham Lincoln Motor Hotel – the kind of place where you could rent a room by the hour and there were waterbeds in the room. There was quite a crowd – it seemed more a regular place for locals to hang out – and we were dressed in the clothes we had travelled in, which probably looked a bit street urchin to them. It didn't make us look like the kind of entertainers they were used to. They all had this look on their face of 'Who – what – the hell are you?' There wasn't a white face in there, and for some reason the boxing brothers Michael and Leon Spinks were there, around the time they were at the peak of their World Champion powers. A strange night, but we just felt lucky to get the gig. The best I can say about the show is that it passed by without incident – and I imagine no one else who was there apart from us can ever remember it happening.

Someone would introduce us at these shows, and they would always say, from London, England, Quando Quango! Sometimes Quando Quando, or Quango Quango. And we'd go, 'Look, can you please say we're from Manchester, England?' And they'd say, 'Yeah, sure, man, sure.' They'd go on and say, 'Ladies and gentlemen, from London, England … '

Simon Topping was with us, always loving a moan, and it drove him mad. 'Yeah, mate, we're from Manchester. Can you go back on and say it properly?' No chance.

While we were in New York the first time, Gonnie and I would go to the clubs – The Roxy, The Funhouse, David Mancuso's The Loft – and of course Paradise Garage and the Danceteria. Ruth was a great help knowing to where to be, on what night, at what time. She knew everyone and had become the booker for the Danceteria, loving that it was a place where 'everything goes'.

She died tragically early at 31, outside The Limelight on 6th Avenue to meet friends when a car crashed into a cab which was flung onto the sidewalk, crushing Ruth as she was waiting. No one else was touched. It was awful – she was the queen of this golden age of a New York underground that eventually had such an impact on the music everyone now knows, and she was so randomly killed on the kind of night out she did all the time – just wanting to see a band, hang out with friends, keep up with what was happening.

She took us once to the Roxy on a Friday night – in this old roller disco ballroom hosted by Fab Five Freddy, with live graffiti art, breakdancing on the floor by the Double Dutch Girls and Crazy Legs from the Rocksteady Crew. Afrika Bambaataa played a never-ending sequence of soul, electro funk, new wave, oddballs and early hip-hop which at one point went from Malcolm McLaren's 'Buffalo Girls' to Foghat's 'Slow Ride'; then later from McLaren's 'Double Dutch' to ESG's 'Moody', from Yazoo to the Pointer Sisters, Tom Tom Club to James Brown, from 'Super Freak' to 'Once in a Lifetime', from Blondie's 'Rapture' to Bambaataa's own 'Planet Rock'.

When he played 'My Jamaican Girl' by Grace Jones – an idea Mark Kamins had based on a Sly and Robbie B-side while working for Chris Blackwell at Island – Grace herself was suddenly there, in the building, looking like she'd just pulled up to the bumper. Over in the corner was a rocky Rod Stewart, on the prowl. It was one of the great mad nights out – New York in a summer of 1983 nutshell – and how I want to remember Ruth, laughing at it all like we were, loving being able to show it to me, knowing it would give me ideas. Which it did.

19
A loud guy in a loud world

In a way, as Rob's mate, marvelling at something miraculous in a New York club, I was working, doing some research, ready to report back to Haçienda headquarters what the club needed to make it more than just another club. Being in the middle of this colossal room at the Paradise Garage, taking in Larry Levan's musical genius through this immense sound system, was a sublime experience. I really wanted Tony to experience what went beyond the physical into the realms of the spiritual.

Surely Tony, with his Buddhist leanings, would understand that it wasn't necessarily about the music being played as dance music, but about the collective nature of it all – the sense of belonging it created and how the music expanded the imagination. At three in the morning, aching from all the dancing and out-of-body experiences, I wished I could call Tony and shout down the phone: 'The Haçienda must be built, but The Haçienda must be rebuilt!'

I might have got him there, but I would have lost him when I said that Larry Levan and Mark Kamins – and David Mancuso and Jellybean Benitez – were proving that DJing was an art form, a unique new hybrid of music fan and maker. That was heretical in the early 1980s outside a very few; the club DJ just played records by artists, one step up from serving in a record shop. (But, Tony, at its best, in the less commercial shops, that was an art form as well …)

With his lapsed-Catholic leanings and interest in the power of faith, I felt Tony would understand how this was a way of combining art, architecture, sound and space to create a sacred environment where people moved as one, flowing freely through imaginary spheres. It was a party, a live show, a performance all in one. The Haçienda was beautifully set up as a backdrop, a space for pleasure, while the Paradise Garage made it clear that it needed to be a new kind of church.

At the Danceteria, I ended up being introduced to Mark Kamins in his booth, which was a hectic place, built in his image. It was the centre of the club, representing how it was a meeting place for creative minds of all kinds, as well as the source of the music. Later, Mark introduced me to his then-girlfriend Madonna in his booth, who didn't seem very impressed with me. She quickly sized me up to see what use I'd be in her career, using a red, amber, green scale. Mark had been green – the hippest in New York – when the unknown Madonna came to his booth with a cassette to listen to, but he was soon to be red. I was grey, possibly from some small East European country she couldn't pronounce. I was dismissed. Keith Haring was there, much friendlier, doing exactly what you imagine Keith Haring doing – scrawling something in a notepad. The guys who became the Beastie Boys were floor sweepers. It was like what you thought Andy Warhol's Factory was: a place for artists, scenesters and musicians to meet, to make things happen.

Mark was excited when he heard I was in Quando Quango. 'I love "Love Tempo" – it's slamming", he roared, slapping me on the back. He was a loud guy – something he'd learnt to make himself heard in a loud world.

It was like almost immediately he invited me into his world, and I would stay with him and his wife when I went over to New York for a long weekend. I dated his sister-in-law, who worked at Profile Records – one of the first hip-hop labels in America. The label had just signed Run DMC, who then seemed as obscure as Cabaret Voltaire, while the mainstream record industry saw rap as a mere fad.

Madonna had just left Mark when I got to know him, moving up a step to Latino DJ John 'Jellybean' Benitez, who was green to go. She was busy jumping from one resource to another, refreshing her sound, which she was very good at. It didn't seem to knock Mark back; he had such joy for life, and he would still help her with bits of advice.

He took me under his wing and loved that I was one of those Factory weirdos – 'Fucking hell, you guys are mad' – which was something coming from a dyed-in-the-wool New Yorker. In Britain, we were seen as pretentious, and The Haçienda was initially viewed as a cold, trendy place – too cool for school and nothing to do with Manchester, a minor celebrity's folly. But for Mark and Ruth, we were a bunch of lunatics, always on the hunt for a good time with our finger on whatever the pulse was. They loved the sound of the records, even the ones dismissed as drab and miserable at home. One was 'A View From a Hilltop' by Section 25 – they loved the combination of sequencers, a driving beat and dulcet northern male voices that sounded strange and special to New York ears. The Detroit techno guys coming through, like Derrick May, loved Section 25, which was quite funny because they weren't so keen on A Certain Ratio, who were trying to be funky. Section 25 weren't trying to be funky, which I suppose to the Detroit crew actually was funky.

I went inside Mark's booth and picked up ideas about how to transition from one record to another, even if they came from different eras, genres, or worlds, as long as the groove – real or abstractly – kept going. He took me to his favourite record shops, including Vinylmania, which was the definition of the ultimate record store on Carmine Street, just around the block from Paradise Garage in New York. It did what great record stores do – reflect an era and become the centre of a community. You'd go in and there'd be a crush of people.

It was more a straightforward rock store when it opened in the late 1970s, but being so close to The Garage meant it broadened into dance music and became a kind of outlet of the venue itself – feeding records in and reacting to the mixes being played. People would queue up in the morning to get in and grab something they'd heard the night before. As 12 inch singles became essential currency, early adopters instantly responded to the idea of records that had only been pressed for DJs and which became rare items, completely collectible.

And they had Manny in there, who was the shop DJ, playing what The Garage had spun the night before – which was what people had come to buy, and some they couldn't purchase, white label promos. Manny helped drive the whole New York club scene. Everyone, including Larry, got their stuff off Manny. He played them, the customers bought whatever was for sale, and it all kept adjusting week to week, making the music change in front of you. There were hundreds of independent labels flying out 12-inch singles all over Manhattan – all at different stages of trying out new grooves and electronics, genres splintering into view, some disappearing, some sticking around. The 12-inch mixes were where you could hear how within the city what was once disco had become tangled up with the uptown Latin scene, the downtown experimental avant-gardists and everything in between.

Mark really wanted to do a mix of 'Love Tempo', which we couldn't believe. He was actually asking us, and we were thrilled. It was his supreme mix of 'Love Tempo' which became the definitive version, grafting shimmering anything-goes New York insouciance onto Mancunian swagger – climbing into the Billboard Dance Charts Top 10. Amazingly to us, it boosted Mark's credibility as a producer, being associated with Factory.

Factory's well-connected representative Michael Shamberg called me one day and said, 'You've got a hit.' My response probably sounded like the reaction of a miserable bugger to him, but I was speechless.

20
A revelation

Quando Quango returned to America supporting New Order in the summer of 1983, who after 'Blue Monday' had spent time logically plugging directly into the New York action, recording with Arthur Baker – who they eventually found, decades before Google, had produced Afrika Bambaataa's history-making 'Planet Rock', which was pretty much New York City central, crossing a ton of boundaries, splicing Kraftwerk-inspired electronics with rap. New Order wanted some insight into how those records were made, how to get the right sound for a particular club – Arthur had the knack. They wanted something outside Manchester, even if they would never leave Manchester for good.

Within hours of New Order mentioning Arthur to Michael Shamberg in New York, Michael set up a potential collaboration. New Order entered the studio with only the vaguest beginning of an idea, and, still more Factory-enlightened amateurs than focused professionals, lacked the slick American session musician cleverness Baker and his co-producer John Robie were used to – Robie himself could play whatever was needed in whatever circumstance, immediately. New Order could do New Order, given time – except Hooky, who could give you Hooky bass instantly.

'Confusion' came out of a confusing mix of Baker's quick-witted no-nonsense New York spontaneity – knowing exactly what sounds to listen for – and New Order's languid jamming and four-way musical instinct, and a studio deadline rushing at them with unforgiving New York speed.

It was a remix of a track that didn't exist, born out of panic and revelation, and Arthur Baker's lucid impression of what New Order wanted to sound like and which club he wanted it played in – which he then turned into a series of mixes once they'd cracked it.

In a way, like me, New Order were in the city on a research and development trip – looking for clues not only about their own music, what it would be like sacrificing their home comforts and their familiar Martin Hannett routine, and where it might go next, but also what on earth was The Haçienda about?

Part of their research was noting how Baker and Robie would take a reel-to-reel tape of a new mix to the Fun House club, where Jellybean, Madonna's latest choice to help her on her way to stardom, would get instant feedback from the lively, deeply discriminating electro-loving crowd. If the crowd danced, you lived; if they didn't, you died.

The video for 'Confusion' itself became part of their research, as Tony Wilson's old flatmate Charles Sturridge, and director of *Brideshead Revisited*, made a kind of after-the-fact fictional documentary of the studio process that led to the single, and its first play in public.

In the video, a music fan finished their workday, ready to go to the Fun House for a night of liberation, scrubbing work out of her hair. Baker and Robie were in the studio, finishing the track, and meanwhile New Order were on their way to the club in a New York taxi to hear their new track getting its first play in public. The happy ending was 'Confusion' passing the rigorous Fun House crowd test – if a dance track could make it there, it could make it anywhere.

Rob and New Order, with me tagging along, would spend a lot of their downtime in New York, checking out the clubs, now that they had one of their own to look after. Oddly, they were making records like 'Confusion', shifting the emphasis of the group further and further into electronic dance, perturbing some of their more Joy Division fans, because they needed to have hits so they could keep supporting The Haçienda. It needed constant cash injection – and they were the only Factory act making money.

Bernard was always baffled by the no-alcohol policy in those clubs. The first thing we did when we went into a club was ask, 'Right, what do you want to drink?' In The Garage, there was no bar, just bowls filled with sparkling water. The club was first and foremost a safe place for the gay community, a place they could be themselves, and it didn't have a liquor licence. It was also about the music, not about getting drunk. Of course, you realised after a while that a lot of the patrons were intoxicated in other ways. Bernard always looked lost without his Pernod. Danceteria had a bar, and that was one of the reasons it was more an influence on The Haçienda than The Garage.

Something else imprinted on our collective memories was a PA Madonna gave on the roof of the Danceteria. Rob was stood right in front of her as she was doing her dancing thing, looking a complete casual wreck in these baggy towelling shorts and Chinese slippers, puffing on a joint. It wasn't clear if he was enjoying himself or trying to stare her out. I said to one of New Order's crew, 'God, he looks terrible standing there.' He said, 'Well, he's going to look even more terrible now', and pulled down his shorts. Being Rob, he had nothing on underneath.

He's stood there bollock naked, baring everything as Madonna's concentrating on being Madonna. She doesn't bat an eyelash. He was never quick at the best of times, and in the state he's in, it takes him time to realise his shorts are around his ankles, and then time to pull them up. His expression didn't change at all. He was getting into the groove. He was thinking, what the fuck are we going to do with The Haçienda?

It might have been the moment it dawned on him that The Haçienda needed to be like the Danceteria. 'This is what we should be doing', he said to me one time we left the club after hours of extreme revelry.

21
A tax bill

There were all sorts of technical and business reasons why The Haçienda was always in financial trouble as soon as it opened. Tony and Rob, with New Order, were badly advised. It was meant to be a smart way of dealing with New Order's tax, as an aside to the main business of giving Manchester this fantastic, world-class club, but it soon became all about the pressure of paying tax – which was really dreary when you think of the early idealistic intentions. He didn't show it, but it really got to Rob. In the end, he did have a boss – the bloody taxman.

They didn't buy the building when they could have done quite cheaply, and when they did eventually buy it, they paid far too much. They got in over their heads, but they could always fall back on New Order – when they had a large bill to pay or got one of their regular winding-up notices, New Order played a big show. It all went to the Inland Revenue.

It was no way to run a business, but I just had to get on with it. The business stuff was all way above my head. In that sense, I really was simply Rob's mate, mucking in to help. Of course, it became much more than that. I lived and breathed The Haçienda for eleven years, getting there early to spend days in the office booking live acts, spending most nights in there watching the acts I'd booked, and in between we used to spend hours in the pub round the corner, The Britons Protection, a classic, historic boozer with this long, impressive wooden bar. It was like our staff room, and Tony in particular loved it because it was one of the few buildings then left in the city centre that stood near the site of the Peterloo Massacre in 1819. It was surrounded by Manchester history, and his mission was always to add to Manchester history.

The issue that had the biggest impact on me was that they decided to open The Haçienda six days a week, which was next to impossible – that was a lot of music to be played and acts to get in. It was a big venue as well, so you needed to get hundreds of people in every night. The big draws at the clubs we loved in New York had their nights, one or two shifts a week. Opening so many nights made it a slog, and we didn't have a series of nights, with a variety of DJs.

It was one of the few things Rob and I disagreed about. We rarely fought about anything. For him, though, he really wasn't thinking commercially. I don't think he could. His original idea for the club was as a meeting place, a social club. 'We built The Haçienda because we had nowhere to go', he'd say. 'It's not just for the weekend.' It might have made sense if we could have carved off a section of this huge cathedral, but to open it up for a few people was such a waste of the facilities.

The first and, to an extent, the only DJ we had at The Haçienda when it opened was Hewan Clarke, who'd DJ'd in the seventies at the late-night after-hours – it opened at 11 – drinking den The Reno in Moss Side, at the centre of the West Indian community. He played brilliant soul and funk American imports he'd be the first to get from Spin-Inn. The Reno was open all week, which I think was one of the reasons it was decided The Haçienda should be open all week too, serving the community, even though The Haçienda community was initially a ragbag of local mavericks, loyal Factory fans and serious-looking student post-punks.

Clarke had done some DJing in the Pips soul room, and had a night at a low-key club called Fever nearby where he played jazz-funk and some purer jazz. Simon T from A Certain Ratio used to go with other ACR members, and they liked Hewan's style, playing and sometimes even dancing himself to a great selection of jazz styles when there might be only twenty people in the room. Ratio invited him on a small college tour with them, and he naturally met Tony, the group's overlord and protector, the manager who put them in baggy shorts and spray-tanned their skinny legs, as if this was the next stage on from Brian Epstein suiting up The Beatles.

Tony and Hewan bonded over a mutual love for Frankie Crocker, the exuberant emperor of disco radio in New York. Tony admired Frankie as an iconoclastic broadcaster, actor and media personality, while Hewan appreciated him as the smooth-voiced disc jockey who filtered Larry Levan's Garage playlist onto late-night radio, where soul met disco, new wave, and synthesised R&B. Tony was also fond of Hewan's style and brought him in as resident DJ. On paper, it was an excellent choice – someone with a cool local reputation who was also in tune with the almost weekly musical revolutions in New York, courtesy of tapes of Frankie's show on WBLS, which prepared Hewan for what was about to hit the cooler record shops in Britain, enabling him to stay one or two steps ahead.

Being at the controls of the DJ booth at The Haçienda was more a responsibility – rather than just being a music/DJ nerd playing relaxed late-night joints unconnected to any kind of ambitious cultural expectations. He also had to deal with The Haçienda's atrocious sound, the eccentricities of its controls, and the peculiar placing of the DJ booth at the side of the stage. No one could see in; the DJ could only see out through a small gap. Instead of being at the heart of the club, monitoring mood and guiding the night, making direct contact with the crowd, the DJ would be in exile.

Hewan would badger manager Howard Jones with ideas on how to help the sound and connect the DJ with the dancers, writing detailed notes about what was needed that somehow went missing for years. Especially after coming back from New York, we all knew what was needed, but first we had to keep the club alive. Friday and Saturday were obviously the main nights when people came, but there was still Monday to Thursday to worry about. Monday could be especially ice cold – this vast building dotted with customers, one or two who might have paid to get in, one or two who might not have personal or even professional attachments to Factory.

Hewan stoically played his carefully chosen records, continuing the soul room of Pips and the jazz-funk of Fever, but also realised he had to cater to the audience inherited from the Russell Club and the Roxy Room, playing electro pop, Gary Numan, Yazoo, ABC, Thompson Twins, the Associates, Eurythmics. It wasn't his bag, and he didn't have his heart in it, really.

Tony had asked Clarke to DJ because he thought that brought the Paradise Garage sound to The Haçienda, but there was much more to what Larry Levan played. Levan set trends but didn't follow any template. His approach was to play any mutant music that took his fancy, some of it still in the process of mutating, never sealing himself inside any specific musical groupings. Hewan was forced to turn to some obvious Saturday night crowd-pleasers, which offended his sense of purity.

The Black audience that followed Clarke to The Haçienda were confused, and those that were giving the club its long-raincoat, miserabilist image were also confused, with their own cutting-edge needs discovered in the fast-moving weekly music press. The one track that perhaps could bridge the two sides, 'Blue Monday', could only be used so many times.

It was as though 'Confusion', haphazardly built for New York's Fun House, an anxious, mesmeric hybrid of New Order's Manchester experience and Baker and Robie's New York knowledge, was the club's theme tune. Co-owners, New Order, including Rob, shouting 'Confusion' on a white indie electro record that passed muster in a niche proto-house club. None of it made any sense, but imagine if it had.

22
A right booker

The groups I was booking carried on the idea of a Factory club as a venue for the kind of new post-punk and independent label acts breaking through, the ones being covered in the more in touch areas of the music press and played on John Peel, some on the verge of being chart acts. As a venue, The Haçienda was regularly putting on some great bands, but the venue was really incongruous – the other extreme from the Russell Club – and it didn't help that it had this reputation for being the trendy home of Manchester's gloomies in their long grey raincoats. The plan wasn't for it to be a live music club, but that kept things going in the first years, or at least put some life into the building, and I loved booking bands.

I was always just happy to be doing anything in music, and I took to booking bands very easily, usually by just following my own taste. Some of the others at The Haçienda thought I was weirdly a bit of a pop freak, but that was coming from my love for Bowie and Roxy Music. I loved obscure, wild music as much as anyone – my central passion was soul and dance – but I also loved great pop music that was connected with glam, punk, post-punk and electro.

Years later, long after it was all over and my place in history was as Haçienda DJ, Wilson at some panel once said, 'Yes, we all know Pickering was a great disc jockey, but what you also must remember is that he was the greatest booker of all time.' He said 'booker', I pointed out, in case anyone misheard the first letter.

Cabaret Voltaire were the first to play at The Haçienda, and history reports that seventy-five people turned up. That would have been ok-ish in the Russell Club, but at The Haçienda it wasn't a good look, and all that empty space gave us the chills. If friends of Factory Records can't pull a few hundred, we're in real trouble. Considering what happened to The Haçienda, taking its place in the history of house music, they were the perfect group to be first, with their own contribution to the pre-house music percolating in the 1980s – combining European electronic experimenters with Black Chicago and New York artists and disc jockeys looking to throw off the disco harness. Some wit observed that maybe more would have come for the Cabs, but they couldn't see the name plaque outside and know where the door was. The other problem was in the first two years, you needed to be a member to get in, unless you were signed in by another member, which created restricted access.

In the first year, we had Echo & the Bunnymen, Eurythmics, Simple Minds, Tears for Fears supporting The Thompson Twins, Yazoo, The Psychedelic Furs, Big Country, Thomas Dolby, The Associates, and Soft Cell. That looks very familiar in hindsight, but at the time it was relatively niche. We'd put groups on for 50p sometimes weeks before they had their first hit. In June 1982, I booked Culture Club for £600, a month after Cabaret Voltaire and three months before they released 'Do You Really Want To Hurt Me'. It would have been three grand within a few weeks of that.

I was there in the club when they were doing their soundcheck. Boy George was gently mocking me for all the moody Manchester bands on Factory that had come after Joy Division, running through all those obvious London jokes about the Manchester weather and our so-called northern habits. 'Is everyone going to come wearing a raincoat?' he wondered. 'Do you wear clogs? Where's your pigeon loft?' He was a wonderful wind-up merchant, but I had work to do. Or I just wanted to get out of the way of his sarcastic jibes about a non-existent Manchester.

'I don't know', I said, 'but if you'll excuse me, I'm going to shoot some windows in at the back.' That perked him up. I had an air rifle to let off some steam when being polite to bands was stretching my patience, and we spent a very pleasant afternoon aiming at some broken windows in derelict buildings overlooking the canal. He had all his Boy George clobber on – the dreads, hat, coat, the whole gothic Rasta thing that would soon be famous around the world – and he was breaking windows, laughing his head off. A little later, he was singing for over six hundred people, and it was a sign of what the club could look like with people and an atmosphere. Don't mention the sound, though.

The joke was that we promised bands at the soundcheck the sound would be better once there were people in the venue. Liz Frazer of Cocteau Twins, a delicate soul with a very gorgeous, radiant voice, burst into tears when she heard the sound during their soundcheck. She was too fragile for me to tell her that the sound would be better with an audience – and, honestly, it was a lie. I couldn't do that to her. She got through the show, but I had the feeling she was crying inside all the way through.

Some bands really got the place or knew how to play it and make it their own. The failing sound and the shape – the combination of bars and alcoves, all the quirks that pissed others off – they really took to it. Frankie Goes to Hollywood from Liverpool turned up on a Saturday night a few weeks before their debut single 'Relax' made number 1 and the group took over the nation, five days before The Smiths' tumultuous homecoming after their debut *Top of the Pops* show in November 1983. 'Our friends from Liverpool', as Tony would say about Liverpool people, with that mix he perfected of affection and slight condescension. Hooky drove Frankie's singer Holly Johnson in through the crowd onto the stage on the back of his motorcycle. You could see we were running our own club and there were no grown-ups involved; it was a health and safety nightmare.

The great drag queen and outrageous muse of the film director John Waters, Divine, appeared in between Frankie and The Smiths, so to speak. You'd never have described the club as failing that week.

The Glaswegian pop beauties Orange Juice came back again and again, and never charged much even as they got more popular. We'd get a thousand fans in and made a lot of money from them, because their singer Edwyn Collins loved the place. Orange Juice's magic trick of mixing slick, chic rhythms with wry Buzzcocks starkness was another clue to the destiny of the club.

The £3.50 Grandmaster Flash and the Furious Five show in December 1982 was another glimpse of a future where The Haçienda could have a mythological sheen. Some of our regular white kids were baptised into a crowd-hyping, party-mad dance music that had its own radical force. 'White Lines' would become a Haçienda favourite after that. Shows like that were when there were loads of legs on the dance floor and a lively buzz in different corners of the place, when the building didn't seem like a chilly chasm hard to fill, but a place where you got moved somewhere.

Maybe forty hardy souls turned up for one of the avant-electro groups I liked when I was in Rotterdam, the German Liaisons Dangereuses, which was seen as an absolute disaster but I took another view – in a way, they played a ghostly, post-no wave disco-not-disco preview of the house that would come to save and make The Haçienda.

In 1982, adrift between Suicide and Adonis, between ESG and Yello, between post-punk and techno, lost in a new building that hadn't yet made its name, Liaisons Dangereuses were seen as dour, tricky weirdos. But then only forty people had turned up to see the Sex Pistols when they first played in Manchester. And sometimes, when there were only fifty people in there, every single one of them was having a ball.

You never know who's in the audience paying close attention when someone like Liaisons Dangereuses played. Someone who goes on to be in 808 State, perhaps, or someone who goes on to DJ at The Haçienda, and could already see where these throbbing rhythms, some of them weird cousins of irresistible Italo insistence, were heading. Yello would sample Liaisons Dangereuses' 'Los Ninos del Parque' – a big track during the early Chicago house years – on their worldwide hit 'Oh Yeah', which was how the 'danceable weird shit' was often being smuggled into the mainstream.

The premise for me became, well, the average attendance for a Haçienda show settled down at around two hundred; they're going to come anyway, so I could book what I wanted. The list represents where alternative, independent music was at the time and where it was heading. Nick Cave, who was splendidly bad-tempered, appeared with The Birthday Party. I booked Julian Cope cheap in March 1984 as part of his first solo tour, but as a chart act he had to be sold behind a pseudonym, which meant we only got our basic two hundred people. His show ended up as a sort of psychedelic lock-in, with acid instead of beer, many of us including Julian falling out into daylight at eight in the morning, one or two taking a few days to recover. That was another glimpse of a future Haçienda – the clues were building up.

Other times, disaster beckoned, which symbolised the recklessness of the place, sometimes leading to mayhem. Extremist madcap Berlin noise artists Einstürzende Neubauten appeared in 1983. Their set not only featured shattered glass flying out into the audience, but group leader Blixa Bargeld, at the peak of his screeching, death-longing powers, had a metal plate installed into the floor that he would ferociously attack with his chosen instrument, a pneumatic drill. He hadn't used that at the sound check.

Suddenly, during the performance, he turned his attention to the column that ran down the middle of the stage and started drilling into it. Panic ensued, as Haçienda staff realised the load-bearing column was central to holding up the whole building. An initial polite if alarmed warning for him to stop was obviously ignored. He attacked the column with more relish. Rob was now at the side of the stage screaming his head off: 'I'll fucking kill you!' He had to be held back from grabbing Blixa, putting both of them in danger of pulling the roof down. Someone a little more qualified for this kind of emergency action finally grabbed Blixa and pulled him away before he caused havoc. The blizzard of noise came to an abrupt halt. The crowd cheered, thinking it was part of the show.

Fate was trying to tell us something. The Haçienda must be demolished.

But the gigs kept coming. I was having a fine time inviting my favourite groups and singers: The Cramps, Burning Spear, Prefab Sprout, Scritti Politti, Psychic TV, Orange Juice, Curtis Mayfield, Defunkt, Hüsker Dü, Robert Palmer, Laibach, Mark Stewart and the Maffia. The Haçienda was dismissed during those early years as 'Wilson's Folly', but it was genuinely trying to do something useful.

There were afternoon film screenings, stealing an idea that New Hormones' experimental Beach Club had started in March 1980, trying to give it arts venue leanings. The Beach in turn had wanted to keep the Russell Club spirit going, when it looked like the flame might be going out.

The Haçienda didn't get many more people coming to the one-off experimental events than the Beach Club, which was based in a squalid pub around the back of Shudehill. There were only so many people interested in the extreme and experimental, but it was part of the same view that those who ran the Beach Club had – this is the sort of thing Manchester should have. You never know where it can lead.

The Beach Club shut down around early March 1982, faced with limited attendance, and The Haçienda inherited that limited attendance, but in premises many times the size. The Beach was reanimating the idea of happenings and performance art of the 1960s in small, ad hoc underground venues; The Haçienda was dedicated to driving the culture of the city from within a purpose-built art house.

The lifeless concrete barn was nearly full when legendary beat guru William Burroughs did a reading in his hypnotic, faintly threatening drawl, as part of a Burroughs-themed series of events curated by Genesis P. Orridge and Peter Christopherson of Psychic TV in London and Manchester, one of the ultimate examples of the club's special one-offs. Those in the audience who were the weird children who had turned into punks, which was most of them, were in their element. (A few hundred yards away, on the same night, the Smiths were playing their first ever show at The Ritz.)

The larger effect was to perpetuate the image of the club as more avant-garde and insular than accessible to locals. In the long run, it left unique cultural traces in Manchester that linger, and had an effect you can't plan. The reality of the situation might have been that actually there was no need for clubs with utopian post-punk avant-garde leanings that were something more than just live events and alcohol, although there were those of us Manchester contrarians who were not going to take no for answer.

Also, that rush of new groups after punk had not necessarily halted, but there was nothing as dramatically new as Joy Division, Buzzcocks, Magazine, The Fall, John Cooper Clarke, Ludus, A Certain Ratio. We put all of those on at The Haçienda, as well as Beach temporary 'house band' Eric Random and the new Factory groups that were being wrongly filed away in the mainstream music press as Joy Division clones – Stockholm Monsters, Section 25 – and Quando Quango also played a couple of times.

Being brutal, the Manchester music scene had levelled out, and maybe that was natural, and maybe nothing was going to have the kind of impact driven by punk and the Sex Pistols again. We did a small season in early 1983, to present what we called the best of Manchester, to highlight some of the newer bands still being washed along by a provocative post-punk energy as the world was taking a more decorative new romantic turn.

It was another attempt to build a scene from within, and put The Haçienda at the centre. James played, some of whom had been pot collectors in The Haçienda, and The Chameleons, who, looking at it one way, had missed the post-punk wagon and, in another, were ahead of the Britpop era. Something was happening, but it was overshadowed by the city's own tumultuous recent history.

I signed James to Factory, in the Factory sense of not having a contract, after Tony pointed out to me that as well as Rob's mate I was also in charge of A&R, responsible for finding new bands. No extra money, of course – Tony probably expected me to pay him – but it got my juices flowing. One or two of James played football with me, and they'd always be in The Haçienda, and they asked if I'd listen to a cassette they'd made. It had thirteen songs and sounded great; they'd really worked themselves out, as though Orange Juice were a Factory band. I put them on an evening called A Factory Outing, with New Order, Vini Reilly and Section 25, christening them Factory before they had a chance to work out what that meant.

Rob and I loved the cassette; it sounded like a complete album, and Tony got interested, as was often the case after the fact, but rewriting things later to put himself in the lead spot. Fair enough.

It was his job. James definitely weren't a dance band, and were the closest to Tony's beloved freaky folk rock as anything on Factory. There were some tough nuts in the group, and also Tim Booth, who had something of the hippy about him, which Tony liked. They were a bit scally, a bit cosmic, and Tony was a sucker for that combination of rough and perversely romantic.

James released *Jimone* as a three-track EP on Factory, recorded at Strawberry in Stockport, and were ridiculously fussy from the beginning about the songs they wanted on it. They'd have been happier not making records, which was beyond even Factory. For some reason, the songs they did choose for *Jimone* were what they considered their worst, so they didn't ruin their better songs until they knew what they were doing in the studio. Fair enough. They had a plan and viewed the EP as a calling card to get some gigs outside Manchester, which initially was a struggle as agents wanted a band that had a single out.

They were always a bit funny about Factory, not wanting to lose themselves in its constant drama and occasional self-importance, and *Jimone* was their sarky comment on the fastidious Factory catalogue system. The sleeve was a last-minute rush to make the deadline and was at the opposite end to the sublime Factory sleeves of Peter Saville, with an aura that was often more his than the groups'. For their first photo session with Kevin Cummins, James turned their back to the camera.

The record fulfilled its purpose by receiving single of the week reviews in the music press, as if heralding a new Manchester scene, made up of straight-faced lyrical guitar bands using common surnames for their own name. Factory released a second EP, *James II*, and the group by now had their suspicions confirmed that Factory was no ordinary record label, and not necessarily in a good way. We were convinced they were even crazier and more uncompromising than us, possibly in a good way, and Rob and I really wanted them to be the next big Factory act.

Gigs were coming, music press coverage was favourable – one critic claimed they were the future of British music – but Factory weren't so good at getting their records into the shops. We combined the two EPs into one, *Village Fire*, which helped James secure a more conventional and lucrative record deal with Sire at Warners.

Being as awkward and untogether as each other should have led to at least one great, lost Factory album, for old times' sake. Tim would always say to me that they left too early; it was a mistake. Rob and I would have happily put out that first cassette they gave us as an album, but we lost it. We searched through hundreds of cassettes looking for it, but it had somehow self-destructed.

The hits and soaring anthems came for James in the nineties, which is what they wanted, but of course not on Factory, and when they were safely clear of any Manchester scenes they might be pulled into. They never wanted to be part of a Manchester scene, in case they didn't outlast the scene. The oddest and most careful of bands became quite ordinary, as if to spite themselves, or Factory. When they left, Tony's pragmatic attitude was, 'Oh well, let's try again', in terms of finding another awkward, unworldly, but one-of-a-kind rock band. Which I did – if not deliberately.

23
A lost soul

Factory's almost undercover jazz-funk group 52nd Street played the new Manchester series, having come to Factory via their bass player Derrick Johnson, brother of A Certain Ratio's Donald Johnson, both also collaborators with Quando Quango. Rob and I were huge fans, and they weren't as anomalous as they seemed – a sparkling dance band among the apparent long raincoats. There was a dance label within Factory, a phantom element pushed by Rob and I that reflected Manchester's non-punk scenes, but it was just never made obvious. Tony wouldn't have allowed it anyway: 'Dance music doesn't sell albums, darling.'

Factory tried their usual tricks to promote *52nd Street* – Tony put them on his Granada arts magazine show, the Factory-friendly music press loved them, and their first Donald Johnson-produced Factory record 'Cool as Ice' was a coveted single of the week in NME. Factory though were, to put it mildly, slack when it came to publicity and promotion, and there was no radio play, which effectively killed it. There was nothing cut-throat about Factory when it came to actually selling records.

There were many things that were weird about Tony's resistance to dance music, even as we to some extent – with 52nd Street, with A Certain Ratio, with Quando Quango, with ESG, with what was happening with New Order as they went more electronic – we were as much a dance label as we were a post-punk label, or a post-genre label. Even Section 25 were using sequencers, and getting played in the New York clubs.

There was a dance dimension to Factory, especially when me and Rob were taking the initiative with the A&R direction. With our taste and long-standing love for Black music, it would have been crazy if it hadn't happened. We signed Marcel King in 1983 – as much as there was ever a signature or contract with Factory – who was very much a part of Black Manchester music history as the singer in a northern Jackson 5, Sweet Sensation, with 17-year-old Marcel and an exquisite falsetto as the Michael Jackson. Barry Johnson, who'd later work with Quando Quango, was also part of the group. They had come through an early 1970s talent show called *New Faces*, a version of *X Factor* where pop producer and composer Tony Hatch, of Petula Clarke's 'Downtown', known as the British Burt Bacharach, was the show's Simon Cowell. Sweet Sensation had a gorgeous number 1 single in 1974, 'Sad Sweet Dreamer', produced by Hatch, which sounded like it could have been made in Philadelphia, a Philly soul classic. It was typical talent show failure after that; a minor hit, a humiliating failed bid in 1977 to represent Britain in the Eurovision Song Contest.

Marcel's fall from grace was particularly awful – he had very little parental care, and in 1983 Rob heard he was sleeping in the back of a car in Moss Side, pretty much homeless. Rob started to look after him, gave him money, and Bernard Sumner and Donald Johnson, becoming Factory house producers – Bernard in that revelatory 'Blue Monday' zone of discovery – produced one of Factory's great lost pop singles, 'Reach for Love', which Marcel wrote.

Mark Kamins did a brilliant mix, boosting the drums, doing all sorts of things with Marcel's voice. It was like some wonderful imagining of New Order as a soul group. It was a Haçienda hit, the perfect NYC–MCR crossover, one of the key moments in the transition of The Haçienda from indie club to dance centre, and we put him on a few times. None of it shifted the needle for Factory's reputation, nor rescued Marcel from his sad fate as a doomed child star.

Marcel began to rely on Rob to help him out, and was badly scarred by what happened after his last attempt to be a star, making him difficult to deal with. Rob and I would have long chats with him, trying to get something going, but I don't think we ever got through to him. He had this great voice, but he didn't put that first – he was always anxious that money was running out. Just surviving was his main drive.

The whole thing fell apart, and Marcel did a couple of things that cost him Rob's trust. Rob, who behind the bluff exterior was a sensitive soul, couldn't keep the relationship going. It was tragically short-lived and Rob was shattered that it didn't come to anything. Rob had his own scars after what had happened to Ian Curtis, and emotionally he was getting a lot of punishment trying to make things work, at the club, and with some of the Factory artists he was committed to. He put on that funny, mordant Rob front, but it was taking its toll.

Marcel was last spotted wandering the streets of Moss Side, destitute and lost, and died in 1995 aged 35, leaving behind one unassailable pop classic, and this glorious moment when the Factory Sound came with a Motown voice.

24
A famous guitarist

For local soul nerds, used to having to fight for wider attention, 52nd Street and Marcel were far more Manchester than the jaunty miserabilists Stockholm Monsters – it was all a matter of perspective – and a few years later, this largely neglected Manchester of funk and soul aficionados would be popularised by Simply Red. It wasn't what was needed, though, to take Manchester culturally somewhere else in the way Buzzcocks, The Fall and Joy Division had five years earlier.

I'd become friends with a chatty, cool-looking 18-year-old kid working in X Clothes, part of a small northern chain of boutiques in a basement on Chapel Walks off Cross Street, near Pips. X Clothes was the best place to go if you were now not part of any of the obvious sixties tribes, and were circling all the street style sub-cults that had emerged after punk. There'd always be great music playing, and people swapping gossip and news – the sort that can lead to the formation of a little scene, that can become a bigger scene.

You had to have a certain confidence yourself to go in there and not look or feel out of place – so it had one of those in-built filters that meant only like-minded people felt comfortable. I was a few years older than Johnny, but I think I got away with it. Tony, when he ventured in once or twice, not so much.

i-D magazine, which didn't separate music from fashion, had launched in 1980 and quickly moved on from being a punk-inspired hand-stapled fanzine. *The Face*, a bold, full-colour style magazine, had just started, edited by visionary ex-mod Nick Logan, who had an innate understanding of the close relationship between music and clothes. Johnny X Clothes, as he was known then, could have walked out of a photo spread in *i-D* or *The Face*, with a wondrous quiff built for him by his close pal and fellow music fanatic, Andrew Berry – the pair would also DJ at a local club. Johnny was very spirited, had already left home – he snuck off to see his first live gig, Slaughter and the Dogs, when he was twelve – and you could mention something musical and he would talk for hours.

He'd been on an ITV magazine show in 1981, *Devil's Advocate*, where a hundred unemployed working class 16–21 year-olds from inner-city Manchester talked about the impact of unemployment, when local school leavers had almost no chance of getting a job. Johnny admitted he didn't mind being on the dole because it gave him time to play the guitar and get better, as his ambition was to be in a band. It wasn't the anger and frustration that the programme was looking for, and the indignant host asked if it was okay that people paid their taxes to support him while he did nothing but play his guitar. 'Absolutely', said Johnny. He said, 'I'm going to be a famous guitarist.' It was so bloody Manchester, and it turned out Johnny had the walk to match the talk.

I knew he had formed a group called The Smiths – which was also so bloody Manchester – and they had played a couple of gigs, their first one at The Ritz on 4 October 1982, supporting fancy London zoot-suited salsa stylists Blue Rondo à la Turk as part of 'An Evening of Pure Pleasure'. Johnny was always looking for more places to play. I told him we'd put them on at The Haçienda. He'd got a cassette he would play in the shop in the middle of all the classic music they'd play. To say the least, it sounded like a real band.

I put them on supporting 52nd Street, which musically made no sense, but made perfect Haçienda sense. The skinny, quiffed singer Morrissey, four years older than Johnny – which was quite a gap then – was someone you'd seen around town the past few years, lurking in corners, watching things from a distance. He had the airs and graces of someone who could see the world for what it was, and he wasn't too happy about it.

Johnny and Morrissey had met because those that knew them both thought they had to. One was good with words, the other good with riffs. Both knew that what they knew was unlike anyone else, and when they came together their individual rare knowledge was multiplied. Johnny had been in other bands with other singers, but none came close to how much he felt he was on a mission. Morrissey, so it seemed as soon as they met and started to write songs together, was also on a mission. At that first Haçienda show he was already acting like he was giving the audience something they couldn't live without.

Morrissey had written a book about one of Johnny's favourites, the New York Dolls, and a few withering reviews for *Record Mirror*. He'd reviewed Depeche Mode at Rafters in 1981 – 'they resurrect every murderously monotonous cliché known to modern man' – which enabled him to slip in a mention of his friend Linder's antic group Ludus, the support act. Ludus wallowed in other people's depravities, he said, so their music offers everything to everyone.

By 1983, he might have missed his moment, having been around plugging away since the Pistols show, never finding the right place, for his own self-regard apart from anything else. He dressed the stage with flowers, feeling that the grey, echoey Haçienda lacked a certain warmth. He was adjusting the controls. And then, at The Haçienda, with hair freshly quiffed, in a white polo neck, Johnny played guitar.

25
A contribution from Johnny Marr

I kind of designed The Smiths taking note of a lot of things not to do. There was a lot of music to copy around Manchester at the time, and I wanted it to be very fresh and unlike the Factory Manchester, or the Devoto Buzzcocks Manchester, which had been done. I wanted to be part of a new community, which actually did involve The Haçienda, which was like the new Factory, and a new place to try things that the old guard didn't have. It was up to the newcomers to do something with it, and in that sense, Mike was one of the newcomers. And I came to The Haçienda through him. He invited me in.

When I went to see Morrissey and I knocked on his door, which has gone down in history, he was still looking very Factory. He was very grey and ACR, and had like an Ian Curtis side parting. My best mate Andrew Berry, who I was living with, sorted out his hair. Andrew DJ'd in various Manchester venues like Berlin, and he would later DJ with Mike, so there was continuity there.

The point was, Mike was into new electro, so I was aware of that as well, and even though there's no obvious influence on a guitar band like The Smiths, it did influence me when it came to the structure and flow of their songs. Manchester to me was always about having a wide set of influences and knowing how to make good use of them – not by copying, but by following their spirit.

James would be a regular support for us, and that was another connection with Mike, because he had brought them into Factory. It's that thing The Haçienda was set up for when Rob first thought of it – a kind of creative hub where young locals could meet and mingle, and make things happen. And as Rob's mate, Mike was part of that – you couldn't define it or explain it, it was just happening. And why was he the one in charge of booking bands? No one would have said it then, and it wasn't even an obvious thing, but he was the one who did it who had taste. He was curating a list – we can use that word now, and I can use it when I am talking about how I put together The Smiths. It was an act of curation based on what turned out to be a specialist knowledge that we all had that at the time just seemed natural and part of our lives.

But some people had taste and some didn't, and if Mike hadn't been booking the gigs and following his own instinct about what was happening and what wasn't happening, it would have been very different. You look at the bands he was booking when The Haçienda was apparently empty and no one went, apart from local students, and it's a history of music from that period. You can also define who Mike was just by saying, well, he booked Defunkt, trombonist Joseph Bowie's group that mixed punk, pop and the avant-garde. I saw Defunkt because of Mike, and that's a special thing. It was almost a voluntary role he had because I bet he wasn't being paid any sort of going rate. That was absolutely the spirit of the place.

It's fallen between the cracks in the acid history of the club, but week in, week out Mike was putting on incredible bands at really important times in their development. He definitely did with The Smiths.

At the time it was just, 'Oh great, we've got a gig', but it did make us feel so good about ourselves. You can look at the video of that first Smiths show at The Haçienda – because Factory, because Tony was a TV man, filmed everything – and what's great is you can really see us feeling good about ourselves, knowing that we'd achieved the basic element for a new group at the time. We weren't ordinary. We were exactly ourselves. People heard that in different ways, but one thing you couldn't deny was you had to wonder – where the hell has that come from? Well, from Manchester, but a Manchester that was always changing, and there were always those, like Mike, who were aware of that change.

Without my musical taste, and my guitar playing distilling all my favourite guitarists into my own thing, and how that fitted with fashion, The Smiths would have been very different. Well, it wouldn't have been The Smiths. The group didn't appear out of nowhere, and those songs I wrote with Morrissey came so quickly because we both had taste, based on our own likes and dislikes and our own dreams.

We didn't talk about it like I can now because part of it was that it just happened, and you went along with it. We weren't actively thinking, oh, this is going to change music; we were just thinking we should try this, and this. By knowing as much what we shouldn't be doing as what we should.

I got lost in The Smiths and then what happened after we split, and then I remember about 1988, my guitar roadie, who I'd known since school, and he was always very switched on, was raving about a new scene. He'd been to The Haçienda, which was something else by then, and he said, 'You won't fucking believe the records Mike Pickering is playing.' And I went along, and I took the appropriate stimulants, and I thought, Mike's taken things by the scruff of the neck and is showing everyone else how to do it. How to make The Haçienda. He'd found another punk. He'd found another Manchester. He didn't talk about it much. I always thought he should talk about it more.

26
A culture clash

I'd become good friends with Mark Kamins, and asked him to come over from New York to do a Saturday night guest spot at The Haçienda, just to see what would happen if we went to the source itself of some of the dreams for the club. He'd always tell me that nothing was planned about the success of Danceteria; it just happened, one thing leading to another. We'd vaguely followed that principle at The Haçienda, but one thing didn't seem to be leading to another.

Maybe Mark had the key, or maybe I was overthinking it. Mark's set made no sense to Hewan, whose nose was put out, and his proof that Mark's methods were no good in Manchester, with its own demands, was an empty dance floor. It was two completely different sensibilities: Hewan putting together a musical set based on superlative, very musical knowledge, leading the crowd on; Mark creating a musical act, looking for a response to his commitment to new music, which had no familiar touchstones.

Hewan didn't feel anything from Mark; felt he was all over the place. DJs like Hewan Clarke had this tendency to approach what they did like an academic, as a teacher, following established logic. Mark just wanted to play crazy new music in any order he felt like as the mood took him. He wasn't teaching the audience; he wanted to work with them, as collaborators.

At The Haçienda he thought he should play a lot of Manchester music, whereas we wanted him to bring his American approach with him. He didn't really get The Haçienda – the layout, the drinking, the switch between live band, DJ, live band, DJ. He tried to chat up local girls like he would in New York, which quickly taught him a few lessons about Manchester customs, none of which he ever got used to.

The one thing Mark and Hewan did agree on was that the DJ box was too small; it wasn't a hub. It was an affront to the art of the DJ, but then Hewan thought the same thing when I came back from a New York trip inspired by Levan, Jellybean, Mancuso and Co.'s lack of a microphone.

'No mikes for the DJs', I announced, and even for the coolest DJ in Manchester, used to talking through the set as part of their hosting duties, this was sacrilege. They freaked out when I said, 'No microphone.' You don't need to tell them what you're playing; they're not all stood around with notepads writing it all down. It was that academic thing; they didn't think of themselves as performers, but musical guides. If someone wants to know, they'll work it out. For the so-called professional DJ, it was like ripping their manhood away. We also needed to open the DJ booth, so the DJ wasn't cut off from what was happening and could actually hear the music they were playing.

Mark would come over a lot, although he wasn't at The Haçienda in 1984 when his ex, Madonna, performed one of her New York-style PAs for Channel 4's live rock show *The Tube*. She basically danced with her brother to four songs from her first album. The audience didn't know what to make of someone doing a dance routine and miming, and she wasn't then Madonna; she was connected with Lydia Lunch and even ESG in our minds, so we were a bit confused. One or two cans were chucked in her direction, and most of the crowd simply stood and stared, as if it was a rehearsal for the real thing. We didn't rate her chances much.

Her tour manager, an old pal of Mark Kamins, took me to say hello in her dressing room, and we had met before, at the Danceteria. She had no memory of that, of course, and, like when we first met, she had no interest in looking me in the eye. The tour manager said, 'Yes, you know, Mark did that mix of "Love Tempo" for Mike's group, Quando Quango.' 'Oh, that dross', she sneered. 'Nice to meet you and all, love', I said.

Later, Rob or Tony offered her £50 to go back out and do an encore. She was really pissed off with the whole thing, and would later claim she had never been to The Haçienda, which tickled Tony, as there were some classic Kevin Cummins photographs of her performing there, making full posing use of Ben Kelly's columns.

We thought we'd show Madonna a thing or two about Manchester by putting on a Factory All-Stars show, with Bernard, Gonnie, me, Donald and Simon from ACR, Beverly from 52nd Street and Marcel. We performed a couple of euphoric Factory 'love' classics, Marcel's 'Reach For Love', which we couldn't spoil, and Joy Division's 'Love Will Tear Us Apart', which was a disaster. We milled about like we were a shambolic charity band, all singing a different song in a different key, following a different tempo. We were torn apart.

Hooky made up some story about Madonna ending up at my house, getting locked out and having to sleep in the porch, which entered local folklore for a while. The evening did end in chaos – Rob banning *The Tube* producer Chris Cowie from The Haçienda for life after some argument – but I can safely say me and Madonna never made up and we never had a housewarming party at my new house.

I had moved out of Rob and Lesley's into the first house I bought on the advice of my dad, shoving me onto the property ladder so I was ready when all this music malarkey stopped. It was a dowdy two-up two-down in Chorlton near the Gretton's that I could just about afford. My dad convinced me that now I was grown up, and earning a regular wage – I didn't dare tell him how little Factory were paying me – I had to take life more seriously. I was hitting thirty. I couldn't be a lodger for ever, as comfy as it was being part of the Gretton unit.

Mark Kamins would stay with me when he came over. He used to roll up at Manchester airport after an all-night flight from New York, having drunk neat rum all the way over. I could hear him shout 'Mikey' before I could even see him as he came through the door into the arrivals hall.

He loved Manchester, but being larger than life, and from New York, he found it small and mostly closed, and when it came to basic home comforts, about forty years behind America. The first shower he took in my house completely baffled him, coming from the land of the power shower. 'Mike!!! There's no water coming out of the shower!' There was, but just a standard miserable Chorlton dribble, not a skin-scalding New York torrent. I told him, 'That's all you're going to get, mate. I'll throw a pan of water over you if you'd like.' He got used to it, but it made him think we were even madder in Manchester than we thought to put up with it.

Rob and I took him to see Manchester City play at Oldham Athletic in the 1987/88 season, when City were in the Second Division, having just been relegated for the second time in the eighties. It was a tough division, filled with tough teams, and the eighties were a tough decade for City.

They'd long lost their Mercer/Allison glow, were usually in some sort of struggle to find form, and their then manager, Mel Machin, was having to work hard to win over the fans, who wanted someone with the flamboyance of Allison. Being City fans, though, whatever the dire circumstances, we stayed true Blue, and even as Rob and I were having our adventures in music and dealing with The Haçienda, the City road kept on rolling through rare triumph and familiar disaster. Mel helped City back into promotion after three years, but as a reward the chaotic City chairman Peter Swales fired him.

Swales, who possessed an alarming comb-over, had made his money in the audio and hi-fi business in the sixties and seventies, and was City's chairman for twenty years. His erratic reign meant that City could be relied on to be as bad off the pitch as on it, which gave long-suffering City fans plenty to moan about – which could be part of the pleasure.

Rob and I once stayed for hours after a dreadful City performance for Chairman Swales to leave Maine Road and swan off in his chairman's typical Rolls-Royce. We waited in the cold, determined to have it out with him. Peter Gardner, who covered City in the *Manchester Evening News* for years, walked out and we asked him, 'Was Swales still inside?' 'Yeah, I think so.' We thought, well, he should know.

After a while, some of the City stewards asked us what we were doing, hanging around when everyone had gone home. 'We want to see Swales', Rob said. 'We want to have a word with him.' 'Well, what do you want to say to him?' Rob replied, as if it was obvious, 'We want to tell him to fuck off.'

The eighties were also tough on the terraces, marked by the era of football hooliganism – or at least the perception of it – which was organised and constant. 'The football fan' was seen as a single anti-social working-class mass, driven by drink to wreck property and attack opposition supporters. Football fans were not regarded as normal people, and the Thatcher Government did all it could to suppress them, treating them almost as a political enemy.

Grounds were primitive. It was the last years before all-seater stadiums, so you'd be crushed into cramped stands, with plenty of spontaneous outbursts between rival fans – these were exaggerated in the media. The whole environment encouraged disorder.

We'd had a chat once with Mark in New York, with Michael Duval of Plan K and Les Disque Du Crépuscule, and they were completely confused by the idea of football hooliganism. We tried to explain there were outbreaks of hooliganism, the culmination of years of violence, of the establishment treating working-class men like scum, so some of them ended up acting like scum. But there was also camaraderie, the fighting against the odds, always the hope and expectation. We tried to draw comparisons between working-class football fans purging pent-up energy and the Black and gay fans in the New York clubs.

When Mark was over one time, we said we'd take him to a match so he could see for himself what we found exciting – even addictive – about football and following a team. Choosing the Oldham–City match away was probably a mistake, as it was a derby, the fans hating each other for the sake of it, confirming the media view that a football match was simply an excuse for a mass brawl. It was the attitude that led to the Hillsborough Disaster in 1989 when the police assumed that chaos on the terraces was hooligan behaviour – not helpless, innocent fans being crushed to death because of typically badly thought-out crowd control.

It was amazing that no one died at the Oldham match. It was utter mayhem as soon as we got to the ground. Poor Mark thought we were taking him to war. There were more City fans than Oldham, and most of them were invading the ground, climbing over fences, no one paying to get in. Mark's face was frozen when a sudden noisy stampede of fans charged right past us shouting something vile at the top of their voices.

Mark wanted to leave immediately, but we said, don't worry, it's just a little scuffle between the police and some fans. You've got to see the match. We managed to get inside, but it was so crowded that we were spilling onto the pitch. We decided to take Mark over to the stand on the other side of the pitch, near the dugout where manager Mel Machin would be standing. We thought it seemed safer, and for a few minutes it wasn't too bad, if a little squeezed. Then Mel Machin came out with the team and stood just in front of us wearing the worst tracksuit I'd ever seen in my life. It made him look like a giant-sized toddler.

All the City fans around us started shrieking with laughter at the sight, making up chants about how awful he looked. 'Did your mum buy you that?' When the match started, there was no way Mark could understand that the game was of less importance to the 15,000 worked-up City fans than hurling abuse at the opposite fans – and even at their own manager, even between themselves. I said, 'Don't worry – it's just a way we keep warm.' Mark stood shivering in the middle of loads of lads bumping into each other and shouting their heads off as if they hated the world. He looked like he'd landed in hell.

It was a terrible day, and we got a shell-shocked Mark out of there long before the end of the match. He was a nervous wreck. 'Never do that to me again', he said. Rob grunted, 'That was quite mild really. I've seen worse.'

It was a one-all draw, but Mark never knew that – and never wanted to know.

27
A challenge

I told Rob and Tony that I wanted Mark to produce the Quando Quango album, and they couldn't think of any reason to say no, even though it was going to be the most expensive album Factory had made, with the travel and the studios Mark wanted to use.

He wasn't a producer, more a motivator, a source of energy, a human catalyst, one of those DJs becoming producers because they knew the sound of the latest thing being played, and treated the studio in a cavalier fashion, which led to wonderful mistakes.

He wasn't experienced at working with vocals, which you can hear if you compare his production of Madonna's debut, 'Everybody', with what she did next. Her voice needed skilled studio work to sell in the numbers she wanted. Pushing the needle into the red and achieving what a professional producer would hear as distortion didn't bother him.

None of that bothered me or Gonnie, or Rob and Tony. We wanted the happening hip New York sound, like New Order did with Baker and Robie, along with all the joyous, unexpected clashing of styles that had happened in New York over the last few years.

We recorded most of his songs for *Pigs and Battleships*, our debut and only album, named after a 1961 film about gangsters in post-war American-occupied Japan, in Strawberry Studios in Stockport, very much a Factory house studio – where Martin Hannett had produced Joy Division's *Unknown Pleasures*. We had a kind of Factory house band playing on the record: poetic guitarist Vini Reilly, the always-groovy Johnson brothers on bass and drums, singer Beverly from

52nd Street, Andy Connell and Simon Topping from A Certain Ratio on percussion, who by now was a regular member.

The last track we worked on, 'Genius', was the album's opening track, so it started with the end-of-the-party sound we made at the close of the recording sessions. I think there was a feeling between me and Gonnie that the group itself was coming to an end. It hadn't been built to last long, and our records were made to celebrate the fact we existed at all. Two or three years of slogging up and down motorways in cramped transit vans, playing soulless college venues to hardly any people, was causing the original fire to flicker.

It was getting harder and harder for me and Gonnie, being married and in a band which became less and less enjoyable for us the more formalised it got. We were arguing before and after gigs about silly little things, and working closely together at The Haçienda as well. If the album had done better than it did, after all the love and joy we had put into Quando, it might have lifted us up into a new dimension. The music we were making needed a reaction from people that we weren't getting.

Factory, as a point of policy – don't force it – never promoted their records, often relying on some form of magic dust to help them on their way. We were getting more of that magic dust in New York than we were in Britain. We'd be playing Paradise Garage with Chaka Khan and Larry Levan, then coming back to play Stafford University in front of twenty people. The heat of one – and the cold of the other – was becoming too much for me.

Our album got its nice catalogue number, Fac 110, and received some positive reviews – and others that were more suspicious of what seemed to be half a Factory album, whatever that meant, and half a dance album, which made Tony panic a little. 'Dance albums don't sell, darling.' It seemed a lot to put into something that wasn't going anywhere, and I started to wonder if it was something I could keep doing when there was everything else going on as a result of being Rob's mate.

At one rambling meeting, we were talking again about what to do with the DJ situation at The Haçienda, which hadn't become any better – even as we fitted the bass bins that boosted the sound a little and, in 1984, moved the DJ booth from its dark, impractical corner up to the balcony. We started to add other DJs, and entered a kind of battle of the DJs which lasted a couple of years as the role of what was then thought of as 'bandless nights' settled into place.

A big signing for us was the well-respected soul and funk specialist Greg Wilson, who played at Legend on Princess Street, which had the closest sound and lighting in Manchester to The Garage.

It was a great home for Greg, with a mostly Black audience taking their music and dancing seriously, and we knew that was something missing in The Haçienda. The idea that dance music was an underground music with its own radical roots and electric innovations. Most local clubs for a Black audience before then were mostly cramped and shabby but Legend's was futuristic and sophisticated, and of course so were the records they danced to.

Legend had a thriving proto-goth Thursday night as well as Greg's night, both proving that traditionally Manchester people lived for clubbing. Somehow we couldn't make The Haçienda, designed as the ultimate venue, click as a club.

Greg was reluctant to come to The Haçienda precisely because its sound system was so weak, and he did not feel any better when he was greeted by the hardcore alternative Haçienda member – unimpressed that he was playing non-stop dance music. In other words, *disco*. It was still that prehistoric. The notion that a DJ could be an artist and performer in their own right – mixing trends, sounds and moods, reacting to and creating the new, pushing back musical boundaries – was in the shadows. Haçienda members mostly had minimal contact with the dance club mentality. It was live bands, and records played as you got ready for the band, and after the show was over.

Greg took it as a personal mission to win over the stubborn white kids ignorant of the kind of grooves and early electro-sounds he was premiering, and the fact that disco had undertaken a fresh start and was now known as boogie.

He continued a Friday night Funk Night that Hewan had started with Colin Curtis in August 1983, and at first it was a club within a club. Hewan's Saturday night slot went to John Tracey, an enterprising friend and ex-house mate of my old school friend Martin Fry's in

Sheffield who had been DJing at the centre of its scene, Penny's. He'd been a Roxy Room Pips fan, and took that into Penny's, filling it in midweek mixing the alternative post-punk music, jazz-funk and the new electro dance, which was something we couldn't do. He had a more trainspotting approach than Greg, and could also be wacky in a way purist Greg would never consider, with sort of post-punk wedding stunts like throwing in some Sinatra or the theme from *Thunderbirds* at the end of the night, which also functioned as an alarm notice for the staff. Greg was great, and helped us so much, but he was like a scholar, a serious collector, whereas someone like Mark Kamins was using disc jockeying to make up a soundtrack to the wild rhythms of his life. He lived his art.

John was more of the obsessive nerd. I think how it worked was that he was coming into DJing as someone who knew all about the variety of post-punk music, was up to speed with the latest NME bands, but was quick to respond to what was happening – moving fast, trend to trend, in New York – and was happy to mix it all together.

He'd taught himself how it all fitted together, and made it sound natural in The Haçienda to a crowd of music paper readers and John Peel listeners who were a little behind him but soon caught up with his taste. His pleading to Rob finally managed to get the bass bins and the DJ booth moved, the controls inside were made DJ friendly, and the acoustics sorted out with some baffling they got on the cheap. There were some cupboards that needed to be built on the balcony, which disturbed Ben Kelly, who thought they looked like black sheds, but the sound needed to be brought up to scratch.

John wasn't ready for the opening which I'd really wanted, but he started in the summer of 1983 on a Saturday night, and he had a Tuesday night slot, The End – a No Funk Night – which had been deathly quiet for us, and was soon the most popular. Greg got an hour of funk on Saturday, in case he felt slighted by the No Funk Night, and the two ends, John and Greg, the regular and the irregular, experts in their own field, started to fuse together in the club sensibility, inching us closer to the New York ideal of brand new sounds that mixed dance and alternative, funk and post-funk.

The Black crowd Greg had brought in were not the type to go with the post-punk flow, but they were bringing the dancing in, coaching the alternative crowd. In September 1983, he brought in a pioneering local breakdance crew, Broken Glass, who used to busk in Piccadilly Gardens and had come out of the youth club scene. Their appearance on the stage was almost like a dance class, teaching The Haçienda regulars and complete amateurs that dancing was nothing to be afraid of, and in itself was a wonderful thing.

Broken Glass meant instant street credibility, which meant the magic dust of media coverage that The Haçienda was oddly lacking. They were featured in the *Observer Colour Supplement*, which helped begin the shift away from The Haçienda being seen as an avant-garde social club, or a Factory-sponsored youth club for local post-punk rock nerds.

Broken Glass would come on tour with Quando Quango, with Greg Wilson DJing. Looking back, it was stunning stuff – something you'd see nothing like in the UK – but at the time, it just felt right. They would dance all around us as we played, and it was quite a show. Sometimes there would be a fair crowd watching, having a lot to process: Latino indie jazz-funk with Black breakdancers. But one or two of the shows, away from the big cities, could be a little empty.

We played in Hickstead in Sussex, and it was particularly quiet. For some reason, a coach turned up bringing these blokes in as part of their stag night. As soon as they staggered into the venue we knew we were in trouble. You could always tell by what people were wearing that they weren't part of your team, so to speak. They seemed very ready to vent their prejudices, and we were far too spicy for them to handle, and far too exposed in such a small venue.

Halfway through it all kicked off – the bored, impatient heckling started, and they began hurling racial abuse at the dancers. They demanded Gonnie take off her top and show them her tits – really intelligent stuff they could be proud of, confirming her worst fears about standard drunken British loutishness.

Broken Glass could handle the ignorant abuse being thrown at them, but once the rabble turned on Gonnie, they were having none of it. They might have danced with balletic grace but they were tough kids from Moss Side, and much to the leering idiots' surprise, they leapt off the stage and chased them out back to their coach. We ran after them as their coach drove off, taking them back to whatever backward place they'd come from. Seeing them flee turned a bad night into something good.

Broken Glass were amazing entertainers, but at the time a radical act. Some at the club didn't want the single-minded battling element of body popping to become a Haçienda staple. Greg left by early 1984 to manage Broken Glass and move beyond DJing, during his brief time giving us more clues about how to fix the DJ problem. The scene was still fragmented – between live music, Hewan Clarke's jazz and jazz-funk nights, with serious Black dance outfits like the Jazz Defektors and Foot Patrol extending the dance education, and John's more post-Pips, post-Penny's, almost conversational sets.

We'd sorted out some problems, borrowed indirectly from Legends and Penny's, which in their own way had borrowed from others before, but there was an integral, subversive Factory element still missing. The elusive originality that cut and pasted its inspirations together in something no one had done before. Kamins – the Levans and Jellybeans – had their own elusive Factory quality, which made them DJs, plus some indefinable, malleable extra.

Rob turned to me at one of those regular crisis meetings, and pushing his glasses back onto the bridge of his nose – the classic sign that Rob meant business – he said to me through the smoke engulfing the room, 'Why don't you do it?' Everyone in the room looked at me. Tony had a wry look on his face – the classic sign that he was witnessing history, and they'll write books about this one day. Alan was lost in thought – the classic sign he was in total agreement.

'Do what?'

'DJ. You're telling all the DJs what you want and don't want. Even nitpicking with Greg. Being a bit bossy if you ask me. You're moving them around from night to night. You know what me and Tony want. You've DJ'd before, you've hung out with Mark Kamins, you've got record collections bigger than any DJ I know, you know the place and the audience as well as anyone. You do it.'

I'd had fantasies of trying it – a new kind of DJ for a new kind of club – but was so busy with Quando, the booking and promotion, and being Rob's mate – for about seventy quid a week, plus free bed and board – that I had never thought it was feasible.

The Haçienda was, putting it mildly, an eccentric project, and I suppose the solutions to its problems, many of them self-inflicted, needed to come from within. It sounds perverse to say that Factory and The Haçienda needed to sort out their own chaos, but they had looked outside, brought people in, and it simply hadn't made the difference they wanted. Maybe someone from the inside, who'd been around since the beginning, who was involved in most internal decision-making – and indecision-making – loops as loopy as they got, wouldn't fight all the quirks and flaws but embrace them, or see right through them.

The absurd utopian ideal would have been for Tony to do it – but the dance club chairman didn't like dance music or, at least, it didn't sell albums, darling. Rob, with his Rafters years, could have been a contender – but he was being driven mad, sometimes with delight, by New Order, and any of the Factory projects closest to his heart. I got the short straw without even knowing it.

28
A new generation

Luckily, I was ready, because I didn't really think about much else at the time outside music. One day, Tony, being Tony, always hustling for attention, had London cooler-than-thou style magazine *i-D* in town, showing them around the club. He was plugging the idea that now The Haçienda featured body-popping competitions and jazz-funk nights, as well as gothic overlords Bauhaus and William Burroughs, it was flowering as a unique multifaceted nightspot.

He dragged me in to the interview, and utilised one of his favourite superpowers by dropping me right in it. It was like I had the job interview after I'd got the job, and not only that, but it would be covered by a magazine. He told them that Mike has some great ideas for The Haçienda's future, which he's going to tell you all about. Tony turned to me, with that look he often had interviewing a stumbling Tory politician on television – wondering what I was going to say.

Maybe he knew what he was doing, putting me on the spot like that, forcing me to speak. I started making something up based on seeing how the New York clubs worked their door policy, making sure they got the right people in who became collaborators with the club. It was another of those sciences we'd been rubbish at. We hadn't got the door policy right, having concentrated on making members for Factory followers and students, which kept the audience mix limited, and weighted it towards the non-dancers. We needed more of what Greg had brought into the club, but also a younger audience, for whom the Sex Pistols show was a distant memory, and Factory some weird elite shit – but not in a good way. We were neglecting a new generation, who would create the kind of excitement we were looking for.

They couldn't get into the main Manchester nightclubs, because their door policy still favoured what we called a thug in a tie – well dressed, shiny shoes, but when they were drunk, they were monsters, and it created a foul atmosphere. These restless, working-class kids were always hanging out around the Arndale Centre looking for something to do and a place of their own. They were known as the Perry Boys, because they'd inherited the Stockport-born Fred Perry polo shirt worn in turn by the mods, skinheads and suede heads. They reminded me of me, back when I was desperate to sneak into the Twisted Wheel. The reality was that there was a whole different culture from the punk and post-punk era, and it needed to be let through, given some space – in the way that somehow happened in the 1960s.

Their trainers didn't get them into nightclubs, but I said to *i-D* it was going to be the other way round in The Haçienda. Polished office shoes and ties would be banned. We wanted the new generation to make The Haçienda their home, and we're going to rename them.

I glanced at Tony, who was smirking that I'd got myself into a corner, making up new door policy, about to christen a whole new fashion sub-genre, nodding for me to continue. 'We're going to call them Baldricks', I said, thinking of the character in the Ben Elton comedy *Black Adder*. I was imagining a fashion that hadn't really happened so we could call them what we wanted, and *i-D* lapped up that kind of stuff.

Baldricks in oversized clothing were a thing for a week or two – sort of proto-baggies, or roundheads as they called them in London – but the point was, we did need to break the membership club rule, and let these new young people in, for whom the club would be a marvel, with its video screens and alcoves. Our regulars were a bit jaded, or took the place for granted, so we needed to find some new energy, from the fans that fifteen years before would have been Northern Soul fanatics.

I called my night Nude, with Johnny's friend Andrew Berry alongside me helping out, who was also running the in-house hair salon,

Swing, where Johnny, Morrissey, ACR, Bernard, Stone Roses and Fall members got their hair cut. They'd moved over from the erratic barber near the cathedral who had given Joy Division and early ACR the short, severe cuts they wanted, inspired by the cool, anti-hippie cuts of Kraftwerk.

Andrew was a classic example of one of those enterprising, multitalented Mancunians who knew everybody and found uses for the club in just the ways Rob and then Tony would have wanted. Rob had asked Andrew in to DJ, but it was hard for him to keep up his day job cutting hair, so he asked if he could bring his day job into The Haçienda. Many club owners might have balked at such an idea, but not Rob. There were mirrors downstairs in the rooms bands used to get ready, and Swing, with its own catalogue number – FAC 98 – to put it through the books, making it as official as Factory ever got, lasted a few years. Some of the bands coming in wondered what the hell a hair salon was doing in their dressing room. Some would get precious about it; others happily tried a Haçienda cut.

Nude took over Hewan's Friday night slot in November 1984, because it felt like we'd found the groove we were looking for. I had an inkling I knew what kind of music the newcomers liked, because you'd see them hanging out at Spin Inn, where the DJs would source their American imports. They loved the electro funk Greg had been playing, the rhythms simmering through synth pop. From the end of 1984, through 1985, they were already onto the first stirrings of home-made house that were coming over from Chicago when it wasn't yet a known genre, just a series of 12-inches wanting to make music better sharing the 4/4 tempo, the 808 kick drum pulse, the synth splashes – Jessie Saunders 'On and On' seemed to clarify it, 'It's House' by Lil Louis seemed to name it, 'Trapped' by Colonel Abrahams, produced by Richard Burgess of 'Einstein a Gogo', seemed to put post-disco pre-house into the chart.

For a while, when there was no one in, or not many, and it looked more like an illuminated underground car park, I could try tracks out, to see how they sounded, working out what worked using the horrible sound in the building almost as a canvas.

By 1986, we were playing Dhar Braxton's 'Jump Back', J. M. Silk's 'Music is the Key', Terry Billy's Mantronix produced 'Don't Lock Me Out'. Something was building. Within a few weeks you could feel the change. The energy was amazing, the numbers were up, climbing over a thousand, made up of half white kids and half Black.

There'd be a little trouble, a couple of incidents – small harbingers of the days to come – and I remember the manager Paul Mason, who'd been brought in to professionalise and rationalise the place from Rock City in Nottingham, became a little nervous. The Haçienda was a different animal from the more organised Rock City and there were early murmurs of shutting down Nude, to be on the safe side. I stood my ground. There was no way Nude was stopping. I understood that Paul wanted to get some sanity into the club, sort out some of the backroom manoeuvring and infighting, but I could see how Nude was where the future was. It was my thing, I'd worked hard for it, and I wasn't going to lose it just as it was beginning to become something. Luckily, I was embedded enough in the club's culture to win that particular scuffle. Paul got a lot right, but he didn't see what was coming. I didn't specifically see it coming, but I did know something was coming. It was why we were there.

29
A house is built

Around the beginning of 1986, Friday night Nude was rock solid, and I was joined in May by 'little' Martin Prendergast, who'd been DJing at Berlin and Manchester poly before The Haçienda, an actual original Baldrick, and we became known as MP Squared. I think it was the bar manager Ang Matthews who gave him the 'little' name when he came in to do the student nights of a Tuesday, to differentiate him from another, taller, Martin she knew. He replaced Andrew, opening the night, setting things up – you'd always have a warmup guy, and Martin was a City fan, which helped, and was completely in synch with the kind of records I was playing. He was a major part in how we built things up during the pre-rave days, there with me until 1988.

Simon Topping had returned from New York, where he'd spent time studying percussion at the East Harlem Music School run by pianist, arranger and salsa guru Johnny Colon, braving the subway trip deep into Harlem. Simon was taking it all very seriously, and more or less the best person in the world to learn from about the history of salsa and its offshoots and the New York Latin scene was Johnny, who'd had a big hit in the sixties with 'Boogaloo Blues'.

Simon was earning money driving a van for avant-garde musician Arthur Russell's Sleeping Bag records, which released Russell's alter ego dance records and secret disco tracks, and early Mantronix, rewiring various connections between the electronica of Kraftwerk, Neu! and Cluster and the sampling of hip-hop. Simon was obsessed with salsa and Latin jazz, and wanted to learn all he could about its

With my mum. The cap was my attempt to look like Bob Dylan. No idea where this was, about 1964

The Bramhall Suedeheads From left: Nick Chambers, Nev Jennings, Tink, Buster Lowe, Phil Mead, Mike P, Julie Pickering, Alan Bell. Bramhall, 1970/1

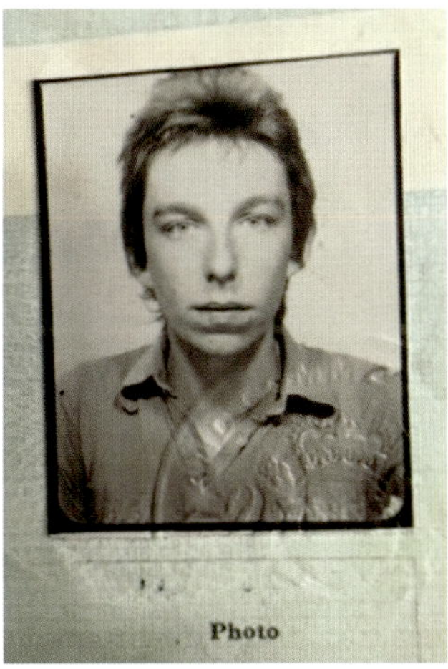

My first passport photo, around 1974. My hair was orange

With the son of the vineyard owner where I picked grapes, 1974/5, near Nîmes, France

From left: Me and Martin Fry, Hyde Park Flats, Sheffield, 1978

Me squatting in Rotterdam, 1980

With Ruth Polsky, at the New Music Seminar, New York, 1983

From left: Me, Mark Kamins, Simon Topping, recording the Quando Quango album at Strawberry Studios Stockport, 1984 (Photo: Kevin Cummins)

Donald Johnson and me in a studio somewhere, mid-eighties (Photo: Kevin Cummins)

Simon Topping, Gonnie Rietveld, Mike P, Barry Johnson, Chinatown Manchester – chosen to look like New York, mid-eighties (Photo: Kevin Cummins)

Martin Prendergast, Mike P, 1985 (Photo: Kevin Cummins)

T-Coy: Richie Close, Simon Topping, Mike P after Granada Studios gig in Manchester, 1987

Me on my rave balcony, Cromford Court, Manchester, 1988

Mike P, Haçienda, 1988

Graeme Park, Mike P, 1988 on tour in Australia. The hats were standard Summer of Love uniform

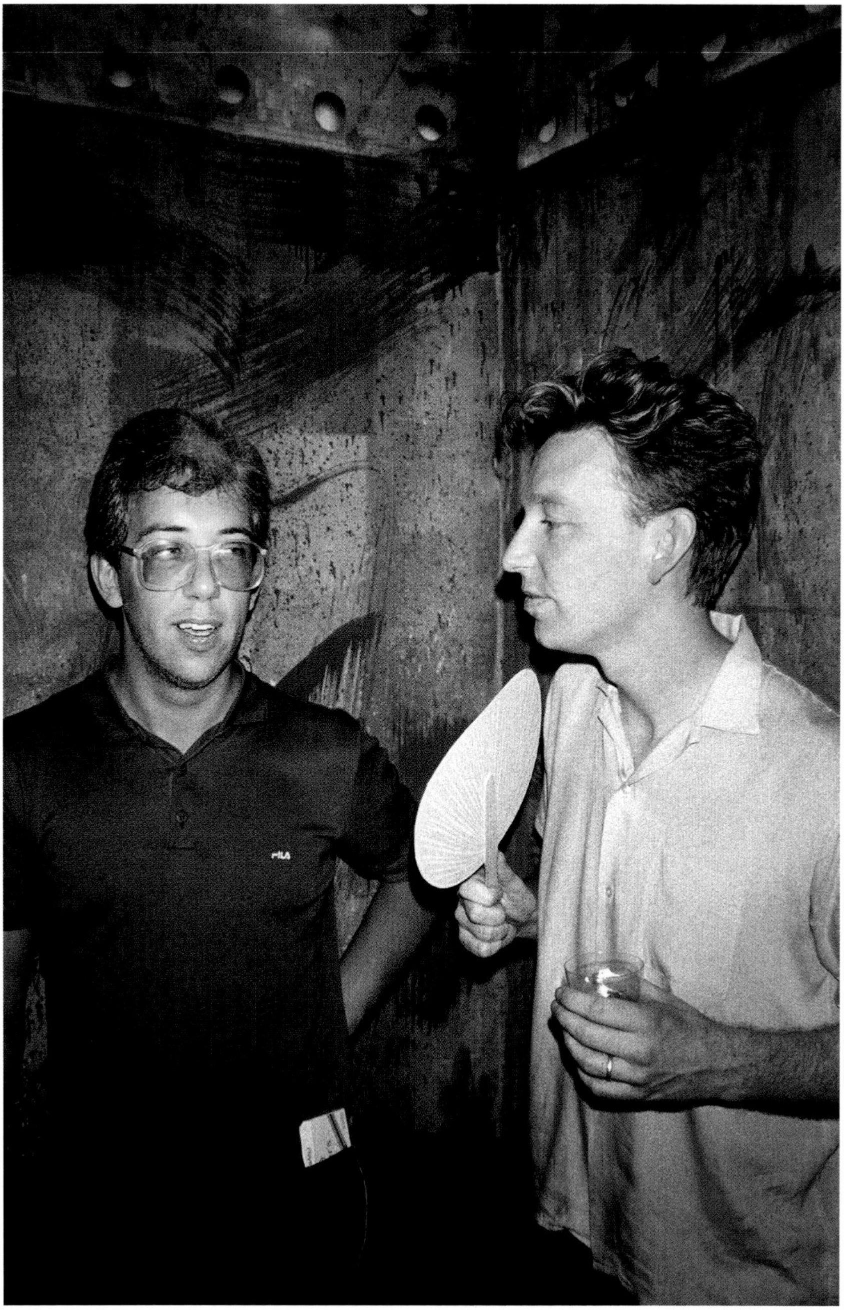

Rob Gretton, Mike P, downstairs at the Haçienda, mid-eighties
(Photo: Kevin Cummins)

Live the Dream rave, Tockholes, Lancashire, 1989

M People: Mike P, Paul Heard, Heather Small, Shovell, winning the Mercury Music Prize 1994. That ruffled some feathers

With Heather Small, Amsterdam mid-nineties

Mark Kamins and Mike P, Havana, Cuba, 2004

Our annual pilgrimage. Grace Pickering, Mike P, Glastonbury Festival 2005

Mike P, Haçienda live, Albert Hall 2015

Charlie Tadman, Calvin Harris, Burns, Mike P in private jet, not sure when

Scully, Pep Guardiola, Mike P, Noel Gallagher, Charlie Pickering, Wembley dressing room. Can't remember the year because we won it so many times

Mike P, Calvin Harris, The Brit Awards 2019

rhythms. He went the whole nine yards as well, adopted the Latino look, from moustache to loafers.

I'd visit some of the Harlem Latin clubs with him. Simon loved being one of the few white people in a club filled with non-whites, rightly reckoning that's where the truth of rhythm lay. His ultimate dream would have been to witness the speakeasies in Harlem in the 1920s, where Black people gathered who weren't accepted by normal society. People on the margins looking for excitement. It all starts there – music, escapism, drugs; some things never change, at least until social media.

There would be between twenty and eighty people dancing in these Latin clubs, and they'd have four bands playing, some young and scrappy, some seasoned and slick. It was relentless.

We saw the innovative Latino percussionist and showman Tito Puente at the Village Gate – he must have been in his sixties but was as on trend as ever, playing for hours with a couple of short breaks, the percussion onslaught getting under our skin. Simon had an incredible collection of salsa and Latin jazz, and when he got back to Manchester he asked for a Haçienda slot. We slipped him on during a Nude night, and he played this blistering selection of salsa, merengue and miscellaneous Latin sounds. The dance floor would instantly clear.

After a couple of weeks, the Jazz Defectors, a collection of top Manchester dancers who accidentally became a band, would start to dance to Simon's records on the empty floor, and other dance crews would do their thing. It became a part of the Nude set, like a floor show – as if it was planned. People liked the routine: take a break, get a drink, watch the show, check out the moves, and then Nude blasted off again.

It showed how The Haçienda fortunes seemed to be shifting. What at first seemed a floor-clearing disaster turned into a real vibe. There was feedback between the crowd and the building – something that happened all too infrequently, or very discreetly, during the past few years. Somehow the crowd had learnt how to use the club.

They start to join in the supply chain of records, as shown when one of the Moss Side dance crew, or someone – I never worked out who would even be bringing a record into a club – slipped me 'No Way Back' by Adonis, with no clue how he'd got his hands on it. It was like magic, it just appeared in my hands, and when I played it, everyone lost their minds. It would have been weird not to.

Whole new dimensions of possibility opened up in an instant. Hands were up in the air en masse, in a way I had never seen anywhere else. The dancers had found something of their own, beyond disco, beyond electro. It was their punk. The bass line tore through the club, the drum, clap, cowbell sounds drove everyone into a frenzy. The metallic vocals seemed to be telling the crowd what they were thinking as they were thinking it, and I was thinking it too.

Too far gone and there's no way back.

I felt like I had been baptised. I wanted more of that. I told the guys at Spin Inn, get me more like this.

The Haçienda had been open two or three years, but that was all preamble. The Haçienda was now properly open. Nude was never a house night before Adonis, but then it became one. He also changed the way I DJ'd. I was never a great technical mixer, but Adonis made me very conscious about what track to go to that would fit the beat and continue the drama. Before, I was often simply chucking things in and out, but after Adonis, I was more disciplined about the pace and structure of what I learnt was a show. And after playing Adonis, the next track needed to be house, and so on – repeat, but change. It was continuous rhythm with no fancy cutting.

In a way I was experimenting with the building itself, making a virtue of the dead sound, using these long, stark tracks like Harlequin Fours 'Set it Off', the Walter Gibbons remake of a 1984 track by American disco electro artist Steve Standard, under the name Strafe. Gibbons was as much a pioneer of the 12-inch mix as Tom Moulton, pioneering the format's use of space, and his 'Set it Off' was like some sort of cryptic spiritual hymn to the very idea of dancing, casually asking the question, 'Do you want to party?' It was carried by this immense insistent proto house hi-hat which found its home in The Haçienda. Sometimes there was hardly anything there; it felt as though it was about to fall apart. It was such a skeletal tune, but it just kept coming, doing the business, as if it was the ambient sound of the building itself.

A record would take off that belonged to the crowd you played it to – it would sometimes take months before the internet for a track to travel to other clubs and cities. Obscure tracks – I remember this with a mix of Circuit's 'Shelter Me' – would become the property of that crowd. The crowd would go ape when they heard it, and want it again and again, and to keep things moving, you had to balance those favourites with always introducing the new. One record could belong in one club, and in that club, it went down like a worldwide smash.

A big sign of the change was when the Chicago House Party revue played The Haçienda on a cold Monday in early March 1987, DJ International bringing in their high priests Marshall Jefferson, Adonis, Frankie Knuckles and Fingers Inc. They were overwhelmed by the crowd, pre-ecstasy but as pumped up as the crowd would be after it hit, and couldn't believe anyone knew who the hell they were. A little Manchester oasis knew all about what they were doing in Chicago. It fixed us as house central, and meant a lot to me and Rob. If no one had turned up we would still have been as ecstatic.

It was the first time they'd been out of America and seen for themselves what was happening with their records. They really couldn't handle it and said it was as though they were playing at home, and had no idea they were being played and loved by what was to them an exotic, far away crowd, and it set up a relationship with The Haçienda that made Frankie especially like an honorary part of the club. He was totally freaked out by it all. And God, those Frankie Knuckles bass lines made so much sense in Manchester.

The music was made for and tested in the clubs, and it was popular music with experimental roots. It was minimal weird shit in some ways, but it made these big community statements and always had the rhythm. It's why New Order ran in parallel with house, the way their particular yearning for togetherness, for safety, combined with the driving drums to create anthems that worked so well in clubs, where people went to find each other, and take it from there.

Chicago House Party poster Hacienda, 1986/87

We had our own connection at The Haçienda with New Order and their association with Arthur Baker. I had my mentor in Mark Kamins who was a direct source to the latest hot New York faves, and there was Spin Inn records, a great importer and supplier of the latest Black dance music for years, the bearer of treasure. The Haçienda was right there as house geared up. It came from outside, but was instantly a Manchester thing, with Stu Allan breaking it on his Piccadilly Radio show, and it was my thing.

House was such a hybrid it didn't get spoiled when I mixed it with all my favourite music: Motown, funk, Ze and no wave, early hip-hop, electro, punk, indie pop, jazz-funk. Nude continued from where John had taken it, with the emergence of house, and by the middle of 1985 it was the busiest night. The Haçienda soundtrack had taken shape. It was an old-fashioned concept really – a cool club playing your favourite music, the expertly chosen and played latest and greatest new music. But what made it new was if you wanted to listen to this mix of music now, you had to go to The Haçienda.

There was a multiracial blend of the new scally kids discovering something for the first time – something they'd been waiting for and which sent them wild – and the Black audience Greg had brought in, along with the sharp new dance crews from Moss Side and Hulme.

30
A meeting of minds

The original regulars had been absorbed, or drifted off, but there were still links to those from the early indie days with Dave Haslam's Temperance night, a soft launch for those for whom dance didn't come naturally. An introduction. Then you could move on to the serious stuff, where the percussion was as hard as fuck.

The Haçienda couldn't lose its basic identity as a live venue, but for me, feeling like an explorer, it was like the early days of glam and punk, when there were only a few records to choose from. You had to fill in the set around the edges. I needed more of whatever it was that Adonis and Jesse Saunders were doing, so I could move the crowd through the night without losing the charge.

The late Quando Quango track, 'Genius', with Mark's production input, was a provisional attempt to come up with an indigenous Manchester-based house sound. Once we'd heard Adonis, Simon Topping and I wanted to go further, realising that house wasn't music to listen to at home or on an album. It was for clubs, a social thing to be experienced with others as part of a whole night of music. We'd been trying to push Quando almost as a pop act, and our managers Pete Hadfield and Keith Blackhurst were playing a track we'd done, 'Bad Blood', to other record labels. Pete had tour managed The Specials, and with Keith was looking after their singer Terry Hall and all his projects, and 2 Tone Records founder Jerry Dammers. They had good contacts, and were well respected for making things happen.

No one was interested in 'Bad Blood'. The band started to feel like an old-fashioned enterprise, packing people into a forlorn-seeming Salford Hire van, hitting the road yet again and trying to sell our wares to almost complete indifference. People were really moving to the Nude night, and no one was moving to Quando Quango outside of New York and Miami. I told Gonnie I didn't want to be in a band anymore, and the DJing was taking off, and I was focusing on the idea of making quick records for the moment. She got it – she had things she wanted to do, other directions to take, things she wanted to write.

One of the best things about Quando Quango was when we were making a track called 'Atom Rock' with Bernard Sumner and Donald Johnson producing, and Johnny Marr came in to add some guitar. It was the first time he had met Bernard, although he'd served him in X Clothes – he graded Bernard as one of the cooler 'older' customers. In 1984, he was now of The Smiths, which meant more than anyone could have ever imagined a year or so before, Manchester still turning up with the goods. It was the first time since he'd formed them that he'd stepped outside the group to play guitar for anyone else. After The Smiths – and no one could have ever imagined that the band would only be together for four years, with Johnny only 23 when they split – he would become one of the great, versatile session players, moving from group to group and style to style with supernatural ease.

In a way, it all began with Quando Quango. As Johnny Marr started playing in the studio, asking what we were looking for and running through a few riffs and sounds, you could tell why he was special. He could lightly yet evocatively outline an entire history of electric guitar playing in seconds – from the blues to post-punk. Scotty Moore? Tom Verlaine? Nils Lofgren? Some Cramps? He told me later that he was nervous, having never done anything like that before, and was a little in awe of Bernard Sumner.

He gave us something like a loose-limbed Piccadilly Bo Diddley funk, and Bernard gave us absolute precision. How New Order made their music was always a mystery to many – how the four of them, in the 1980s, gelled, how what each brought to the group found its balance. But seeing Bernard concentrate as if nothing in the world mattered other than what he was working on showed me how he worked.

It was the first time Johnny worked with electronics, and he was fascinated by how Bernard used machines to put things together. When he arrived at the studio, they were just finishing off a Section 25 mix for 'View From a Hill', mixing it down, and Bernard was trying out some new techniques with the emulators and sequencers he'd been buying – essentially pushing the boundaries of this Kraftwerk-inspired sound. Despite all that experimentation, it still ended up sounding very much like Bernard.

Johnny told me it got him thinking, even as he was the guitarist in one of the great guitar groups of all time, that one day he'd like to be in an electronic group. After The Smiths, in 1988, it happened, when Bernard and Johnny – with help from the Pet Shop Boys – put together Electronic. At first, Bernard seriously wanted to call Johnny's first group after The Smiths 'Sell Your Body'. Johnny would have sleepless nights thinking he was going from one of the great group names to one of the worst. Bernard saw reason, and the name Electronic hit that 1988 moment when things weren't rave or acid house, but rock and electronics, which was beginning to mean computers, were making sense together. They didn't want to admit it at the time, but they'd found a sanctuary from New Order and The Smiths.

I like to think it was all helped by Quando Quango putting together Johnny and Bernard in the studio.

31
A decoy or two

With our own, humbler 'supergroup', Simon and I stripped everything back to our punk roots and decided to make a Latino house record with minimal equipment in a cheap demo studio in a basement in Didsbury, south Manchester. We had envisaged a cross between Tito Puente and Adonis, having seen what caused such a reaction in The Haçienda. Latino Manc Simon was now New York-trained and, for a grumpy sod, could really swing, and I'd learnt, watching Bernard, how to programme the drums.

Simon came across our version of Arthur Baker's multitalented studio musician John Robie, Richie Close, a versatile session player adept at all sorts of styles, while he was playing with a talented local Latin jazz group, Apitos. Richie was a bit older than us and had never been to The Haçienda, but he was a brilliant musician and had written infectious TV themes for programmes like *Danger Mouse* – made in Manchester – and *Question of Sport*. He was exactly what we needed to bring our roughed-out ideas to life. We had the concept and the vision, and Richie filled it out musically.

I'd learnt how session players are so important – the ones that can play anything with real style – and even New Order needed session players to get that tightness that elevates the great soul and funk records. Together, as what we called T-Coy, we came up with 'Carino' – ten minutes of sunshine and hypnotic pulse with a no-nonsense good-time-jack piano motif on top, no vocals, no frills, no problem.

It was an experiment to see if we could make a club record that could actually be called house, or at least could be played with early Chicago house without clearing the floor. Hip-hop wasn't a good look if white guys went down that route – not unlike reggae – but house had been warped into existence by disco, soul and funk freaks adapting European styles, so for us to have a go seemed part of the back-and-forth transmission between cultures.

We didn't even think of it being on Factory Records. Rob's time as a Factory director was coming to an end, and we had Tony's mocking voice ringing around inside our heads. 'Dance doesn't sell albums, darling.' Maybe that's where the title 'Carino' came from – Spanish for 'darling'.

We didn't want to sell albums, just make something for The Haçienda from the inside. We felt like we were an important outpost of house, and Manchester had form reacting quickly to punk. We were thinking like the Buzzcocks. Something revolutionary had happened, and we needed to move before the magic dispersed.

Tony backed the track, made by two Factory old timers, on his *The Other Side of Midnight* TV show, where he had a different set of priorities. With his Granada hat on, he was a music enthusiast revealing diverse interests and happy to promote his friends and colleagues. With his Factory hat on, he had different standards. It was so Factory in a way – put together by Factory loyalists with their own integrity – but it didn't become a Factory Record. Which is also so Factory. And being so Factory was part of their downfall.

We mainly wanted to stay in the shadows, even when we played live, following the directives coming from Chicago, where records were being released behind various slippery fronts and pseudonyms.

At first 'Carino' wasn't even on master tape. The basic Didsbury studio didn't have those kind of facilities. We had it on cassette only, the way a lot of those early Chicago house records seemed to make the rounds, and we gave a copy to Stu Allan, who in July 1986 had started his own show on Piccadilly Radio. He was the latest in line at the station after Andy Peebles from 1974 playing the latest soul and funk, and then once Andy had jumped to Radio 1, the influential Mike Shaft, who did a great Wednesday night at Legend, fronting the more dance-orientated Taking Care of Business. (T-Coy was from take care of you, so you could see where the name came from. We were also being a bit coy about who we were in case it put people off.)

From the very start, Stu was responding to the enigmatic 12-inch mixes arriving at Spin Inn from Chicago – he'd had the same experience as me with his live gigs, in his case seeing the response to Steve 'Silk' Hurley and his 'Jack Your Body', and Farley 'Jack Master' Funk and Jesse Saunders' 'Love Can't Turn Around'.

Stu started his first new show with the Jackmaster Funk track, causing consternation 'upstairs' at the station – it was a big jump to start playing this rawer, stranger soul, with this track seeing the result of an Isaac Hayes song from the 1970s being passed through the deconstructing electronic Chicago process. To non-expert ears, to conventional radio programmers, it was as though Radio 1 started playing the Normal and Fad Gadget as soon as they were released. Usually, for radio play, it took time for something new to soften and familiarise itself, if ever. With house, there was no time to waste.

Fearless Stu had a house hour during his Buss This hip-hop show, and we got the cassette of 'Carino' to him, which he played non-stop. He ran a Top 10 house music chart and kept it at number 1 for weeks. If we had released it as a Quando record, and it was definitely a continuation, it probably wouldn't have made such an impact. Being a no-label, no vocal, no song, no detail, out-of-nowhere track – a blank cassette with some biro on it – something emerging from hiding, made it house. House came from all over the place and from nowhere. The lack of image was its image. It was all about the music, man. Everyone in early house had at least one alter ego.

When we did put it out as a record – re-recorded and ready for action – we released it through Deconstruction, an initially temporary-seeming label my managers Pete Hadfield and Keith Blackhurst had formed with and around me. We were fed up with having to rely on others to put out the music we wanted to, that we could see had an audience ready and waiting. We'd talked about not wanting to go with Factory, and the trouble we'd had finding a label for Quando Quango. Factory were like a record label that didn't act like a record label – especially now Rob was pulling out – they'd sign good things, package them in a world-class way, but do nothing to promote or plug their records.

Pete and Keith had signed one of their acts, Hothouse, to the UK-based subsidiary of a German label, BMG, which gave them an in. We went to see BMG's A&R man John Lloyd about some sort of deal on the back of T-Coy to reflect what was happening at The Haçienda – Chicago house becoming Manchester acid house. John had never heard a house record, so I blagged it, playing T-Coy and a couple of obscure Chicago twelve inches I'd got – nothing to do with me, but useful as apparent demo tracks – and he said, great, go and make an album, and gave us a budget of £18,000. Modest, but under the circumstances, quite miraculous.

Deconstruction became a label by accident. Clearly influenced by Factory, Pete especially adored Tony, but it would be run like a business, with a clear musical house style. It would be a hybrid label – smart, modern artwork mostly done by Mark Farrow, who'd worked with Peter Saville – and with its own dissident attitude and understanding of the volatile relationship between music and fashion, but run with the intention of getting its records properly promoted and noticed.

'Carino' got reviewed well as edgy, elusive northern house – funk given the 'Blue Monday' treatment, house as though caught in the current including the short-lived Washington take on hip-hop, Go Go, and Latin bop. Down in London, the Cold Cut crew loved it and alerted sound system maestro Norman Jay.

He played it on the early Kiss FM he helped found – the first dance music station in London, launched in 1985. The pirate radio stations were another vital part of the ecosystem of house, transmitting the excitement before it all got taken by the fashionistas into the mainstream. I went down there early on to do a set for Kiss FM from the top of a block of flats in south London. You could see the city at night and imagine the music sneaking into people's homes, into their bloodstream – tracks you couldn't hear anywhere else. It was a great feeling.

'Carino' was a big underground hit, but too fluid, genre vague and instrumental for even any of the braver independent labels to take on. There was no obvious hook; the hook was losing yourself in the whole ten minutes.

With Deconstruction, I could still act as though it was a Factory project – one thing I could never understand about Tony was that he had created the perfect setting for subversive, shape-shifting dance records made by underground spirits who loved playing with identity as much as genre, but he couldn't bring himself to go there. Somehow, the relationship between Manchester being a great home for people who loved to experiment and the experimental nature of keeping dance music ahead of the times never clicked with him. I had to make it click another way.

For the £18,000, we put together what was essentially a T-Coy album – a sampler of northern house music, an invented mix tape of imaginary performers. We made *The North – The Sound of Dance Underground* as a document of an underground Manchester scene with a bunch of acts we mostly made up. T-Coy stood for decoy.

Simon and I became Frequency 9 and Masters of Acid, I hid behind DCB and ACR using the kind of diversionary alter-ego tactic we'd used with T-Coy were represented by Donald Johnson and Martin Moscrop as ED209 – I discovered that Martin had been an apprentice electrician at Mirrlees Blackstone in Hazel Grove a couple of years below me. The pseudonyms messed up the royalties, so it sold quite well, but I never made a penny from it. I failed to persuade the PRS royalty collectors that the songwriters on the compilation of different 'groups' were mostly me, Simon and Richie.

There was some actual truth in the notion that the mostly self-invented *The North* was reflecting a new Manchester scene. Leading it from the shadowy edges was an underage Black kid called Gerald Simpson who had bluffed his way into The Haçienda as a young dancer from Hulme, not looking to drink, but to soak up the atmosphere and listen to the beats. He saw the club as a thing of wonder, and for him, the sound was stunning, hitting it at that moment in 1986 when things were changing fast. He'd gone to clubs like Legend, Playpen, as well as The Haçienda on his own, teaching himself the new world of Manchester, which contained a dream world of soul, funk, jazz and electro, and to go with that, a world of new moves.

He was a trained dance obsessive, one of his teachers was from the Northern Ballet, and he'd seen Foot Patrol dance at The Haçienda. The club had the effect on Gerald we'd always hoped would happen locally – as if it was some abstract version of a university campus – and he had such an intense mind, such a need to know. Music wasn't entertainment; it was a way of life. He was absorbing everything: Hewan Clarke playing jazz-funk, Miles and Herbie Hancock at his local youth club; the jazz breaks Mike Shaft was using on his Piccadilly show; Mantronix playing electronic drums live in performance; New Order's discoveries about how the whole body could be used to dance to house.

He was also an electronics obsessive, interested in how technology worked, and he would scour dusty second-hand shops for discarded Roland machines. He got a second-hand TR-808, which had a life of its own, working at McDonald's to pay it off. He found a 303 bass line machine, accumulated loads of old records to scratch vocals from, and built a rudimentary four-track studio in his parents' house where he still lived. He taught himself to be a producer – but a rare one without DJ experience – who made records directly for clubs, made to blast out of a great sound system. He started out calling himself Jackmaster G.

Making loads of cassettes experimenting with his second-hand machines and his primitive studio, he'd drop them off at Piccadilly Radio reception for Stu Allan, or get them to him via Spin Inn, which sponsored the show. When Allan played some of these solo electro-jams he only knew that someone called Gerald had dropped them off. On air, he called him A Guy Called Gerald.

Gerald's learning and his hunger, his knowledge of some strange audiopsychic map of what Manchester was in the mid-eighties, it all fed into a *Voodoo Ray*, a sharp edge, mesmerising Moss Side synthesised meltdown of classy jazz-funk.

It was like this tunnel between Chicago house and the Detroit techno of Derrick May, Juan Atkins and Kevin Saunderson and the British dance music that stretched from acid house to drum'n'bass and jungle. Five hundred white-label records were produced by a local label, and one of The Haçienda DJs, Jon Dasilva, got hold of it.

It landed in The Haçienda like there was nowhere else it should be. Gerald was in there one day when it played; he wasn't expecting it and had no idea how it happened. It was like it had just leapt from his mind into the very place that had given him the ideas in the first place.

If I was creating the illusion that the *North* album was a comprehensive survey of where Manchester dance music was in 1987, 1988, then it had to have 'Voodoo Ray' on it, and Gerald was also with us in spirit, and more directly, on other tracks.

We had this track called 'Dream 17' that Gerald had worked on – a genius at generating all these wobbly, spine-tingling bits and spaces and freaky effects that made it very acid house before that was anything. Gerald was in 808 State at the time, with ex-Biting Tongues member Graham Massey and motivating DJ Martin Price, giving Manchester more claim to being the UK home of house. He created the framework and rhythm pattern for The Haçienda's second Summer of Love classic of 1989, 808 State's 'Pacific State', helping more than most to drop the acid into house and the sunshine into a nation drained by the Thatcher years – I really wished he was a full-time T-Coy member.

I'd written some vocal lines for 'Dream 17', numbered because that was Richie's house number in Heaton Moor, but we didn't have a singer. To be honest, as we were playing it, lost in a world of our own making in a traditional semi-detached in a back street of Stockport, we also needed a smoke machine and strobe lights. It felt like it could last for about three days and you'd never be bored.

We were sitting around at Richie's house drinking tea and wondering what to do with it next when the doorbell rang. It was Simon's latest girlfriend, and when she heard what we were talking about she said, 'Well, my mum can sing'. We asked what her name was, and she said Annette, which for some reason was enough for her to pass the audition.

She only lived nearby, and she was round in a few minutes, a lovely grandmother in her forties, and she was soon singing on it and it sounded perfect. Luckily, it still sounded perfect later when we listened to it and we had come down to earth a little after taking a trip through our own creation, which sounded so magnificent to us we couldn't stop giggling. Everyone thought Annette was this cool young lass, a Denton Donna Summer, but she was a housewife from Heaton Moor who never sang on anything else. It proved in its own way that house was the new Northern Soul, and there were no rules.

There was a big launch party – an absolute bells and whistles acid house circus at The Haçienda for the album when it was finally released on Deconstruction in November 1988 as a CD and double album, with the exuberant Central Station Design-designed cover blown up and hung around the club. Their wobbly lines, disorientating, garish colours and slapdash cultural appropriation for the late eighties Factory sleeves were at the other extreme to Saville's straight lines, minimal colour palette and cryptic imagery. Manchester was always mad – for pleasure, for change, for making connections, for showing off – but the madness at the beginning of the eighties was another level of madness altogether at the end of the eighties.

Tony congratulated me on the album, and I said, 'You know Tony, this could have been on Factory, or some Factory sub-label.' 'Darling, he said ...'. You can guess the rest.

Central Station Design were doing the record sleeves for Happy Mondays, and in late 1989 they would design the Madchester logo for the Happy Mondays sleeve to their *Rave On* EP.

The lead track, 'Hallelujah', at last gave The Haçienda its irresistible, celebratory, made-in-Manchester anthem, and a barmy house band that had enjoyed cult status for a couple of years would soon become a household name, somehow keeping their balance dancing on a very thin wire between triumph and disaster. As Tony said, more or less, yesterday's weirdness had become tomorrow's reason why.

Hold on.

What the fuck.

Mentioning the Happy Mondays makes me think I've missed something.

I must have taken something that did something to my memory.

Let me put 1985 to 1988 another way.

32
A scam and a racket

There is a point – and you might have been thinking as you read it that it's bound to come, it must have already – as the lawless early Haçienda turned into the house-y Haçienda of myth and fractured memory, when things start to get a little messy in terms of remembering when and how it all happened. Who was there, who said what, who fell out with whom, who had an idea that changed everything. I'm not sure of the exact order.

When the events started to blur, when time looped into itself, when it becomes difficult to recall how the one fantastic thing led to another – what The Haçienda faithful behind the scenes had always hoped for, crashing through chaos, mistakes and revelation, sometimes all but disappearing into the smoke, the herb of Manchester that dulls the pain and awakens the senses,

Especially when the herb of Manchester was supplanted by the appearance of ecstasy – some kind of cosmic reward visited upon the folly, the challenge, the absurdity of making it so far. You have passed go, collected your ticket – your tablet – and broken through the looking glass. The white kids started to dance a little better, and then they got even better, and it dawned on me why, in New York clubs like The Loft and The Garage, there was no alcohol, just bowls of water, and everywhere you looked there was fantastic, body-bending dancing.

It would be obvious to say it all got a little wobbly after E arrived, as if someone in a lab somewhere, hearing the consequence of combining stark electronic sound with rhythms flowing out of funk, soul, jazz, electro pop and disco, had worked out a formula that would enhance and expose every drop of sound, every ethereal pattern, every damned constant beat and bleep and whistle and effect and drop through space. My memory gets pulled all over the house after I joined in with the ecstasy crowd and discovered a potion that made house music in particular seem like an alien creature that spoke your language.

I'd have to go back before the ecstasy came to town to locate the moment when things took a turn for the unbelievable, and it all started with Twisted Wheel alumnus Phil Saxe, who had married my Blackley neighbour Jean, who leapt out of the car driven by my mum desperate to see The Beatles, prepared to brave a thick Manchester fog. Time twisted around itself. Jean had become part of the Pickering family, and had herself moved to Bramhall near where we were. Phil was Jewish, and his family were upset that he was marrying outside the faith, so my mum and dad acted as his parents during the wedding between Jean and Phil. We had become that close.

Since the Twisted Wheel had shut and sometime spinning at Placemate, Phil had done some ducking and diving, got a part-time degree in marketing and worked as a marketing manager for toy paint makers Humbrol. A real job made no sense and he quickly moved on. In 1983, he opened a stall with his brother, Somewear, selling clothes on the market underneath the Arndale Centre in central Manchester.

There were piles of cheap, shapeless jeans and loose jumpers for the local scallies, nothing particularly fashionable, or so it seemed. Some of the jeans were semi-flared, which was a brave move at the time. Punk and then post-punk and 2 tone pop ska had pretty much destroyed flared trousers. But what goes around comes around.

Phil told me a couple of young girls had started asking for flared trousers. He was shocked at first, especially when they were after twenty- and twenty-five-inch flares, but when fashion comes knocking, you better not ignore the call. Especially when you're twice as old as the ones doing the asking. He asked them why, and they gave him a look as if to say, it's none of your business. He knew enough from the sixties to sense there was some new fashion emerging and at 32 it was going to look strange to him. Being Phil, he was quick off the mark.

It was in early 1985, which is as close as I can pinpoint it, when I went round for a drink at his and Jean's place and, after a couple of beers, he said, 'Hey, Mike, come and have a look at this.' He took me to his garage, pulled open the doors, and inside from floor to ceiling there were stacks and stacks of flared Wrangler jeans that he'd discovered some local distributors had stored in their warehouses – dead stock, small enough around the waist for the teenagers who were his customers. He'd also got hold of hundreds of pairs of long-lost flared Levi's for a pound a pair.

The jumble of flared jeans were a casualty of the punk years, and he was selling loads of them to kids he said were the hippest in town, because they were making up their own style. He had all these plans – he was telling me how to take them in here, let them out there – so that they would fit baggy on the hips.

Phil had always been note perfect as a mod – understanding the crucial details right down to the steel comb in the Crombie top pocket and the white tights on the girls. He had an instinct for how the young put themselves together to belong in one place, work themselves out, and separate themselves from the ordinary world. Phil sized up his trouser treasure squeezed into his garage with a look of satisfaction. I was witnessing the birth of what became known as baggy in a garage in bloody leafy, affluent Bramhall.

Some of those kids buying the flares at his stall looked to him like Scooby Doo characters, with their baggy sweaters, stringy hair and wispy facial bristles. One bunch of ne'er-do-wells who'd been among his earlier customers, and looked like they had customers for whatever they sold, told him they had a band, and, knowing of his music past, they asked him to go and see them rehearse on Cheetham Hill Road.

They'd been banging and messing around for years, getting nowhere but sticking at it for something to do. He became their manager, not least because they sounded like a band always on the verge of falling apart with words you couldn't quite make out, which was his kind of thing. And he was the kind of manager that just decided to become a manager – loving music but not musical, finding a way to be part of a band without being in a band. He started giving them the clothes they were after so they looked like a group, a gang, dressing the same way – the manager dressing the band he's discovered routine.

Phil would tell anyone who asked, or even didn't ask, that they were the new Velvet Underground. They weren't. But it didn't matter, because they were the new Happy Mondays – the name coming from the day one of the band members' giro cheque would drop through the front door. Or something murkier. Phil had been out of the music business for a while but hadn't lost his knowledge, and he was full of ideas.

He gave me a cassette of demos that he had paid to have done, and they sounded scratchy and primitive, but not ordinary, and the singer had this sweet, quavering voice, a little like Feargal Sharkey of The Undertones singing with The Skids. They were a scrappy but lively pop group really and had no qualms about that, and I wasn't looking for another weird, low-key Factory band. I wanted pop! As weird as it wanted to be, but pop.

The Smiths had taken unique made-in-Manchester music into the mid-eighties, and who knows what was going to follow that. It could be anything. It could be this group who were still learning how to play but were wearing the right clothes. And, if I heard right, were taking the right drugs. I mean, they believed in what they were doing. That's always a good sign when you're looking for the next big thing, and before I saw them, Phil promised me they looked like a group – another bonus when a lot of groups in their early days can look like each of them is in a different group. I won't mention the early Stone Roses.

I played it to Rob at The Haçienda, and it passed the Rob test, for now, resulting in a flicker of a smile. He said, 'Play it to Tony.' He was in The Haçienda Hicks bar, where they sold the cans of lager. I went and found him, twisting someone's arm about some scheme or another, schmoozing a journalist, and said, 'I've found this band. It might be a James situation, but more punk, more scally. I don't think they will be as difficult to deal with, though.' He looked at me, working out if that was a good or bad thing.

He asked me what they were called. He rolled the name around in his head and shrugged. 'Happy Mondays. I suppose I can get used to it.' I told him I think they should be on Factory. He was in a good mood, or two spliffs in, and after all James wasn't a totally flop signing, so I had credit. He said, 'Darling, if you like it, that's good enough for me.' I thought to myself, you could have at least listened to it. This was too easy.

Well, it wasn't that easy. I went back to Rob and he referred to the Factory rule that we had to see a band live before we signed them. He put them on with New Order in the Maxwell Hall at Salford University on 17 April 1985 – one of those classic Rob sink or swim actions.

There was a review in the *Salford Student Magazine* that had absolutely no idea what they were. Were they American? Yobs? They were dismissed as 'instantly forgettable'. You couldn't trust the review – it failed to notice the flared trousers, which was seismic at the time. If I had been writing about them in *Modern Drugs*, I would have spent some time on the flared trousers.

The Factory professionals noted that they looked like a gang of nefarious casuals, the frantic guitarist knew some interesting chords, the bassist seemed to have studied Peter Hook's one-finger playing, the drummer was trying to play funk and punk at the same time, and the bolshie-looking singer was either making everything up off the top of his head or he was some kind of freestyling street poet who made Mark E. Smith seem like Pam Ayres. They were selling madness more than music in a way.

Ramshackle but pretty good, concluded Rob, sagely, flicking his specs up the bridge of his nose.

Perhaps only Factory would have been daft enough to decide it was worth having such a group of felonious misfits and reprobates on the label. It was either total innocence or total cunning. We got them some other gigs, some with Terry Hall's Colourfield, because I shared the same managers, and then it was decided to make a record.

We had a meeting about who we should get to produce it – one of those sequences of events which happened in New Order, Factory and Haçienda meetings where all the sensible, practical options are laid out, and then they go up in smoke, and somehow the final choice is none of those.

Which is how I ended up producing the first Happy Mondays tracks, not Bernard Sumner and Donald Johnson, and not Martin Hannett – he hadn't produced anything for Factory for a few years after a catastrophic falling out with Tony, but Tony, who had visited the Mondays and bonded over their shared Salford roots, detected singer Shaun Ryder, if not the rest, was a world champion drug fiend connoisseur, the kind of amoral vagabond Tony would naturally adore. Shaun and recovering heroin user Martin would work well together, both having seen things most people rarely do.

Or Tony and Alan came up with the idea together – put the old team together, Hannett working on the newest Factory group, a return to the good old days when Factory made classic albums.

Manager Phil wasn't so sure – Martin had totally lost direction, and technology had moved on, something Martin knew more than most, as the big argument with Tony was based around Factory preferring to invest in a nightclub than in the latest studio equipment. Phil could see the time and money he was investing in the group going up in that Factory smoke. He could see chaos coming. Add Factory logic to the logic of the Mondays, and you're asking for trouble. Or, you're making an unfathomable connection that makes a glorious mockery of time and space.

Times had changed since the Hannett-produced albums Alan was thinking of, by Joy Division and The Durutti Column. The drugs had changed. Weed was the main drug of choice right up to the mid-eighties, then coke turned a few heads, and Hannett got lost in heroin, but there was something new in the works, a psychedelic stimulant that made everything seem absolutely glorious. Best not let Hannett into that world.

Maybe me as the producer was an Alan suggestion which he seemed to pluck out of the air, and Tony found no reason to challenge it, maybe put out that his dream Hannett/Mondays plan was not going to happen. Rob went along with it as well, because he had other things on his mind. As the smoke cleared after the decision was made, they might as well have handed me a mug with 'Mug' written on it. But I was game. How hard could it be?

We used Square One Studios in Bury, a clean, decent, cheap studio, and I got Tim Oliver to engineer – an early assistant to Martin Hannett who was working with Kamins at the time on the Quando Quango album. He'd had prior experience with Shaun, doing some demos with him when he was 15, which showed that Shaun, for all his shady, larking demeanour, was serious about his music from an early age as one route out of Thatcher's bitter, narrowing Britain.

The Mondays turned up in a rusty, dented old car like something out of *Wacky Races*, and I said to Gaz Whelan the drummer, 'Where's your kit?' Most drummers in my experience had a kit, but not Gaz. We used an old set in the studio, which wasn't a great start. Tim still managed to get the Hannettesque–Strawberry Factory drum reverberation, which he'd had first-hand experience of, especially in the opening of 'Delightful'.

It was 1985 *NME* time, plenty of groups sounding DIY and purposefully unpolished, so 'This Feeling' was pure, gleeful jangle, like the Scottish Postcard sound of Orange Juice and Josef K and Bernard's New Order strum, with its roots in the Velvet Underground – Phil would be beaming away as this belted out of the speakers. Shaun was sort of setting out his stall – 'What do you want me to say? What do you want me to do? Whatever you want, I can get it for you. Roll up, roll up.' I didn't need to be scared, but if I didn't know them by then, I might have been.

The studio quickly became their playground, like they'd found Disneyland in the back streets of Bury. They didn't want to leave after the first night, because it had a pool table and a telly. Mark, the guitarist, said, 'This is better than where I live!' It was soon littered with cans and boxes and scraps of paper, enveloped with smoke from giant joints, like they were making a nest.

The studio had to kick them out in the early hours – they were having such a good time. Three days of that and somehow we got three tracks. In his own way, Shaun was very determined, he was the boss, and he would tell them all what to play. He'd tell me what sound he was after, a reference to Sly and the Family Stone, to

Echo & the Bunnymen, to Public Image Ltd, to Can. He had something in his head which we could get nowhere near in three days. We did well just to get it down as it was, and we weren't using any synths or drum machines.

It wasn't in the realm of possibility to make it into a dance record, not even as I was making them for my own group and had a handle on the new rhythms I was playing in the club. The idea of putting modern dance bpm with white indie rock might in the end have been only a couple of years away, but it didn't seem it then.

If I had thought of putting some electronic block beats under a languid indie shuffle and Shaun's comic grotesquery, Tony would have sacked me or locked me up. 'Dance doesn't sell albums, darling', and at that point, Happy Mondays seemed like a new Factory album band.

Working with them, I couldn't decide if they were just in it as part of an overall grift to con the world into handing them a living, a long, paid holiday playing at being a pop group, blagging what they could while they got the chance, or whether their music and the antsy, capricious wordplay was how they were going to change their world and make a confounding escape from scamming and racketeering.

When Tony did get to hear what we'd done, he wasn't thrilled. 'Not your best work, Michael', he said. I love you too, Tony. The reviews weren't bad, and the first music paper journalists to come across Shaun and his pilfering rabble knew they had struck interview gold. As one interview in the *NME* noted, Shaun says things when he's being interviewed he really shouldn't say. He had the sort of future that might involve not having a long future.

Actually, it now seems the perfect first record by Happy Mondays, recording exactly where they were at that moment, straight out of Salford, with tantalising hints of a new hybrid of attitude and rhythm. I wish I'd thought of saying, 'Well, Tony, it is what it is. It's a start. And actually, they'll be writing about it in books in the future.'

In Shaun's autobiography – once he became an unlikely middle-of-the-road national treasure – he said he felt the EP didn't quite work. They were all too nervous – that was one way of looking at it – and the songs sounded too fast.

For the next record, the single 'Freaky Dancing' with B-side 'The Egg', it was Bernard's job to work out a Mondays sound, a clean, hazy mess of driving rhythms, post-jangle guitars and Shaun's sweet and sour dreams, his woozy hipster haranguing.

It's still pre-E so it's still an unformed, bleary Monday morning Mondays, on the cusp of something Manchester and new that was in the air that no one at Factory could put their fingers on. Bernard got close, but an ingredient was missing that he had no control over because it had nothing to do with sound.

For Tony – and me and Phil were with him all the way – the answer to who should produce their debut album was obvious. We'd had a couple of experiments within Factory and had a band who might peak with an *NME* cover; let's get serious.

The answer was John Cale. Of course! Pretty much the absolute opposite of me producing them in Bury, and somehow the Welsh icon agreed to two weeks at a studio in London at the end of 1986. We were all fanboys, and it was the answer of an older generation, the answer of fans of the Velvet Underground and his solo albums, and his collaborations from Nick Drake to Brian Eno, but most of all, of Cale as a producer. It seemed fate.

He'd produced the debut albums by The Stooges and Patti Smith, two of the all-time great albums for Tony, me and Phil, and I'd add the debut solo Nico album *Chelsea Girls* and the tracks he worked on for the debut solo album by Mike Heron of the Incredible String Band, *Smiling Men with Bad Reputations*, especially 'Feast for Stephen'.

Phil and I had been such Cale fanatics we had once followed him back to his hotel after his June 1974 show with Ayers, Nico and Eno at the Manchester Palace. We tried to talk to him, but I think he thought we were going to rob him or something, and he wasn't very friendly, mumbling something incomprehensible we interpreted as 'fuck off'. Which of course made him even more of a hero.

As the Factory arbiters sat in a smoke-filled room getting carried away about the thought of John Cale, Tony said, don't forget he produced the greatest debut single of all time – he had a few – and one of the songs that seemed enshrined as where punk rock began,

'Roadrunner' by Jonathan Richman and the Modern Lovers. That sealed the deal. Tony knew how to get hold of him – he'd appeared at the tenth anniversary of punk shows that Factory presented in the summer of 1986, what would now be some sort of festival 'legend' slot.

The Happy Mondays were ok with it, because their drug-taking versatility was getting more intense and unflagging, and around that time their favourite occupation was cutting coke tins in half, stuffing them with hash, and making them into bongs. They figured John Cale, of the uncanny Velvet Underground, of 'Heroin', of the Stooges with self-flagellating Iggy fucking Pop, was going to be a drug fiend with access to pharmaceutical-grade narcotics who could teach them a few new tricks.

When he arrived, he was more like a sedate professor of classical music with a very disciplined view of how to make a record. And he was completely clean: mints and fruit seemed to be his addiction. He was on a health kick and the Mondays thought he must be an imposter, some elaborate Tony Wilson practical joke.

He was used to working with some of the best musicians in rock, and even when he worked with self-described non-musician Brian Eno it was with a conceptual artist who had musical ideas. He heard the Mondays working out a song, and looked distraught. As people, he absolutely hated them. Possibly the first words he said to me were 'They're a bunch of bums.' Yeah, John, and you were well and truly bummed.

After hearing them have conversations among themselves in what seemed some internal slang – maybe a discussion that ended up with the album title Shaun was convinced by, *Squirrel And G-Man Twenty Four Hour Party People Plastic Face Carnt Smile (White Out)* – he often had to nip to a nearby pub to clear his head, spoiling his health kick a little. I was sure he was going to walk out, but I think he took a weird shine to them, and didn't want to let them down any more than not being the lord of debauchery they hoped for. They thought he was strange, but not the strange they wanted. He gave them certain exercises to keep things on the straight and narrow, like always getting them to count 1, 2, 3, 4 before they started a song, to ground them in reality. He also asked them to leave if they wanted to smoke.

Cale was very amused to the point of stunned watching Bez try to play the tambourine, which took a considerable amount of effort to get hand to hit instrument. Maybe he decided Bez was some form of performance artist, or perhaps a semi-professional clown rehearsing his act.

The professional pride of a serious musician made him stick around, but the Happy Mondays debut was not one of the greatest debut albums of all time that Tony was wanting. It was a middling to good Cale production, one of his lost gems, locating the evil glitter in Shaun's voice, because he still had the touch for anyone still interested. Maybe Tony shouldn't have warned Cale, tongue slightly in cheek, that what he was letting himself in for was scum, absolute fucking scum. Cale didn't fully appreciate that Tony meant it in a good way.

33
A rock group you can dance to

It was written in the stars that the Mondays, after a trip to Amsterdam, would find their way to ecstasy. They were naturals, as delighted everyday takers using it for a morning mooch or late-night flights, as forward-planning sharers, and out of The Haçienda alcove they made into Acid Corner, dealers.

From their fortified corner of the club, their crackpot office, the ecstasy spread throughout the club like wildfire, causing a sensational shift in focus. You could almost see it roll like a Mexican wave across the dance floor. Twenty, then forty, then sixty, and on it went. Previously awkward white kids in ill-fitting baggy jeans were suddenly dancing with dazzling Northern Soul fluidity.

In the middle of all this, as though it had been carefully timed, after three attempts at finding a producer for the Mondays, which went from the neophyte to the label darling to the living legend, Martin Hannett ended up producing their second album. He was either the last resort, or Tony impressed on everyone his original feeling that it simply had to be. 'Aut aleam iace aut perde fortunam', he said – 'throw the dice, or lose the chance' – if my memory serves. The pairing was also in the stars.

Lanky streak of piss and Shaun's berserk pal Bez was now part of the group, perhaps his audition being when he would do limb-flailing laps around The Haçienda shaking a pair of maracas to Adonis or Gerald like some kind of surrealist hype man for the wonders of ecstasy. Just as it had on The Haçienda dance floor, ecstasy spread through the album the Mondays made with Hannett, *Bummed*.

Basically, the group were asking Hannett, who had conceived some of the sounds and effects that infected house via ESG and hip-hop, to help them make a house album as they devoured ecstasy, figuring that the essentials of making a great album were the drugs consumed. Production experts could tell you back then when a mix had been made on cocaine, or marijuana, or speed, or maybe just cups of tea – and now there was the ecstasy era, with Happy Mondays as the advanced guard, bringing Martin back to some kind of studio life where he'd dabble in a drug he'd had no experience of. Heroin had killed his creative drive; ecstasy brought it back in flashes that were enough to locate the spirit in the group.

The Mondays had also come across house, the music the drug was made for, or vice versa, and they loved those primitive early 12-inchers we were playing at The Haçienda on Trax and DJ International, picking up on the cartoonish pseudonyms – Sleezy D, Mr Fingers – and the way electronic music could have a rough edge, a sublime crackle.

Hannett didn't need ecstasy to hear music the way the new consumers were suddenly doing. The facility to hear the granular detail of sound, explosions of matter and the open interstellar spaces all around it, came naturally. He did join in sampling the Mondays latest high, and now and then their incomparable northern knowledge would be pooled.

But he didn't dance – at the time he'd surprised the Mondays with how big and cumbersome he was – and he didn't know how a club DJ works, the way they move a crowd and structure a set. House couldn't be made by a non-clubber, only an interpretation, a version, occasionally, accidentally, for the hell of it, pushing the needle into red on the bass, guitar and bass drum, the stars aligning, and, on 'Wrote for Luck', a near bulls eye.

He gave them his drums, his precious time folding reverb, he gave them desperation, he gave them room to bang and shout and cackle and act like they'd just woken up and were still dreaming.

He gave Shaun these open, and cluttered, spaces to parade a fractured, inside knowledge of low-life creeps, addicts, hooligans, losers, pushers, perverts, users, junkies, deadbeats, scorers, lovers, pals, bums and cat burglars. He let Shaun Ryder play the role of great damned soul, of sleazy seer, even if that wasn't what Shaun was after.

He didn't give them house though, and therefore he didn't give them dance, but he gave them nightlife, he gave them free-range psychedelia, which would slip into the next stage, when the remixers came in, including quiet beat genius Vince Clarke of Yazoo, and fixed and found the rhythm that helped them sound like a night at The Haçienda not a night in a war zone.

Tony – and Alan – was right about Hannett being the one to produce the Mondays; from the chaos and the darkness, and occasional emergencies involving guns and real fear, Factory produced one of those intense, forward-moving albums that changes things. They liberated another collection of enlightened amateurs to go places that no one else was.

Phil Saxe was right in another way. Most nights in the studio, there was a riot going on, and two realities clashing. It was like Martin knew he was heading for the end. The Mondays were just getting going.

It took The Stones a fair few albums to get to the feverish debauchery and decadence of *Exile on Main Street*. It took the Mondays just two.

Before the ecstasy hit – funnelled through the Happy Mondays around The Haçienda, which turned out to be the perfect venue for their irregular entrepreneurial activities and alternative community welfare – my production of their first record was like a wayward day at the beach compared to the sinister, out of control hi-jinks of *Bummed*.

We'd tried in-house producers and living-legend producers, and the living legend's debut album only sold about 4,000 copies, and Martin's second not much more. The Happy Mondays were intermittently sounding like what Happy Mondays should sound like – the titles 'Freaky Dancin' and '24 Hour Party People' were quite a clue, and just about every word Shaun sang and chanted and misspelt, tapping into the illicit frequencies of a strange and exhilarating world.

Shaun's own instinct about what was needed involved the house music Bez would go into a trance dancing to in The Haçienda. Shaun himself was fond of waggling his ass to the insistent delirium. He knew that things needed to change for the group.

Happy Mondays stuck with Factory, so the casualty was Phil, who Shaun reasoned didn't see the importance of what was happening at The Haçienda. He had other skills. Phil's ingenuity at playing the system ensured the band, except full-time postman Mark, were able to claim the Thatcher-initiated Enterprise Allowance Scheme while they knocked themselves into shape during 1987.

A guaranteed income of £40 a week, and a year free of dole check-ups, was available to those unemployed who set up their own business. You needed savings, and Phil temporarily supplied those for each member. The Tories either missed that you could get someone to lend you the grand you needed to get going, and then, as soon as you were on the scheme, you gave the grand back. Or maybe they did know it was bollocks, and were just massaging the unemployment figures.

It's not clear what business Shaun and co said they were going into. You could be pretty vague about it, a little like it had been for me in Rotterdam. It was an unlikely, unplanned Thatcherite success story, leading to the emergence of numerous artists, record labels, musicians and comedians over the next few years – the anti-art Tories indirectly responsible for Britpop and Britart.

It was a smart move by Phil, but there were enough scammers, schemers and unlikely capitalists in the band. They needed something more than the £40 a week, which for one or two of them was just part of their income stream.

'Wrote for Luck' on *Bummed* initially sounded pretty warped before everything fell into place, revealing that the ecstasy flooding the venue was transforming the house music into epic versions of itself – its meticulous repetition turning into transcendent anthems. This was somehow the solution to finding the Happy Mondays sound.

The band, armed with their vast stock of pills, were creating conditions that made them sound like the most important group in the world. It was somewhere between conceptual art and one of the greatest entertainment cons of the twentieth century. For a year or two, from 1988 into 1989, as my Nude night became more and more a house night and The Haçienda was gripped by a collective fever dream, the group existed within this world, yet their sound remained outside it. The crucial connection hadn't yet been made.

Factory friend Nathan McGough took over as manager, immediately formalising the band's relationship with the label and focusing on finding the answer. The great thing about Nathan was that he was not only crazier than Factory, but possibly crazier than the band. That's the kind of manager Happy Mondays decided they needed – one who could keep up with their mysterious movements and also come up with concepts.

Nathan noticed that Bez was not only caught up in the pounding beat and all-night madness of Haçienda house and the raving party scenes he and his mates helped fuel, but he was also driving two hundred miles – sometimes with Shaun – to visit clubs down in London that, after a delay, had finally caught up with house music.

Yes, being from Manchester and, at that time, caught in the throes of a drug resembling a truth serum where everyone's truth was different, we claimed house – at least its northern UK outpost – as a Manchester first.

For a while, at the end of 1987, I didn't know whether what I was playing was happening anywhere else in the UK. It felt like a Manchester secret. There was no internet to sling everything everywhere immediately. There were rumours and random sightings, but it was only in 1987 when I saw a Top 10 in *Record Mirror*, compiled by a DJ at Nottingham's Garage called Graeme Park, was full of the same tracks I had been playing that I realised it was all bubbling away elsewhere.

Certainly around the North and the Midlands, in Sheffield or Leicester, but I don't think anywhere as big as The Haçienda. We were doing it on a grander scale.

That's where The Haçienda and the 1,400 or so it could hold came into its own – it was a prototype superclub. If there were pockets of activity in various places, The Haçienda was there at the centre of it all, drawing people in through its sheer ludicrous presence.

I invited Graeme up from Nottingham to do something with T-Coy on a Northern House Revue I put on at Nude in February 1988. His pseudonym was Groove, for a track he'd released called 'Submit to the Beat'. He couldn't believe the difference between his Nottingham crowd, still self-conscious *Face* and *i-D* readers clutching onto fashion, and the Manchester mob, dressed for movement and mayhem in dungarees and loose t-shirts. He looked a little scared for a few minutes – and then he got it. Manchester people were hungrier for finding new ways of celebrating on a night out, which is why we got to house quicker than anyone else.

We played some tracks together, and he became part of The Haçienda roster. I asked him to replace me for my Nude slot when I went on holiday in July 1988. Martin Prendergast had got into some trouble with the police, which eventually got sorted, so I had to find someone else.

The Haçienda DJ line-up was growing all the time, as the idea of becoming a DJ rather than forming a band became increasingly attractive. The Haçienda, positioning itself at the centre of what was happening, became a launching pad for a new kind of performing DJ, playing the house music that communicated to everyone and was now the future.

The power to make people dance was becoming something special, and Sasha of North Wales and Laurent Garnier from France were knocking on my DJ door, like I'd knocked on Mark Kamins, asking, 'What the hell are you playing?' They soon joined in playing at The Haçienda, on their way to their own pioneering years.

I was fully aware that house, and its acid sequel, were Black American inventions, as Detroit's techno supremo Derrick May in no uncertain terms told Tony Wilson and temporary nutcase sidekick Keith Allen at the 1990 New York New Music Seminar conference. There were definitely European editions, harder, darker in Belgium, lighter, dreamier and sunnier in Ibiza, but it didn't seem to have hit London.

It was essentially all hypnotic music given bendy, bleeping twists and turns by the way you could manipulate various Roland machines, mainly the 808 and 303. It had come from all corners of the earth and from all electronic genres, and Chicago was where it had got all mixed up into house.

Manchester was where it got turned into a thriving regional variation by musicians like 808 State, A Guy Called Gerald and T-Coy. It first hit me that it hadn't spread south, at least outside a few small areas, when in early 1988 I went down to play a night at a club called Fever at the Astoria in Central London. I played my latest Manchester set of what at The Haçienda were out-and-out guaranteed hits, and was greeted with guys staring at me with faces like thunder and arms folded.

The crowd was mainly Black, and it made me realise why the Black audience at The Haçienda was melting away – ecstasy wasn't the right drug, they didn't like chemicals, they didn't like the house tempo, and nights out required a commitment to some local urges that weren't where their heads were at. The white kids invaded their space and they moved on. Black Manchester got knocked out of the timeline yet again.

The guys surrounding my booth at the Astoria got particularly agitated when I played a track I thought was a straight score, Derrick May's 'Strings of Life'. They looked like they were in pain. I didn't realise it at the time, but this was a track that had come into the UK via the gay club Heaven, where Mark Moore of S'Express would be playing it and whipping the crowd into a frenzy. I'd cleared the floor.

A message came through, which at first I thought might be them asking what the track was, as it wasn't yet officially released. On it was scrawled, 'Why are you playing this Chicago homo house music instead of rare groove' – which is where they still were. Things were getting territorial. In response I pushed the speed up a few beats and the booing started.

In July, I was back at the same place in the same booth. The club was now called Trip and the whole place was in lysergic technicolour and had gone rave mad. They'd put podiums in the space which elevated dancers through the dry ice up towards the heavens, which we copied for The Haçienda, striped of course.

At Trip, there was the same kind of end-of-the-world, beginning-of-life Haçienda wildness. Everyone was in baggy smiley t-shirts, bandanas and bright colours, blowing whistles to the same tracks I'd played months before to total antipathy.

House arrived in London as acid house, mainly because of a trip DJ Paul Oakenfold took to Ibiza in the summer of 1987 for his 24th birthday with other DJs including Danny Rampling. At after-hours parties full of beautiful people, they discovered house music with ecstasy as a channel to pure knockout pleasure. They had their Paradise Garage moment in the Balearics, where the party didn't start until around four in the morning.

The DJ who unleashed their wild, eclectic side was an Argentinian called Alfredo, known as the Levan of Europe. He played everything from The Residents to Mandy Smith, Morricone to Keith Hudson, Art of Noise's 'Moments in Love' to U2 – anything that told a story carrying dancers to other places without them even knowing why or how.

He'd been quick to take in house, and would stick to that for an hour or two, but made sure he returned the freedom of a more eclectic mix of slow, rock, pop, soul and dub. The mix of house with other music, feeding in and out of it, always worked best in clubs, including The Haçienda, before it started to get too rigid and non-stop house.

Paul started playing house as part of his set at his Project club in Streatham, then turned the frenzied Ibizan vibe he'd experienced into Future, and then Spectrum at Heaven. Danny Rampling, with his wife, opened the candy-coloured Shoom in a gym south of the river, a mellow madhouse for people with attitude which could stay open until 5 am.

It was places like Spectrum and Shoom where holidaymakers who had led the London house charge gathered – Bez and Shaun were heading there from Manchester to experience something extra after spending a night at The Haçienda. The rooms were filled with people who looked like already devoted Happy Mondays fans, dressed the part and, for obvious reasons, at the right energy level with the elevated head space to consider that what Shaun was singing was deeply spiritual and Bez was their representation in space.

In London, they had taken the gaily coloured Ibizan motif head on. We'd always done wonderful birthday parties at the club – it was part of how we were self-consciously The Haçienda, throwing a themed party every year. We had a sporting theme with a boxing ring, a funfair one, and we built a pontoon bridge out to the derelict land at the back. We spent a fortune; it was completely financially stupid, but it all made sense when the London clubs imported the Ibizan parties and turned clubs into environments.

Paul Cons, the enterprising promotions manager at The Haçienda, went to Shoom to see what they were doing. He'd been running a Haçienda art, cabaret and comedy night called Zumbar, an exotic variety show with acts like iconic *Coronation Street* star Liz Dawn as Vera Duckworth singing in fur coats, and comedian Julian Clary when he was the Joan Collins Fan Club with Fanny the dog as a sidekick. As The Haçienda fever was rising, Paul used July 1988 as the day to launch the Hot night with a beach party, which took the Shoom vibe to extreme levels – he bought in a ton of ice pops, beach balls, and installed a twenty-foot swimming pool. Most turned up for a day on the beach in swimming costumes and brightly coloured plastic sunglasses.

Tony Wilson off the telly hosted a spin-the-wheel game with prizes, most of them modest, but one of which turned out to be 'free bar', which blew the profits for the night. Leroy, the bar manager, was not happy, always suffering especially when the ecstasy hit and the bar takings plummeted as the punters switched to water, which Rob insisted should be free. (Leroy used to drive ACR around Europe a few years before, neglecting to tell anyone he didn't have a driving licence.)

The pool burst, there was water everywhere, but it was a big visual part of what became known as the Summer of Love. The Haçienda had completed a five-year journey – from the brain-splitting drilling of Blixa Bargeld to the hedonistic crowd participation indoor beach of Hot.

Hearing about Bez and Shaun's long drives to London, Nathan didn't understand their dedication to a good night out at first, especially when they had The Haçienda. When he experienced it, he understood that Shaun, and Bez – if he only knew it – apart from loving the berserk energy and the outlaw spirit, were on the hunt for the answer to the question: what should Happy Mondays sound like?

The answer was hidden in plain sight; a rock band – and the Mondays were effectively a rock band – used real drums, and real drums were no good in a dance remix. They couldn't be made to attack a nightclub. A rock band didn't use electronic drums, and even Hannett's magic drums were still a rock band's drums. The rock band's concert venue needed to tangle up with the nightclub's sound system.

Tony's stubborn insistence was that a rock band was always at the centre of a cultural eruption, but at that moment dance and its electronic insides meeting the dream of ecstasy were where the action was.

DJs were becoming the stars, sometimes against their instincts – I know I was meant to be almost behind the scenes, but by 1988 there were a couple of times, getting off on the tracks I was playing, that I would stand with my arms outstretched, like some deranged conductor, and the audience responded like I was claiming credit for simply finding and buying a record. I'd forgotten I was playing the records, and just started dancing, carried away with the joy of it all. There was an unusual energy at the time, and it could get a bit mystical. That accidental superstar DJ pose would have consequences on those later DJs loving the messiah kick they got from being in control of such a collective experience. We were a little humbler up North.

The DJ became the face of the acid house explosion and could adopt Christlike poses, but they didn't have a voice – they weren't a lead singer. Tony was faithful to the idea of the heroic lead singer rock star. Everything changes, he reckoned – fashions, politics, entertainment – but nothing really does. There was a new music, but it still took putting the focus on a front person to lift it into the popular imagination. How to turn a rock band with a rock star singer into a dance act tapping into the new house excitement?

If a rock group's rhythms were electronic and synthesised, would they still be a rock band? The answer, after all that, was it didn't fucking matter. Any young rock group that didn't factor acid house into what they did lost their audience overnight.

Replace the drums on a Happy Mondays track – even those heavenly Hannett drums – with drum machines, and let it all fly in the hands of the remixers. With Shaun's gleeful, strung-out, stream-of-consciousness abstract reality thrown into the mix, a sample of his jumpy, grumpy brain, you reach a new point: a rock group you can dance to, a rock group given spooky, spaced-out house proportions.

The answer they needed was, to some extent, in London.

34
A rave

It was also, obviously, still in Manchester. I'm sticking with my view that we got there first, or at least were the best party people – the most elated, the most dedicated to clambering free of Thatcher's soulless, money-mad eighties. Not that it was a competition.

Martin and the Mondays pooled their ridiculous knowledge about the relationship between sound and getting high one more time for the *Rave* EP – four songs that seemed to break out from deep inside Shaun's illuminating experiences, switching between The Haçienda, Shoom and Spectrum. Dedicated to people who can't keep themselves or their minds still, it created the templates and set the stage for the remix EP. The limited rock drums were replaced by the mighty, thumping, radiating punch of the electronics.

Martin had done his job for the Mondays. During the session, the group rationed his intake of Es to two a day, so he felt happy and only dimly aware of the approaching abyss. He gave everything he had left to this gang of light-fingered Salford savages at immense personal cost. It was his final major work, a wonderful swan song, and I'm glad he got to do it – there was a last gasp, the exhausted production of The High, one of those second- and third-generation floppy, baggy Manc bands London record companies were panic signing, trying to recreate the incongruous trippy dance/rock hybrid of the Mondays and The Stone Roses. For me, *Rave* was his great farewell.

He'd created the perfect Factory sound, but he couldn't take it where he hoped to because Rob and Tony decided to invest in a nightclub and not the groundbreaking Fairlight digital synthesiser he wanted. He dreamt of a high-tech Factory studio, not a bloody dance club. Records were the key, not a stupid disco.

This had led to the legendary 1982 Factory meeting at the Manchester Club, when Rob, Tony and Martin were having this mad argument about it. Martin was on the phone and we could hear him through a speaker, and in the middle of the row Martin fired an air pistol, which he happened to have lying around. Which was followed by silence. Rob feared the worst and started to panic. 'Are you alright, Martin?' I was saying, not completely convinced, 'Of course he's alright, he's not shot himself or anything.' He hadn't, but he'd made his point. Rob shouted, 'Oh, for God's sake, I'll buy you your fucking Fairlight, but we're still opening a club.' Martin never got his Fairlight and we never got to hear what he might have done with this revolutionary sampling machine.

After he did *Rave* for the Mondays, I only saw him once more. He came round to my house one day in 1990. I rarely saw him, but he only lived in the next street in Chorlton. He was in a terrible state, looking for some money, I think. I walked him back home and we didn't say much. In his front room, the floor was covered with newspapers, piles of rubbish and dirty plates. The drugs had caught up with him again. He died about a year later in 1991, aged 42.

Based on Shaun's journeys to London raves with Bez and his growing friendship with Paul Oakenfold, Nathan had asked Paul to remix 'Wrote For Luck', which he did with engineer Steve Osborne – the first time they worked together. The result was 'W.L.F (Think About The Future)', the loose, pulsating, swaggering sound of Happy Mondays: a rock group in a groove, with a lead singer chopping his life into frazzled bits of truth and reflection, nailing the end-of-decade zeitgeist simply by singing 'ah aah ah ah aah ah'.

Oddly, for a turning point in history, it wasn't even definitely the best remix of the song. Vince Clarke's charged, dreamy electro-sonic mix might come out on top if you're choosing, possibly because that was the one used for the video, shot in the Legend club by the Bailey brothers through the silver mist of dreams.

Shaun the boss is surrounded in the video by Mancunians perfectly off their trees, blissed out bug-eyed Bez lost in the endless mental now, all of them stars of the speeding up/slowing down show. You couldn't believe that anyone dancing around their leader was ever going to grow old.

It's a reminder that around about the time this was shot, for a couple of years – the final two of that turbulent decade – I was the happiest I had ever been. So was everyone in this video. Cross cut to the future that Shaun was asking us to think about in 'Wrote For Luck', and the digital age of the 2020s, and it's as though it was some kind of party for the end of the pre-digital age – everyone being together and touching and taking off. It was no wonder that no one wanted it to end.

The video should be in any documentary on the history of dance, the history of rave, the history of language, the history of pop videos, the history of drugs, the history of the best time to be young, the history of Manchester, the history of the relationship between chaos and creativity, the history of The Haçienda, the history of 1989, the history of the answer to the question: what kind of group were Happy Mondays?

Fucking Hallelujah! was the collective response in the group and at Factory to the finding of the answer, and on 23 November 1989, Happy Mondays were playing 'Hallelujah' and The Stone Roses were playing 'Fools Gold' on *Top of the Pops*, one of those David Bowie 'Starman' moments of life change for those blessed young of the right age and the right taste. 'Never in doubt, darling', said Tony Wilson, the newly crowned king of Madchester, even as ruin and retribution was just around the corner.

The Mondays, and the Roses in their Manchester story, with their own eighties search for what they should sound like, absurdly teetered on the edge of the mainstream – bringing their ragged sense of transcendence to a wilder world. If it all went belly up – and what were the chances of it not, after such mental commitment to their cause, with such self-destructive impulse – they at least put their unique input into what an ideal pop group should be like.

Surely nothing else as Manchester could possibly follow them, and their unlikely rise to fame.

35
A contribution from Noel Gallagher

It was in the *Manchester Evening News*. There's this thing happening at The Haçienda that looked like it needed checking out. The first time I went and heard the house music Mike was playing, I couldn't make head or tail of it. I stood there with my can of lager thinking, what the fuck is this? There's no singing, it's just tsk tsk tsk tsk and these squelches and a couple of words. I couldn't work out what everyone was dancing to.

The next week I went back and I took half an E. I took the half because honestly there was a rumour when it first turned up that if you took one you'd die. Some said it was a killer drug.

It was twenty-five fucking quid so I wasn't going to waste it, and I snapped it in half, so I wouldn't die – maybe just a bit of brain damage. Let me just get maimed first. In hospital for a long time, maybe forever. It was worth the risk.

It was good gear in those days. After taking it, I got it. Those squelches, tsks and the constant beat made more sense with the E than the lager.

I remember going to the Kitchen afterward, two flats knocked together in desolate Hulme Crescents. You traipsed up these stairs, knocked on the door, and someone opened it and let you inside. Mike will fill you in. And I was stood on one of those balconies in the morning thinking to myself, I've never noticed before how beautiful Hulme is.

More people started to come to The Haçienda and Nude, which helped. At first it was five hundred, then over the next couple of weeks another five hundred, then another five hundred, and the week after six hundred are being turned away.

I've got them all on cassette now, all of Mike's Nude nights from 1985, the later nights he was doing with Graeme Park. Every single one that I've put on a hard drive. I've been going through them at home meticulously, it took me ages to stack them in order, and you can hear a real musical journey as the music changed. It begins almost calypso-like electro and then over time it builds and builds. You didn't notice it as it was happening, it all just flowed, but now there's a story that you can hear taking shape. By 1987, 1988, there's a music revolution every month, it gets more sophisticated, and you can hear what became acid house getting its own sound.

On one of them, when you turn the cassette over there's this loud crackle. Someone must have pressed play and record at the same time and you can hear Mike go 'That sounds fucking mega', and Graeme says, 'I think you're taping over it'. Mike goes, dead annoyed, 'Foooocking heell'. More crackle, and then the track kicks in. How on earth they DJ'd in the state they were in I have no idea. It was like two lads messing around on their own, but they would be playing for nearly 2,000 people.

I'll play these cassettes on a ghetto blaster to my mates sometimes who are like ten, fifteen years younger, and I tell them, 'That's real, that is. That's human beings putting that together live – playing vinyl, it's not computers, it's not pre-programmed on a USB stick. It's as live as fuck. You can hear the pops and scratches. You can hear them using their hands to speed up or slow down a record to get it in time with the next one.' I've got an app on my phone now that can cue tracks.

At the time, you used to hear Tony Wilson crack on about The Haçienda like it was the greatest show on earth. I used to think, 'Give it a rest, you big fanny.' But as you get older, you look back and you cannot overestimate how much this collective of mavericks had this idea and saw it through – even as it was losing money. They really were doing it for the city and the people, and the madness that made it what it was couldn't have happened if they were in it to make a profit. It was almost, if they were making money, something was going wrong.

I remember in 1988 and 1989, you'd walk around Manchester and see all these people you'd seen at the City match the day before, high on ecstasy, and you'd think, this cannot fucking last. We had the Roses, the Mondays and New Order all at the same time doing their thing, and a few years before that it had been Buzzcocks, Joy Division and The Smiths. In that tiny fucking little city centre. People are always asking me, 'Manchester – what's it like, how did this all happen?' Don't ask me. I don't fucking know. The rain? Because we're stuck indoors doing shit and taking shit? Because we were poor and needed something of our own to celebrate?

What I took from The Haçienda when I joined Oasis in 1991 wasn't a conscious thing. I wish I could claim I was being this consciously clever, but when I started to write songs it dawned on me – from going to The Haçienda, especially during those two years – 1988 and 1989 – that the music was all about what it made you feel, not what it was about.

The generation before – The Smiths, Joy Division – it was all, 'What are the songs about?' And Manchester had been blessed with the most outrageous lyricists: Devoto, Shelley, Curtis, Morrissey, even Shaun. You name them, there was no point competing after all of that. What was I going to say?

I wrote words that when they went with the music made you feel something. That's what I took from acid house. Not the rhythmic side of it, or the electronic side, but the memory it left you with that something incredible had happened.

Acid house was all about bringing everybody together in the moment – and that's what went into 'Live Forever' and 'Rock and Roll Star'. It's all of us in it together. It wasn't about the subject matter. It was what you felt when you heard it and the register they're in. In all those great acid house tracks they're soaring, there's nobody mumbling, but if you wrote the words down on a piece of paper, they don't mean anything, they're not saying anything.

I'd also remember being so impressed standing on Kippax Street when I was 10, 11, and a song would start, and the crowd would join in, and it would get so euphoric, like an acid house track. You can hear that on 'Don't Look Back in Anger' – by the end, there are thirteen voices singing it. It was all subconscious; you don't get up one morning and think, 'Oh, I'll do this and that.' It doesn't really work like that.

I remember hearing 'Ride on Time' by Black Box for the first time in The Haçienda when Mike played it and thinking, 'That's it, you cannot get any better than that.' It's a song, but it's not about the words, but you'll remember the words. And the crowd exploded on first hearing because of those three words that didn't mean anything but meant everything at that moment, because of where you were and what you were doing. It was that feeling of community that went with it. Everyone being as one – not because the song means anything but because we're all listening to it as one. That's what the song means.

I still say to this day that 'Ride On Time' is one of the best things I've ever heard in a nightclub. It's got barely any words, it just repeats ride on time, ride on time, ride on time from beginning to end. It's nonsense, but the energy isn't. It makes you feel something. It's all you need. It broke out of The Haçienda. How the fuck did that happen?

36
A ride on time

There's no one story of how 'Ride on Time' ended up the biggest selling single of 1989, but mine is as good as any.

Sometime in the summer of 1989, I got slipped a white label of this obscure Italian house track, a little like I'd been slipped Adonis, but this time by an Italian guy in a ponytail who turned out to be a DJ and house producer from Bologna called Daniele Davoli.

He'd put the track together with studio musicians Mirko Limoni and Valerio Semplici, messing around with an Akai sampler he'd just bought and chopping up a Loleatta Holloway vocal from a 1980 track mixed by disco lodestar Tom Moulton called 'Love Sensation.' He thought a lot of Italian disco records lacked energy, so he had gone to the other extreme, and imagined what house music would be like if it had the power of Led Zeppelin or Deep Purple. It was ferocious, and unbelievably addictive. They'd accidentally or out of desperation created this mighty, raw masterpiece.

I immediately wanted to play it, and I told him to come back at midnight, and we'll see how it goes down. He was a little nervous, as he said it cleared the floor in some clubs back in Italy. To me, that made it seem even more exciting.

He came back, and I put it on at midnight, peak time, and, Jesus, it had one of the greatest reactions to a new tune I'd ever had. People were banging on the DJ box demanding to know what it was. You had to be there. Those who never experienced it in a club had no idea what its appeal was. It got inside our heads and it was the sound of getting something out of your system when sometimes all you wanted to do was scream with joy.

I lost track of where Daniele was in the usual after midnight Haçienda mayhem, and it was a little bit Cinderella – he'd left behind the record, but I didn't know how to get hold of him. My manager Pete rang me up the next day from the Deconstruction offices in Islington, under Madness's office, and said, 'Did some Italian DJ with a ponytail come up and see you at the Hac?' We all remembered the ponytail. It made sense of something in the track that was a little Eurovision.

He'd had a meeting with Daniele who was looking for someone in the UK to put his latest track out. Pete was already interested in another Black Box track he'd come across. He had a listen but he wasn't sure if it was my thing. There were those who felt that the sample of the singer shrieking 'ride on time' – some heard 'right on time' – non-stop would frighten people. I said, 'Pete, it's amazing. It's hook after hook after hook. It's a Haçienda smash already. We have to sign it now.'

There were all sorts of problems with the track legally. We sent Dan Hartman, the writer and producer of 'Love Sensation', a cassette, and he said he loved it, and would never have thought of doing it like that. He generously let Black Box have the rights, asking for thirty per cent. They weren't happy until we pointed out Hartman could easily have asked for a hundred percent. The track they had sampled wasn't as obscure as they thought to those who knew their disco.

I said, we have to re-do the vocals or clear the sample. Daniele had made it with the same wild west sampling spirit from ten years ago at the beginning of hip-hop, before the lawyers got involved and set up some laws and restrictions. He convinced Pete and Keith that the singer was not Loleatta Holloway but some Italian girl he had hired.

I played the original 'Love Sensation' and the Black Box 'Ride on Time' together and I said, look, it's obviously a sample, and Loleatta's scream is one of a kind. No Italian singer is going to have that kind of gospel fury. It was clever how they'd done it, and spliced it with the Korg piano, but the vocal was definitely a sample. Not, as they said, just three words, because the whole point was they pummelled you with it throughout the track. It was the track!

We said, Daniele, you have to tell us the truth, or we're fucked. He had an old school outlaw spirit, assumed Loleatta was dead, and he promised us it was not the original vocal but a copy. We were in a rush, we needed to get it out for the summer, and so we trusted him.

It came out on Deconstruction on 31 July, and Paul Oakenfold and Danny Rampling were already playing it in their clubs non-stop. I found out they had bought up a load of the original Italian release. By the end of August, as The Haçienda market research had shown me, it went to number 1 in the mainstream charts, where it stayed for six weeks.

Of course, becoming such a big hit meant visibility, and suddenly, money, which changes everything. It put cultural and legal attention on what was originally made as a kind of underground test for a new piano sound and style with some vocals cut and pasted from a relatively obscure track. It was probably going to be at best a summer club hit, passing through relatively unknown, not disturbing any pesky lawyers.

After it had been on *Top of the Pops*, with French model Katrin Quinoi miming the vocals in her own time, playing the role of singer in artwork and video, Loleatta hears about it – definitely not dead, and a gay icon. She was playing shows introducing 'Love Sensation' and saying with some righteous indignation, 'I heard some skinny bitch stole my voice!'

It had originally been released by Gold Mind Records, a subsidiary of New York-based disco and early high-energy specialists Salsoul Records, which was owned by the Cayre brothers. That had us in a panic, as they were as tough as they came. They didn't mess about.

They'd been at the forefront of making 12-inch singles commercially available, not just promotional white labels. You didn't want to mess with them, and you didn't want to mess with their music. Loleatta had been their prime disco diva, although she was never directly signed to the label and was often hired in to sing on various records, so Black Box in their innocence had stirred a hornet's nest. They'd picked up on something that Loleatta had essentially improvised herself around the original lyric, so from the very beginning it was a moot point who wrote what and who should get a credit.

The Cayre brothers were used to pushing boundaries, having produced as Good Times Home Video a load of animated films with very Disney-like titles, which got them noticed by Disney, who then went after them. They didn't mind appropriating other works themselves and testing legality, but they definitely didn't want it done to them. We paid them a significant amount of money, naively assuming they would pay Loleatta, which was beyond our control. Loleatta was not going to come on board after the miming model and the missing money, although it would have been great.

We replaced the voice using Heather Small, the powerful singer in a band Pete and Keith had signed to Deconstruction called Hot House. Deconstruction sent her to Italy to record the vocals on the original song, confident she was able to make it sound as momentous. It was top secret, even Black Box didn't know who did the replacement voice. Heather never told anyone, following some sort of vocalist code of conduct. Who was singing what version as it got to number 1 was never clear, even to me, and Pete and Keith at Deconstruction were quick to put out full-page music paper ads poking fun at the controversy with the slogan 'Who Sings? Who Cares!' In a way, Heather as the singer was the furtive beginning of a group I was just beginning to have thoughts about. For a while I only had a name – M People.

Yeah, how the fuck did 'Ride on Time' happen? It certainly wasn't because RCA gave us a load of promotional money – at the time, they showed their bias against dance by deciding to fly-post the latest Dave Stewart album, which sold about two copies – although don't fact check that. They didn't put any money into promoting 'Ride on Time', clearly seeing it as some kind of gimmick.

It was a massive mess of a song that sort of flung disco at the walls of house, and it helped shift the axis of pop towards Europe and a Europop and Eurodance that wasn't seen as inferior anymore. It led to

Euro superstar DJs giving their steamy, seaside take on house. I just remember playing it at The Haçienda at midnight at the beginning of the summer of 1989, and by the end the reverberations had reached around the world.

During its run at number 1, Tony Wilson and Alan Erasmus launched Factory Classical, a typically capricious Factory adventure possibly at the absolute opposite end of the spectrum to acid bouse and Madchester. The Kreisler String Quartet played something lovely by Benjamin Britten and then Tony gets up to give a speech.

A little way through it, he said, 'We happen to have a couple of people in the room who have the number 1 record in Britain at the moment.' Everyone politely applauded me and Keith – the kind of people who would have considered Black Box a vulgar and possibly deeply offensive piece of throwaway pop. I thought, you bastard, you know how much I like to stay in the background! He was actually being generous, genuinely pleased for me.

Typical Tony. Factory's running out of money – it can't pay its bills – and he's happy to draw attention to the fact that a record that could have been on Factory and brought some money into the label was not on Factory, which was doing something completely obscure for the good of their soul. He said to me, as it was staying at number 1 week after week, dance music is probably making money because he always said it would never make money.

Alan did ask me why I was playing these records at The Haçienda that were available to sign and were selling millions and not releasing them on Factory, but I didn't really have the answer.

It never occurred to Tony that I would deliberately take 'Ride on Time' away from some Factory dance subsidiary, as he knew I knew he would not want it on his label. It was not so much that dance did not sell, but more that he could not see any meaning in it. There was no way on earth he would want 'Ride on Time' or T-Coy, and his way of underlining this was to release albums of oboe pieces and interpretations of baroque composer Monteverdi.

He might have enjoyed the chaos, and at times Black Box did seem like Factory chaos – ripped-off artists, mad, haphazard Italian fantasists, uncleared samples, sharp, threatening New York entertainment entrepreneurs, scandalous miming incidents. In the end, by 1990, Tony had plenty of chaos to deal with, and the classical label was a typically eccentric, defiant distraction. He had the Happy Mondays to deal with, and that was his kind of chaos, his kind of dance.

37
A fake me

When it came to the Happy Mondays, by 1989 I'd done my job, got them as far as I could, loved them when they hit the heights as high as a kite, and then let them get on with it. The last contribution I made working with them was to introduce them to Rowetta when they were looking for a female singer.

I made a record with Graeme Park in 1989 for Deconstruction under the name Dynasty of Two – after the early, purest of the pure Dynasty ecstasy available in The Haçienda that would set you back £25 a pill (well worth it). Dynasty essentially fuelled the Second Summer of Love. The track we did was called 'Stop This Thing' and we sold it as the first Green house record – don't ask – with all profits going to Greenpeace. God knows what state we were in when we decided to do an eco-house record, but definitely one where it seemed like a brilliant idea. We needed a female singer, and I found a demo with Rowetta singing an obscure soul song. She could certainly belt out a tune.

Rowetta was dead straight at the time, but years of Happy Mondays association sent her on a few tours of the twilight zone, and now she styles herself as the Queen of Manchester. Sorry, Rowetta. Or, you're welcome, Rowetta!

It would take its own insane course, the Oakenfold and Osborne third Mondays album *Pills 'n' Thrills and Bellyaches* that was as pure, dream come true as the group would get, and the epic farce of the follow-up album that helped bring down Factory, who, it turned out, like the group, hadn't learnt much from the ups and downs of smash-and-grab eighties. It was Alan who had the bright idea of getting the group away from temptation by sending them to a recording studio in Barbados. He seemed to have no idea it was difficult to spend time there without being offered drugs, especially if you looked like an obvious target. Happy Mondays had targets on their foreheads.

This time, the drug in question was crack, so miracles would have been needed to help make a coherent album. Instead, the gentle, life-loving Tina Weymouth and Chris Frantz, ex-Talking Heads, somehow ended up producing, mostly in a state of shock as Shaun, Bez and co enacted a Hunter S. Thompson journey to oblivion. Alan didn't know what had hit him trying to sort that out, and quickly went into retreat mode.

Things were more unpleasant and fucked up than the ecstasy years, which had their moments, and I was happy not to have been involved in their downfall. Before the disaster, when they were breaking through and everyone involved could pretend it was all under control, I would go on tour as a before-set DJ along with Paul Oakenfold. That was the light side of nightmarishly funny, and we had access to Nathan's American Express card, which was seriously abused. Nothing, though, compared to the self-abuse coming from inside the band, who used the freedom given them by being on tour, feted, celebrated and indulged, to take the booze, pills and powder party to the limit.

There was something admirable about it, as horrible and deranged as it got – their determination to be who they were whatever the fallout. Hanging out with Bez could be charming, and you would usually find yourself in some bonkers scenario, as if chaos followed him around – or maybe he followed chaos around. We were in LA at some point – don't press me on dates or even year – and we saw a flyer for a warehouse party that said Mike Pickering of The Haçienda was playing. It happened a lot – those organising rave parties sticking names down on the promotional material to get people along, who would usually be so far gone by the time they arrived as to forget who they'd come to listen to. You could put anything on a flyer; my name would forever be advertised as taking part in some night I knew nothing about.

Fake rave flyer 1988

Bez thought it would be funny to take the real Mike Pickering of The Haçienda to see so called 'Mike Pickering of The Haçienda' play a set. When we got there, 'Mike Pickering of The Haçienda' with lots of curly hair was finishing his set. Some records the Mike Pickering of The Haçienda with a Manchester fringe on top would never play. Bez went up to him and said, 'Good set, man, what's your name?'

'Mike Pickering.'

'Of The Haçienda in Manchester?'

'Yeah, that's right! You know it?'

He had an English accent, although not a Manchester accent, and Bez said, 'Well that's fucking weird, because this is Mike Pickering of The Haçienda right here.' It all got a bit tense, and I tried to calm it down: 'No big deal, you're all right mate. No biggie. No real harm done. Just don't do it again.'

Bez was not so forgiving. 'You can't be fucking Mike Pickering of The Haçienda with a haircut like that!' 'Look at his hair', he kept ranting. 'Look at it!' That told him.

At the same time and place, there was the famous story – which got turned into Bez at Johnny Depp's Viper Club in LA turning down the chance to go home with Julia Roberts – but which was more him getting into an argument with a woman who he thought was claiming to be Julia Roberts, and he refused to believe it. We heard him arguing with her, 'You're not her from *Pretty Woman*, no fucking chance!' We told him, 'No, it is Julia Roberts; these Hollywood actresses love to hang around dirty English bands!'

Once the bad drugs started to come in, Happy Mondays wasn't so much a friendly space anymore. There were murmurs starting about how much Paul and I were being paid. We said, 'You wanted us on tour, don't get funny about how much we're being paid!' It was becoming clear that there was no role for me – and Deconstruction was picking up as a label. The constant drugs were putting a big space between them and anything normal, to put it mildly.

They're ok now. Better when they're clean. They've worked out how to make money out of being who they are. They were ready for reality television before it was invented, and while they were waiting, cooked up a hell of a backstory.

Somehow it's a story with a happy ending.

38
A glow

Funnily enough, it wasn't Happy Mondays who first gave me ecstasy. It was Paul Oakenfold, in Barcelona, when I was there with T-Coy. When you took it, you felt it was your duty to introduce your friends to this astonishing new world. You couldn't bear that people you liked or loved were missing out on the experience of a lifetime. Drug dealers tend to give away a drug at first, to lure a potential customer in, when they start charging. With ecstasy, it was nothing to do with being a dealer. It was a slice of heaven, and one of its benefits was putting you in a state of loving grace, and you loved everything, and everyone was beautiful, in their own way, and you wanted everyone else to love everything and be beautiful. If we wanted to find a way for everyone to get on together, we had to give them ecstasy. It didn't even seem a drug back then – it wasn't in the hands of seedy drug dealers or even friendly drug dealers. It was given to you by a friend.

That first one didn't do much. I thought, maybe it's not for me. Then, one night after a Haçienda set, early 1988, so insanity was already in place, we went to a party with Lesley Gretton – at Bernard's in Handforth on the Manchester–Cheshire border. Jeff, the chef from The Haçienda, gave me one. Forty minutes later everything stopped and started in a split second, and it was one of those tremendous, 'Oh, now I get it' moments.

I totally understood. In seconds I was on top of the world with my brain reshaping itself, and the walls seemed so wonderful, and everyone's face made me smile like an idiot. A little later, I took it in Ibiza, almost like going to the source, which wasn't true, but felt like it. I stood on the terrace at Amnesia, the open-air club where the whole multicultural world seemed to come on any given night, hardly anyone English, certainly no one from Manchester, and there was a plane flying overhead. I was with a few friends, and we all started cheering the plane and waving – that's our plane! We lost it completely. Boy, did I dance that night. Part of me is still there, dancing to whatever Alfredo wants to play. Everything made sense. Everything was aglow.

For a few weeks I kept ecstasy separate from the DJ booth. Then one night I thought, sod it, everyone in the house seems like they're on it, I better join in. The temptation was too much.

The first time I took one I went through one of my five-hour sets and it felt like two minutes. The place went haywire. At the end of it, absolutely soaked, my brain still humming, the air around me on fire, I thought, that was one of the best nights of my life. I seemed to know what record to play three, four ahead, knowing exactly where the crowd's mood was and where they wanted to go next – once I'd chosen the first record, the rest followed in the perfect natural sequence, moment to moment, lift off to lift off.

I would play a little riff of something, and the crowd would surge, and then I'd hold off, arms in the air, calm before the storm, and you could feel the crowd cheering and whistling and shouting, and then I would drop the needle right into the rhythm as it punched forward and everyone started shaking and rolling. It was beautiful. I'd learnt to play the crowd. Fat Boy Slim would later say of the moment he would stop the music for 15, 20 seconds, and then, bang, back to the beat, and thousands would go ape-shit – 'I got that from you, Mike.'

The next time Tony would say to me dance music is never going to happen, I made sure I asked, 'Have you seen your own fucking club?' He'd have an answer, of course. The acid in acid house was his answer. It wasn't the dance music, it was the *feeling*.

You could see the change among those in the clubs in different ways. It changed the way clubbers did things; it wasn't this mad dash to get drunk or smashed. I did another Trip in London at the Astoria, and there were some rough and tough-looking lads blocking my way to the toilets, Millwall hooligans by the look of it, and I thought it was going to get a bit dicey. But they were all loved up – 'How are you mate, nice one' – and almost started hugging me. I mean, it didn't go that far, but everyone was so euphoric, and there was no need to make things tricky. You couldn't be anything but nice.

Ecstasy wasn't cheap in the early days, but it was pure MDMA, and you would still be high the next morning, but you didn't feel bad. It was a risk to take it, but not as risky as it would be later when it was adulterated and people started feeling bad, and worse.

It was initially coming from within the scene, and it wasn't yet under the control of the criminal element, or at least the criminal element out there in the dark corners of Manchester. They would soon be sniffing about, taking advantage, cutting it up, charging deluxe prices, but early on it was almost just something we passed among ourselves. All the good guys, the characters who were as much part of the scene as they were dealers, were eventually pushed out. They disappeared, threatened with death if they hung around. It got nasty.

For those first two years ecstasy was one of those born-again moments for whoever it hit at the right moment, when it still seemed connected to the music, and the people you were sharing it with. When it was part of some dream you were in control of, not part of some trend, or tabloid frenzy, or Madchester nonsense, or dealer violence, when it made you see everything in a new way. For once you were in charge of your own destiny.

It worked for me. One day I'm living in my crummy two-up two-down in Chorlton with my girlfriend Maria, and everything was ticking over. The two-up two-down where some believed I'd had an odd evening with Madonna involving some lost keys. Then I have an ecstasy experience at The Haçienda and I'm lifted elsewhere. Maybe I did have an odd experience with Madonna after all! That would be something for the memoirs. Maybe I can twist it to say the first time I ever had ecstasy was with Madonna.

Ecstasy wasn't like any drug I'd taken before. Things were different. You made decisions out of the blue, and that could have been dangerous. But you had this feeling of, 'It's now or never.' It might be irresponsible, but what have you got to lose? The message was in the music, and you understood it as clear as a whistle when you were high.

I met a girl – and before I go any further, let me say, I met Laura, who I was with for sixteen years, and who I had two children with.

I met a girl at the end of one of the raves that were starting to be thrown – in car parks, in tucked-away railway arches, in random houses, abandoned shops, packed basements, someone's flat in the early morning to keep the party going – because The Haçienda shut at 2 am, for licensing reasons, and one thing that New York and Ibiza had taught us was that you don't have to stop, just like that. The party moves wherever the party has to move to.

The parties started to move out of the cities once the police cottoned on. At first they were oblivious. They didn't have a clue. It's what made the Second Summer of Love in 1988, a name paying homage to the hippy-driven 1967 San Francisco Summer of Love, particularly amazing. It all seemed like a secret society, beyond the rule of law, picking up cryptic messages about where to go next, this eruption of untraceable love vibes making the government panic.

The police raided one called Sweat It Out that we did, which was originally meant to be underneath Store Street arches on 8 October 1988. This one was properly organised as their first warehouse party by Haçienda regulars the Donnelly Brothers, Christopher and Anthony, whose sister Tracey worked with Tony and Alan at Factory. There was a stage, security, generator and lasers, and me and Jon Dasilva were scheduled to play.

We first came across them as lads causing a nuisance at the door, bootlegging Happy Mondays t-shirts. Tony took a liking to them, another bunch of ingenious Wythenshawe kids working out how to earn some cash in Thatcher's unemployed country, and got them doing official Mondays merchandising.

Tony loved the idea that the bootleggers became the official sellers – and that the bootleggers were connected to the notorious local criminal family, the Quality Street Gang. He liked the contrast between music and fashion on one hand – and fashion and crime on the other. Tony was drawn to the glamour of his romanticised version of the Manchester underground – until it came to knock down the house.

The police became aware that something was going on with these elusive raves because the idea of acid house was getting mentioned in the mainstream media, often portrayed as some kind of drug-fuelled orgy that was going to bring civilisation down. The Donnellys used Store Street as a kind of decoy, spraying a smiley face at the original venue and giving Alice in Wonderland instructions – wait here.

It seemed like the whole Haçienda crowd had moved over and were waiting when the Donnellys turned up with information about the real venue, on Temperance Street next to Mayfield bus depot. The police got there in the end, but only in the morning, after it was all over and we were sweeping up the water. I was mainly worried they were going to confiscate my records.

'What's happening here?' they asked, and we said, 'We were just having a party, but we've all been well behaved. There was no alcohol, it was all water, coke and orange juice, no one needed alcohol.' They were poking about, really dubious. Then I mentioned that Tony Wilson off the telly had been there – which he had, filming it for *Granada Reports*, always on the spot to see Manchester make history, often making the history because he was on the spot with a camera crew. That impressed them. 'Yes, we've had a few people like that, it's all very respectable.'

For Tony it was of course the greatest thing that had happened in Manchester since the last greatest thing that had happened in Manchester. There were tears in his eyes as he told the youngsters all about the time the Sex Pistols played at the Lesser Free Trade Hall, the old-timer getting that thrill once more. The police warned us that we were on Railtrack territory; we pleaded innocence, and they let us off with a warning, telling us to say hi to Tony.

The parties began to move into the countryside to avoid the police presence. News would spread around The Haçienda about some barn in Cheshire, and a convoy of cars would set off, snaking down narrow roads past fields and trees towards that night's venue. Sometimes you'd head to a car park where there was a phone box, and at a set time you'd receive a call. Some place by a B road, off the A6 or wherever. Then the convoy would depart, cars full of kids playing music at full blast, sometimes having to evade a police car in pursuit.

You felt part of a movement – people united into a community, something built from within, with no influence from business or media. When they got involved, dragging the police with them, that was when it was all over. The Second Summer of Love was this great mix of people who never usually mixed, finding ways to outwit the system and do something just for themselves. It was such a change from the segregated clubs. Soul boys, football yobs, punks, funksters, hip-hop heads and hippies were all in it together.

Apart from anything else we were doing, we were in the process of making Britain an all-night country – at least in the cities. It was still fixed into post-war hours, where shops and pubs closed at weird times and life and city centres emptied out. We wanted to keep going – and we'd keep the music playing and the minds and bodies moving. Sometimes you'd come out of a night at The Haçienda, and if there was nowhere particular to go, a few of you would squeeze into a car, and we'd just drive around playing the set we'd just played in the car.

Pretty much every genre of music you hear these days in a bar, restaurant or cafe, at a sporting occasion, on the beach, on TV ads – all the dance genres and evolving electronic and techno rhythms that emerged at the turn of the century and survive into the 2020s – were born in those fields and warehouses. It all comes from the house four-on-the-floor.

Inspired by the entrepreneurial, clandestine energy, Rob thought there should be an after-hours party for the completion of the recording of New Order's *Technique* album – where they finished their eighties as a complete changeling pop group, up to speed but still in their own space with the acid house, rave and unhinged Second Summer of Love that was happening around them in their club.

Against all the odds they had created a club that helped them keep up with changes in electronic and dance music like few of their peers could – and helped them create a masterpiece, their first number 1 album, mixing their natural melancholy with haywire all-night mania.

Being Rob, he decided not to hold the party in their own club, or somewhere out of the city centre in a warehouse where the raves were happening – but in Peter Gabriel's deluxe Real World residential studios where the group had moved away from Manchester distractions to finish it off, after recording it to grab some of the spirit in Ibiza. Real World was like a five-star hotel with a world-class recording studio attached in this gorgeous Cotswolds village near Bath called Box.

Gabriel was away, so two coach loads of excited, whistling Haçienda workers and regulars – off their heads already – set off for the two hundred-mile journey to the West Country. We were less ready for action along the way, but the closer we got, the energy picked up. It was a hard place to find, and one or two ran off when they saw lights in the distance. 'There it is! There it is!' I'm not sure whatever happened to them. We eventually got there and set up in the barn studio, and New Order's tour manager, Andy Robinson, was walking around with a tray full of ecstasy: 'Here you are'.

I was DJing, of course. If there was a party, I always had a job to do. A couple of minutes after I started – or so I thought – Graeme, who was going to take over, tapped me on the shoulder and said, 'It's my turn now.' 'Fuck off', I screamed, 'I've only just started.' 'Mike', he said, 'you've been playing for six hours!' Jesus Christ. Graeme took over – in much the same six hours in two minutes world as me.

I'd passed ecstasy onto him after he'd come up from Nottingham to take over from me while I was away on a much-needed holiday during July 1988. I figured he had to know. He was a bit nerdy then, as DJs often are when they start out – never really losing it – and he nervously giggled, 'I've never done drugs.' I explained that, in a way, it wasn't a drug. It was kind of part of the house DJ equipment.

We don't think Peter Gabriel knew for years about Rob's rave, if at all. All the staff were off their rockers. All we were doing was dancing, so no harm done – and, like good little ravers, we cleaned everything up so no one would ever know. We didn't leave as much as a fingerprint.

Rob didn't take ecstasy. He stayed up for the whole time we did, though. He was a freak of nature. He just watched everyone with a loving smile on his face. It had been a hell of an eighties. I didn't take the bus back up. I drove Rob back to Manchester on a long, slow curve north – and we talked and talked and I can't remember a word we said. Except: 'What are you doing?' 'Nothing.' 'What should you be doing?'

39
A spontaneous decision

After I met Laura at one of the inner-city parties – within minutes, feeling I knew immediately this was important – I was saying to her, 'Look, I'm playing in Paris this weekend, you must come.' She said, 'Well, don't you live with someone?' This didn't seem a problem. 'Yes, I do', I said, 'but I will go right now and tell her I'm going to Paris with you.' She looked like she didn't believe me.

But I did. I went home, I told Maria I was leaving. It might have come down to the fact that she didn't take drugs, and wasn't going to take ecstasy, and I was. I didn't belong there. It wasn't a world where in a couple one took it and one didn't. You would be on different planets.

I told her, 'I'm going to Paris at the weekend with this girl I've just met.' You can imagine how that went down. It didn't help that I was feeling so friendly and happy I was probably coming across as far too happy and friendly considering the circumstances. She told me what the fuck I could do with my fucking weekend in Paris. It made sense, but I was making my own sense by now and was convinced I had to make this change.

I gave Maria the house and everything, because absolutely it was my fault, but I was having one of those moments that led me to Greece, to Rotterdam, to Rob's side, to the DJ booth. Now, something was leading me another kind of change in my life – another beginning. I just needed my records and a few belongings, and I was off.

Yes. I had taken ecstasy and seen the light. Time stretched. Everything you did seemed amplified in your head. The secret of life was within reach. Whoever I was in the morning would change a few times during the day.

I wasn't the only one. There were others around me making a change to their lives, as though your social life was becoming a euphoric time of discovery and revelation but your everyday life was stuck in a rut. You got to thinking... what if this life is just a test? For what? I don't know. But, you know, it's a thought. It's why you passed ecstasy on to your friends – we didn't talk much about our feelings, and this was a way of saying, this will make you feel good. If you already feel good, you'll feel even better, and so on. We'd discovered some kind of instant all-round therapy that knocked anxiety on the head and made house music sound like you'd found God.

Because it seemed the decent thing to do, I told my main record supplier at Spin Inn, Russ Marland, that he had to try it. He knew the music better than anyone, but without the drug, he didn't know the half of it.

There was still a little trepidation about this new drug in 1988. It took him a few weeks to try, but then I hooked him up with the internal Haçienda delivery system, and he took it for a Wednesday night Void set, and was last seen after hours walking towards Jamie Nicholson's Kitchen in the unpoliced and lawless Hulme Crescents. The police didn't go near it. It was off bounds and they wouldn't have known what to make of it if they had managed to find it. When I next saw Spin Russ he didn't say much, just sort of nodded at me with a knowing look in his eyes and handed me a bag of records. They meant even more to him now.

The Kitchen had been going for a while, an intimidating, dimly lit edge-of-reality place where Manchester's counter-culture outsiders would spontaneously gather; music heads, local nutters and sundry outlaws – and a few of the new local celebrities – could mix and jam in what became the after-hours illegal club/squat, paradise/hell of choice during 1988 and 1989. There'd be fifty, sixty there, maybe more – you could never see through the weed. You could easily disappear in there for a night or lost weekend. I know I did, but all I've got for you in terms of remembering would be a blank page or two. I took Mark Kamins there once, and it was a cold, frosty night, and we made our way through this endless concrete wasteland and he was going, 'Where the hell is it?' And then there was this one sign of life, all this smoke and steam and sweat billowing out of this one crappy looking concrete flat. 'This is the joint! Fucking hell, Mike', Mark twitched, with a panicky look on his face I remember from when I took him to see City play Oldham, 'Where are you taking me?' 'The heartbeat of the city, Mark.'

After confessing to Marie, I threw my things into the back of my shitty little Renault 5, stayed in a B&B for a couple of days, and then went to Paris with Laura. I was on a high all the time, because of the ecstasy, but also because I was having such success as a DJ, beyond the days I was working at The Haçienda. I was also working around the country spreading the message, and it was all cash in hand, so for the first time in my life, I had some spending money.

And being a Haçienda DJ, as the E shot through it, and the wider world started to notice, it felt, for a year or two, like I was at the centre of the universe. Once the wider world started to notice, and Tony the impresario, the myth maker and culture jammer, went with the media-friendly Madchester, it started almost immediately to get darker, messier, as if there were suddenly rules and regulations to follow, and uniforms to wear. But for a couple of years, 1988 and 1989, the Summer of Love years – which created more ultimately counter-productive attention – I felt nothing could go wrong, and I could do no wrong, even as some things were going wrong.

In a moment of my madness – or utter, spellbinding clarity – I thought, 'I don't need anywhere to live! I'll just move from place to place, and make more connections, and play more places. Perfect!'

Laura and I squatted for a while in an absolute horror show in Hulme, near The Kitchen and what became known as the Joy Division Bridge because of Kevin Cummins' 1978 photographs of the group overlooking an early January snow-covered Manchester. These bleak flats had been condemned because of the asbestos, and they were extremely unsafe, and we knew we had to find somewhere proper to live. Our sudden new rave-inspired romance deserved somewhere better.

Someone told us to try the housing association, and we went along and gave them a whole spiel about our sorry situation – we were homeless, living out of the back of a car, and we really wanted to start a family. We must have sounded as desperate as we actually were, as they responded very quickly with something that sounded like they were having difficulty getting tenants for, or were very choosy about who they let in.

It was an affordable housing association flat amid sixty others with well-kept communal gardens in Cromford Court, a hidden village on top of the Arndale Centre, right in the centre of Manchester. I never knew it existed. We were lucky, and seemed to be the type they were looking for to replace the original, older tenants who were dying out.

This was a time when barely a thousand people lived in the centre of Manchester, in various small places dotted around, and it would become a ghost town after working hours. The original Cromford Court was a Victorian street just off Market Street, which had been demolished to build the centre in the mid-seventies.

It was where some of Manchester's great 1960s venues and clubs were found, including the Magic Village, which Twisted Wheel founder Roger Eagle opened in 1967 to cater for the new psychedelia. He was actually a tenant at Cromford Court – although it was brutalist, mostly concrete, with the gardens adding a little green – and it was brilliantly discreet. You were in a kind of gated community right in the city centre, but you'd never have known from the outside.

We told the housing association we'd take it before we'd even seen it – the location was enough. They said, 'No, please do have a look', and we couldn't believe it when we saw it. You entered through a door on the fifth floor of the Arndale Car Park just off Shude Hill, and you'd emerge amidst the gardens with all these neat two-storey houses, like something from a 1960s science fiction film. We were at the far end overlooking the Corn Exchange, and it was the most beautiful urban setting you could imagine. Our flat had a big lounge with a balcony looking out over the city. You could see Piccadilly in one direction and out across Salford in the other.

We could see all the lights, helicopters and rooftop dancing during the twenty-five day Strangeways prison riots and the sometimes naked protests against dreadful conditions in April 1990 – a public spectacle that, somehow, echoed the carnival spirit of Madchester, as if the place were an outpost of The Haçienda. Any film of the rooftop antics could be cut to a Happy Mondays track, and you'd have a blistering, real-life Madchester moment – pandemonium with a purpose you could dance to.

40
A police raid

It felt like the end of it all, really – the peak of Madchester. There wasn't another Summer of Love after 1990. It was a turning point – this isn't the eighties anymore. Not long after, Thatcher was out, the Hulme Crescents were demolished – the two things weren't necessarily linked – and within a year or two, Factory Records went bankrupt, and The Haçienda began to feel like the set of a Scorsese crime drama. Laura and I lived in Cromford Court through the two Summer of Love years – 1988 and 1989 – and into the early nineties, and it was perfect, like the city had somehow arranged it.

During 1990, our spot at the top of the Arndale took over as the after-hours choice from the Kitchen, which was losing its base as the dangerous Crescents were demolished. Things were changing anyway – the same lurking professional criminal types watching Haçienda activity began to drift in, sensing opportunity among needs and vulnerable customers, and darkening the atmosphere. Utopian ease was more the spirit at Cromford Court – it was still about letting the music and the buzz carry on.

Laura and I and a few others would wake up on a Saturday morning after Nude and just wander around the city centre going, wow, isn't life amazing. It would lead to me buying some of the worst clothes ever – like a big brown furry tracksuit with stars all over. A day later, when my mind had settled down, I'd look at it and wonder what the hell I'd done. And exactly where had I been? For a few hours, you thought you were wearing the best gear in town – then when everything wore off, you realised you looked like a clown. I had to go back to the shops and tell them not to sell me shit on a Saturday when I was still living the Friday night before.

We were getting increasingly on the radar of the police as well. The police crashed into our flat one Saturday morning and arrested me. They just booted the door down and acted like I was some sort of drug lord. There was debris everywhere – but they didn't seem interested in any of that. I said, 'If you'd knocked, I would have opened the door.'

Some illegal rave in Rochdale had my name all over the flyers, and it had come to the attention of the local council. The establishment was getting uncomfortable about the raves and ravers gathering in mysterious ways to actually dare to have some harmless fun – surely it was a sign the revolution was coming. The flyer didn't give much detail, but of course, I was named on it, without knowing anything about it, because they needed to draw in a crowd. I was from The Haçienda – I was top of the bill.

It was a Donnelly Brothers event – but, of course, their name was nowhere to be seen. I was the face of it, and on Monday morning I was in court in Deansgate to defend myself. Tony was there, having a good time in the public gallery, sat next to the brothers, the picture of innocence. Tony did get me a lawyer, to be fair. Rochdale Council wanted to put me under a restraining order for twenty-four hours around the apparent date of the rave.

The judge admitted it was all a bit unfortunate for me, caught up in this, and he couldn't really get his head around this new phenomenon – but he was afraid he'd have to issue the order. I was to leave the Greater Manchester area for twenty-four hours. I was banned from Manchester! My picture was in the *Manchester Evening News*, and Tony, naturally, interviewed me on *Granada Reports* as some kind of rebel. It was a laugh for everyone, and no real harm done and all that – except for our front door. I didn't want to go to Rochdale anyway.

Laura and I were not only living in the centre of Manchester, we were at the centre of Madchester, a place made in the media, and that became a kind of tipping point, along with the access to ecstasy switching to the criminal gangs who were beginning to take over.

You could see their type coming in one by one like shadows during 1989, sussing things out, beginning their tactics of intimidation, looking to control the dealers and get their cut.

I saw someone I recognised as one of the gangs around town, Gooch Hill or Pepperhill, as unfortunately I was getting to know them. He was lurking in the background one night before I went on an American tour with New Order in 1989, and when I got back a few weeks later there were dozens of them among the crowd. Some local gangs keeping the peace, some from out of town trying to disrupt things and grab territory.

The criminals brought the police, and the freedom of the two Summer of Love years was destined to quickly crash into harsh reality. Manager Paul Mason was forced by 1990 to introduce a dress code of no tracksuits and no trainers, intended to filter out the gangs, but it also had the side effect of keeping out the kids, Black or white, who had given the place its essential energy.

The Madchester thing quickly turned Manchester into a kind of marketplace and a source of scandal for the media, mad for the characters who were once lively, quick-witted local lads trying to get a break and were now photogenic headline makers. The complex mix of signals and sources, the collision of Black and white sounds and styles, the spontaneity and eclectic power of the music were all simplified down by a media turning Madchester into a tabloid headline machine.

There were camera crews everywhere looking for whatever the hell it was. I'd be interviewed by TV and radio from America and Europe, many of whom were puzzled that the club could play so much music by these few Madchester bands. I had to explain that so-called Madchester music was coming in from Chicago, Detroit, Germany, the rest of the UK. Madchester came to mean just baggy, and the Blackness of it got whitewashed.

'A lot of this Manchester music is made in Chicago', I would say, which reminded me of a time when I played some of it in a club in Chicago, and someone asked, 'Is this music from Manchester?' I said, 'No, it was made about three hundred yards away the other side of the railway tracks outside this club.'

I was getting impatient, with acid house becoming its own monolithic trend, with gangsters in the shadows and sometimes just in plain sight, with the increasingly visible police presence trying to dampen down our collective exuberance, with being asked stupid questions. I was getting bored with ecstasy and how it was becoming a kind of crutch. I didn't want to rely on it like some people were.

It made me realise how much I didn't like being pinned down. As soon as I was too visible, and too stuck in a rut, it was time to move on. I was having the time of my life, but it wasn't sustainable. Noel got it right when he said The Haçienda was the centre of the universe until New Year's Eve 1989, when the clock struck twelve, and it seemed as though everyone stopped taking ecstasy and started taking crack and cocaine.

I started to make sure I had an exit plan in place.

Part III

Working

41
A cliched crime drama

Just like that, the bubble burst. You could say there were a few bubbles, from a happier time, and one by one, incident after incident, they kept bursting.

By 1990, the drug use at The Haçienda was, as the saying goes, becoming a problem. The original routine – having some drugs and then selling them to your mates, a vague criminality that didn't cause much trouble – was being replaced with a turbulent in-house marketplace. It wasn't so much the drug use as everything that comes with it, the outside forces and consequences as it becomes almost institutionalised, that are impossible to control.

What was defined as the first ecstasy-related death in the country cast a dark light on the club's thriving drug culture, which, to an extent, had been self-governed – however chaotically – and did not seem connected to crime or disorder. Certainly not to guns or knives, nor to any sense that violence was in the air. In July 1989, 16-year-old Claire Leighton collapsed at the club and died thirty-six hours later after a rare allergic reaction to ecstasy that caused massive internal bleeding. She wasn't a regular Haçienda visitor, or a drug taker, and had come to the club to dance, which she loved doing.

It was awful but an anomaly, having nothing to do with the club's culture, although it shifted the emphasis. Dark spirits seemed to enter from outside. Coverage in the tabloids quickly spun from celebrating the loved-up smiley brigade with their whistles and silly hats to sounding the alarm over a new killer drug and, inevitably, a new kind of youth culture menace. One month it's the most important northern club since The Cavern of the early Beatles, the next it's a dangerous hotbed of drug-taking and sundry complications.

In 1989, the club had reached a peak of freedom – an exclusive, life-changing new religion centred around ecstasy, which had become a pop icon in its own right, breaking down all kinds of barriers and bringing unity and optimistic dissent. It was too good to be true, and too good to last. I remember, in the late eighties, seeing kids wandering around Manchester with silly grins on their faces, looking like something from a Scooby Doo cartoon. Three or four years later, a new kind of kid was hanging out in the city centre wearing gun holsters.

The Haçienda was detached from the violence that sometimes plagued Manchester, but then violence came to its doors – and eventually made its way inside. Ecstasy had seemed to destroy hooliganism altogether, only for it to return, somehow wilder and messier because, for a while, it seemed to have disappeared. The rougher, more intimidating side of Manchester joined the party – and fucked it up. For a time, few clubbers had much contact with the gang element, but those on the door were facing a losing battle trying to keep out those who saw the club as a source of easy money within a busy night-time economy.

When The Haçienda licence came up for review in May1990, the police strongly objected to a renewal because of the 'continued use of controlled substances on the premises'. Tony Wilson went into full on defence mode, writing a piece for the *Manchester Evening News* describing the club as the reason for a new civic confidence in Manchester. It was a major part of how the city was renewing itself and being seen internationally. It had used Manchester magic to put the city at the centre of the universe, and the police should help protect it from the gangs and their threatening tactics, rather than treat it as a constant crime scene that somehow the club was in on. Manchester council supported Tony's view, that it was a positive feature of a revitalised city, and when it was working, a safe space that needed help.

The Greater Manchester Police disagreed, a force then built in the deeply reactionary image of its born-again Chief Constable, James

Anderton. He was coming to the end of a mean-spirited, anti-gay, religious moralist reign with a full-on Old Testament beard and cranky claims he was driven by divine guidance, brilliantly described in Happy Mondays' nicely fucked-up fantasy, 'God's Cop'.

The police saw the club as a central part of the city's inner-city problems, in no way the answer to those problems. In a weird way, the police and the gangs colluded in making The Haçienda what it hadn't been before. In Wilson's world, it was the dream of a new venue representing a utopian city through music and a self-governed creative community, and that dream had, to some extent, come true. For the police and the local gangs, with no understanding of Tony Wilson's cultural visions or the true needs of the city's youth, it was something out of a cliched crime drama.

Their only rational explanation for what was happening inside The Haçienda, and increasingly beyond, was that it was the centre of a drug world where they could play cops and robbers and underground war games. And that's what it became. You make, you choose, your own reality. The only nightclub reality the police and the criminal firms could understand was drugs and violence, and that became The Haçienda reality. The two sides met on the same side – which had become the dark side. It was quite a crash in such a short space of time, from the nights of pure bliss and indoor swimming pools to the nights when there'd be blood on the dancefloor.

With much pleading from an expensive QC at the licence hearing in November 1990, the police gave us another six months to see how things went, which was marked in traditional Haçienda style, where the positive still existed, with a ThanksGiving night featuring the debut live show of Bernard Sumner, Johnny Marr and Neil Tennant's Electronic. Things were back to normal, except there never was a normal, so things carried on as before, the DIY spirit getting crushed by a need for professional grown-up discipline beyond any of us, and after a brief time in the sun, disaster was leading to disaster.

At the end of January 1991, a 'sick and tired' Tony Wilson, with New Order, announced at an overflowing press conference at The Haçienda that the club was going to shut down for between two and four weeks. They were in talks with the police about how to move forward. Control needed to be regained, and its staff and clients given some security in the face of an increasingly unhinged gang onslaught.

One of the security team had just been threatened with a machine gun, and one time there were actual gunshots. It was madness. I never thought I would have to be thinking about gun violence in Manchester, but the local gangsters who were usually hidden in their own world started to see it as part of their territory. Those outside the inner sanctum were having to deal with this so that the dancers now coming in from outside Manchester – causing other problems – could get on with their night out, innocent of the terror behind the scenes.

Tony was trying his best, but he was a poetic media artist and social activist at heart, a political idealist, and he was out of his depth having to deal with this savage, unruly alliance between police and thuggish heavies. Trying to maintain truces and help set up murky underworld deals was not something he was prepared for. Of all the ideas he had – some magnificent, some their own kind of madness – one of his most absurd, because it was so ridiculous, was his decision to put a local gang on the door as security. 'To fight fire with fire', as he said.

The pressure wasn't good for him. It mirrored the movement within the club itself as drugs other than ecstasy became part of the menu, while the gangland salesmen and various dealing opportunists made themselves at home, pushing cocaine as their main drug of choice. I couldn't stand cocaine – it seemed like the Antichrist next to the spirit of ecstasy, and I could never understand when people took an ecstasy tablet and then some cocaine. It took the special high away and replaced it with this bitter, narrow darkness. You could sense the mood change and it inevitably led to the violence. With ecstasy the last thing you wanted to do was pick a fight. On cocaine, and the crack that came in with it, there's all this suspicion and paranoia, and a really irritating hyperactivity and lack of empathy. You tend to drink alcohol as well as taking the coke, and the mix is horrible. E took away the compulsion to drink, and it's alcohol that is often the real instigator of violence.

Tony stuck at it though, and refused to give in. The Haçienda, even during the difficult days, was his kind of adventure, or at least, it made his life interesting, which was always his thing. He liked to be where the action was, one way or another. He liked to think he was making history – Rob too, who would always say, after some drama, or incident, or beautiful moment, 'You can't buy history like this.'

Tony once said to Bernard that as the violence and gang rivalry grew and the chaos kept ensuing, 'I bet if there was a button you could press that would mean none of this ever happened and there was no Haçienda, you wouldn't press it.' Bernard, quick as a flash, said, 'Where's the button?' I wouldn't have been so sure, but when the violence came close to me, and my friends and family when they came to the club, you had to wonder. When you've had a knife pulled on you when all you are doing is wanting to play some records and have a good time, it's time to check your career path.

In the end, I would have pressed the button, but with the proviso that the club from 1982 to New Year's Eve 1989 did exist. It was just the gangster-run mayhem of The Haçienda of the nineties that I wouldn't have minded disappearing.

42
A temporary contemporary table

Apart from it all getting very weird and uncomfortable, Laura and I had a baby on the way, and the police banging our door down in Cromford Court really soured things. I couldn't keep up the pace of that past couple of years, and taking ecstasy was getting a bit boring. It was becoming a routine, which was a contradiction in terms and took off that early shine.

It had felt like a special secret society, which gave you space to move in, and the ability to take control of your lives, and now it wasn't a secret, it was the absolute opposite. It reminded me of punk, which for a few months, maybe a year, as a mixture of cultural experiment and personal adventure, seemed the most important thing in the world, and then was suddenly turned into just another fashion to follow.

I hadn't been greedy with ecstasy. A lot of people were greedy and took it a lot, and burnt themselves out seeking the original revelations they experienced, which could never be repeated. I had a certain regime: one, maybe one and a half, and that would keep me going for ten, twelve hours. I didn't see the point of taking more, but others did, and they started to lose track of their life. I like to lose myself in the moment, in the music, but I also liked to keep my wits about me. I'd been around long enough to know not to make it everything in my life.

I was always quick to spot when something was losing its momentum, its edge. There comes a moment when you think, well, that was unbelievable, but I don't want to be doing it for the rest of my life. I like the original energy, and then I don't want to get lost in the crowd. I have some kind of built-in limit, and then I want to try something new. I've always liked a new challenge, a new beach, a new shoreline. As soon as it's done, it's done. Move on.

I had a lingering loyalty to The Haçienda, and to Rob and New Order, whose own loyalty to both the club and Factory was amazing. They had so many lucrative offers from major labels to leave Factory, and the club's demands on them, even when it was doing well, were constant, but they never wavered. It's difficult to overestimate just how committed they were to what in many ways had become a real drag on their resources and energy. It's astonishing they kept making music with all the distractions.

Eventually, their reluctance to make another album for Factory in the early nineties, along with some ordinary post-baggy signings and the catastrophic failure of the Happy Mondays' farcical baggy buggering attempt to make an album in Barbados, led to the bankruptcy of Factory. In that sense, the group delayed the inevitable by continuing to hold the label and the club together until, in the early nineties, reality finally had its serious say.

I think Tony poked reality one too many times in the eye by deciding to borrow money to open new offices on Charles Street off Oxford Road near the River Medlock, what is now known as the Innovation District. The new offices confused me when I went for the first time, because everyone in these shiny designer premises was sat in front of computers, staring at screens. 'It's the future, darling', Tony grinned, somewhere between smooth talking estate agent and overexcited social agitator. That was when enthusiastic apostles like Tony felt that the incoming information age was going to lead to the breakdown of hierarchy and authority. At least that's what he told me as he proudly showed off the people at their computers in their own world, which would soon become very familiar, and lead to a shrinking of the human spirit.

He'd also made sure when Factory opened their European-style bar Dry on the then run-down Oldham Street by Piccadilly Gardens in 1987 – when there was no such thing as the Northern Quarter, soon to become Manchester's bohemian district – that it had the first internet connection in the city. Dry was another claiming of neglected territory for others to follow, just as The Haçienda had been over on the other side of the city centre.

In the new Factory offices, there was also the specially commissioned Temporary Contemporary Table, built before a more permanent table could be chosen, based around Tony's hatred of endless meetings – he wanted a meeting table built to make meetings difficult to go on for more than a few minutes. He put more thought into this table than many of the records Factory were releasing at the time by the likes of the Wendy's and Northside. The designers Andy Woodcock and Ed Jackson took Tony's pleasantly stoned brief and constructed some apparently floating, unworkable edifice that was more a sculptural representation of the fragility and formlessness of Factory than an actual table. It was made for about £2,000, but Tony liked to exaggerate the amount. Wildly. He told a shell-shocked Erasmus it cost north of £30,000, making him panic, knowing full well the tremendous instability of Factory's finances. If Rob had been up to it, and hadn't lost a little of his younger edge, they might have come to blows over it.

I guess Tony wanted to demonstrate that however perilous things were for the label and the club, there was always room for the Factory impractical and magical. When he showed it to me, announcing it had its own Factory catalogue number, I burst out laughing. Was he joking? Yes and no.

There's sometimes talk of a Tony Wilson statue in Manchester. I think they should just hang a version of the Temporary Contemporary Table outside the town hall. It was Tony in a nutshell – brilliant and bonkers.

43
A superclub

The Haçienda shut down for longer than a few weeks after Tony's 1991 press conference, which cost a fortune. A few changes were made, a new lick of Ben Kelly colours to freshen things up, and some extra airline-type security and closed-circuit TV on the door.

On the dark side, there were furtive negotiations with gang members from Salford, Cheetham Hill and Moss Side, which in the long run didn't stop all hell breaking out regularly until the club staggered to an end in 1997, bloodied and finally bowed, owing millions. It was in such debt that for all the drug-related problems, the batterings and stabbings, the rumours of severed dog heads being delivered as threats to rival gangs, the unbelievable gun shots, the shocking police raids, the end came as much because of changing musical trends and the fragmentation of the nineties dance scene, and the more prosaic fact that the club never sold enough alcohol.

There were promises made to me when it reopened after the shutdown that the gang elements were under control. I needed persuading, as I had more or less made my mind up that I didn't want anything more to do with it. I went back for my Friday night set, and at first, everything seemed fine, if a bit nervy to be back in the club after a few months. There was an odd, strained atmosphere for those remembering what had suddenly become the old days. I finally decided to go back as it had been such a big part of my life, and Tony had been so bravely determined to get things up and running. For a few hours, that return night seemed fine. There was tension in the air, but by eleven, things seemed to be settling down and I was getting into the swing of things, lifted by the music I was playing.

Suddenly, there was a violent bang on the door of my booth. I opened it up and there was a stern-looking police inspector stood there. He aggressively gestured for me to turn the music off. I stood there stunned, not reacting quickly enough for him. He shouted at me to turn the fucking music off, and realising something serious was happening, I stopped the music in its tracks. Usually, when the music stops clearly not on purpose, there's a lot of desultory booing, but this time there was just a stunned silence, and then everyone was hustled out of the club. Menacing police lined up in anti-riot uniforms banging their shields, replacing the music with an absolutely frightening sound of violence.

At the entrance there was blood all over the floor, and when you emerged outside there was a helicopter low in the sky shining a spotlight on us as we were funnelled down Whitworth Street, some of us questioned by the police. It was like being in an American film, one that seemed to be filled with cliches, until you witnessed it happening.

The club was shut down a few weeks later, when one of the doormen was run over out front, and it was basically more carnage and police vans and menacing riot squads. To be honest, it was difficult to know who was making more of a meal of it – the gangsters or the police. One night, when I got home after another horrible evening of police and thieves acting out, snarling dogs, random disputes kicking off, choppers circling, I was shaking, and I thought, that's it, I've had it. No more.

There was one more bitter-sweet return before it was over and out for me. I went back to do the eleventh birthday party on 20 May 1993, because in clubland terms, away from the underlying mayhem, The Haçienda was worth celebrating as a new Manchester landmark, and as a pioneering superclub. It had been the inspiration for the new breed of superstar DJs that were beginning to emerge.

The eleventh birthday party was in many ways the crescendo of what made The Haçienda what it was, featuring eleven DJs associated with the club, including Alex P, Frankie Knuckles, Graeme

Park, Tony Humphries and Brooklynite David Morales, one of the first signs of the new breed of global superstar DJ/artist/producer/remixer, as the club mixes that were originally feeding the dance floor became part of the mainstream. Already a house master, replacing Larry Levan at The Garage, Morales first played at The Haçienda in 1990, and loved it, said it was one of the best clubs he'd ever played, with a lively personality all of its own. We were good friends, and he said to me, 'I've heard you have given up DJing. Why have you done that?' I told him I hadn't quit DJing, I just didn't want to do it at The Haçienda anymore. He looked a bit puzzled.

There had been a few incidents, and the whole feeling had changed for me, but I had started playing Cream, for instance, in Liverpool, which began – inspired by The Haçienda more than the more formalised Ministry of Sound – in 1992 as a small underground club. James Barton and Darren Hughes started it, with distinct graphics and a great logo designed by stylish Saville acolyte and Deconstruction graphic designer Mark Farrow, and made it into the kind of successful business – with slick merchandising, attached record label, festivals, Ibizan extension – that was the exact opposite of The Haçienda trajectory. Cream was a great club from the beginning, openly learning from our experience and the Nude night, and James Barton and his brother Scott in particular nurtured its growth from exciting local nightspot livening up a city and bringing in outside energy, and the best DJs, to an internationally famous entertainment brand. Its name and logo took on a life of its own.

But then the word 'brand' would have made Tony and Rob feel sick. They would protest they were punk philanthropists, not measly entrepreneurs. These sharp new entrepreneurs seemed to belong to Thatcher's Britain, and even her successor John Major's back-to-basics regime, more than anything dissident and self-governing. Branding sounded like they were doing something wrong. Brand didn't stand for freedom. It might have stood for them becoming millionaires, though.

I also worked a lot at Renaissance in Mansfield, which was a classic example of a club in the middle of unlikely nowhere giving people a chance to experience something exotic and international.

It was a great space, but it was in a shitty part of bloody Mansfield, and almost off the map there. It showed that a really good club can transcend its immediate surroundings and become a portal into a placeless but captivating world, just like those clubs in lower Manhattan in the late seventies and early eighties that were in really derelict and unpromising parts of the city – in the end it's all about the records being played, the taste of the DJ, a crowd that is prepared to go with new sounds, and of course the right drugs in a non-threatening setting.

Geoff Oakes at Renaissance, like the Cream owners, had learnt from The Haçienda the importance of art and style, of spectacle, of dressing the space, putting some flair and personality into the flyers they produced, summing up in visual ways their values and attitude. It had been a battered old working men's club, but he did it up to hide the paint-peeling grottiness.

The Haçienda blazed a trail and then hit a brick wall – but that helped Cream and Renaissance know what to look out for, how to produce pleasure in a more professional way. Morales had fond memories of the unique club that inspired the ambitions of others, so he couldn't understand what I meant when I told him I didn't want to play there anymore. He soon found out.

He did his show downstairs, which they opened especially, and towards the end, he had a bottle thrown at him because he was only doing a short set and some coked-up goon wasn't happy. He was staying with me in Chorlton, and afterwards, he was stunned by the new, darker atmosphere. He said, 'Wow, I see what you mean.' I'd had a knife pulled on me that night, which for me was the final death knell. You don't ever want to experience that, especially when you're working, and that work happens to be about giving people a good time, even hopefully a better time than they'd ever had. I never set foot in the club again, and David also never went back during its final years when it got even shadier. We were chased into the night and fled the battleground. It was time to beat a retreat.

David came back to it, like I did, when The Haçienda entered another realm – as a travelling show in the twenty-first century – memories of the spirit of the place represented by the DJs recreating

Renaissance 1993 flyer

and updating their original sets, materialising in various venues as a nostalgic recreation, a euphoric orchestral reinvention. The Haçienda had to leave behind the building to become The Haçienda again.

Before it had an afterlife, it had to be recreated a few years after it had been demolished. It was remade in 2002 for the *24 Hour Party People* film, directed by Michael Winterbottom, that made the chaotic stuff of Tony Wilson's life and work and friends and foes into a rumbustious and immodest comedy film. The film remembered the ideal Haçienda, the dream space, the lost time, by producing an exact replica in a local warehouse, and stepping into that film set was a very weird experience, like the most vivid flashback imaginable. The only thing missing was the broken bottles, knives and punch-ups, thank God.

Haçienda workers and regulars were in tears wandering through this immaculately rendered alternative reality. Bernard ordered a drink at the bar from Leroy, the original barman, as if he was back serving. It was a Manchester that plenty wanted to stay inside. It was The Haçienda where there was no violence, no drugs and thugs, just drugs and bliss, music and comradeship, and always more to come.

The Haçienda did in the end become the kind of fluid, evolving brand those clubs it inspired, like Cream and Renaissance, became. Part of its power was the strength of the branding, even if Tony might have said, 'Well, no, not branding, simply affirming the city as a laboratory of a playful revolution in everyday life. We are creating processes and atmospheres that allow room for the unfolding of individual freedom.' Shame about the gangsters' individual freedoms ...

Whether The Haçienda becoming an efficiently marketed business was what Tony and Rob originally envisaged doesn't really matter; that its innate spirit can still exist in some form thirty years and more after it shut at least meant it got itself free of the Gunchester it became part of. Maybe legend is a better word than brand, but Tony would have had issues with that as well. 'Never look back, darling, never look back.' Which was funny, because after Factory went bankrupt, a few years later, he launched Factory 2.

The Haçienda had its afterlife, an after-party, continuing well into the twenty-first century, not so much because of nostalgia or heritage, but because the very idea of it had become embodied into Manchester. It wasn't just for ageing ravers – the grey-vers – being all sentimental. Manchester had its industrial history, its innovative image, its weather, its defiant character, its hard, sharp wit, its clubs, its legendary groups, and now it had a constant dance soundtrack and an enduring cultural landmark.

44
A songwriting project

The daughter I had with Laura, Grace, was born in May 1991, and we realised we had to leave Cromford Court above the Arndale Centre. It was great as the centre in the city centre of our late eighties lives, where the party mostly never stopped, but in the cold light of day, once the buzz was wearing off, it was really like living in a car park. There were no shops for miles where you could buy things like milk. I'd have to jump in the trusty Renault and head out into the suburbs to buy food. There were no Tesco Metros in the nineties.

It wasn't the place to bring up a child and, God help me, I was heading towards 40. Forty in the early nineties was a very different 40 than what it became thirty years later. It was deep into middle age, at least as far as it was perceived in the outside world. I didn't feel middle aged, but something changed in me, and I couldn't live the way I had been the last few years.

As soon as Laura was pregnant, this working-class thing kicked in and I thought I have to work, work, work. I've got to build a castle now. I'd been making a bit more money, even if getting it out of Tony hadn't exactly been easy, and it certainly didn't reflect the change I'd helped bring to The Haçienda's fortunes.

I'd had my eye on doing something else even as The Haçienda was rocking, because I was thinking, well, being a DJ is a young person's game, your main job is spearheading a party, and I can't do this for the rest of my life – not to the extent I had been, with the substances that had also become part of the way of life. There was no sense that in the next few years, being a DJ was going to be a route to a kind of stardom, with the money to go with it. Within a few short years, a DJ like me would be paid like a prince, but for me it was still a hard if enjoyable way of earning money. When I was at my peak, there was no sense that you could become a superstar by being a DJ.

After the superstar DJ boom happened, I likened my situation to being like a First Division footballer in the 1980s – paid well, but no way extravagantly – compared to the Premier League footballers thirty years later, literally paid millions a month. I'd more or less stopped being a full-time DJ by the time the money and adoration turned up, having to be told by those glamorous creatures doing more or less what I'd been doing that I was their inspiration, even down to the way they held their arms in the air. When I did it, no one was looking at me doing it and raising their arms in the air – usually because the dance floor was crowded and there was nowhere else to put their arms – and I was doing it not as a performer but really as a fan of the music.

When the superstar DJ did it, the whole crowd would be looking at the DJ, who was by then a performer taking charge of the whole event. I missed out on that, although I'm not necessarily bothered that I did – seeing thousands of dancers worship the DJ always made me feel a bit queasy, especially when the DJ wasn't actually playing records but simply sticking a USB into a computer with the music all programmed in. I didn't think of myself as any kind of messiah. I thought of myself more as a selector. I was the interface. It suited me.

Before the DJ big time, it took a lot of commitment, and you were not considered central to anything. It wasn't a steady income, and even if you were in demand, it wasn't a good living. You were just part of a process, playing records for people, and even as you judged mood and directed energy, you were not necessarily doing anything creative in your own right. That was changing as the DJ took on other responsibilities, and I was learning to do studio remixes of records, like many DJs were at the time. I made use of my experience in the studio with Quando Quango and T-Coy to do mixes for other people, working with Graeme Park – although that was also becoming something of a chore, where you'd do a mix for some act, and then it would just disappear into the world.

You'd never hear anything from the record company once you'd delivered it, and certainly not from the artist, who probably hated what you'd done to their song anyway. It didn't necessarily seem creative either, and everyone – dance act or not – wanted a remix for a while. Really, it was purely a marketing tool, a promotional device. You'd be trying to add the house beat to pop records, novelty records, even rock records. It was disco all over again. I remember in 1990 remixing with Graeme 'Pineapple Face' by Hooky's Revenge offshoot, and we thought we did a good job, but essentially made up a completely new piece of music, then put about three words of the original vocals on top. Even Hooky seemed to have no idea I'd done it. It felt like being a chef again, making meals to order.

You were just another small part of some business chain and, however exciting it could be, you were effectively working for others – although it was fantastic to do a couple of mixes of the New Order England 1990 World Cup song, 'World in Motion', working on Paul Gascoigne's voice, and a great lost ABC track, 'One Better World' from their 1989 *Up* album. It contradicted the Gretton principle of not having a boss, even if it wasn't the usual kind of boss. Or your boss was your old pals, Martin Fry, or Factory Records.

Stopping taking the ecstasy led to other problems, because I needed to find different ways of creating the charged-up feeling I needed when doing a set. I started to lean on alcohol, vodka in particular, which led to stomach lacerations and other problems – because I was working as hard as possible with a baby on the way and stress levels rising. The DJ as the ultimate social animal needs help getting social, and the stay-up-all-night thing I thrived on in the late eighties was beginning to take its toll. From someone who had never given a second thought to security, infected by the Factory way, I went almost to the other extreme.

It wasn't a cynical or deliberate decision, more subconscious than that, but I started to feel that actually writing songs would be a way of preparing for the future. I feel less worried about it appearing mercenary now I've read John Lydon talking about Public Image as his pension scheme. It's a working-class thing; the need to make some money doing what you're good at. You might make a lot of money doing it but it never really makes you middle class. You're still working class, but you can buy expensive things.

I mentioned to my manager Pete Hadfield in early 1989 that I was getting fed up doing these remixes. It was becoming a bit of a routine. I also wanted something other than just playing other people's records. He said, 'Well, write some songs. You've done it before.' I hadn't thought of it, as I didn't have a band around me, and T-Coy seemed a moment that had passed. I certainly didn't want to sing; that's what had ruined 'Love Tempo' for me, hearing my glum voice all over it.

I realised I missed making songs as I had been doing with Quando Quango and T-Coy. I just wanted them to be more popular. Martin had done it with ABC, and New Order records were selling really well. I wanted any songs I wrote to be sung by proper singers.

Pete said, 'Well, think of a group as a project, and work out what you want that project to be.' He more or less laid out a plan for me to follow: get some musicians in, make a demo, think of some lyrics, and do a guide vocal, then work out who you want to sing it. He used Jazzy B's Soul II Soul collective as an example of the kind of thing I could do – put together an album of songs with different singers so that the overall sound was mine, the rhythms and mood, but there was a collection of guest singers.

I had a relationship with Strawberry Studios after Quando Quango and Factory, and they had built a small writing room over the road from the main studios. I used it to put together three songs, which seemed to work out pretty well apart from my horrible voice. That made me even more determined to find great voices to sing the songs. Songs seemed to be coming. I don't know how or why, but somehow I had them inside me, waiting to come out. All those tracks I'd played at The Haçienda had imprinted something in my mind. Looking back, I can see how I was using the idea of M People to maintain the rapture of the acid house days, which for me was being disrupted. It was like the mutual trust that had been built up because of shared values had been smashed.

I knew Lisa Stansfield through her boyfriend and now husband, Ian Devaney, who'd played on some Quando Quango tracks, and she came down and sang on them, just to get them into better shape. It was just before she'd released her own solo album after being in a group called Blue Zone with Ian and Andy Morris, and singing on Coldcut's 'People Hold On', when she was on the verge of having a huge hit with 'All Around the World'. She'd been working for ten years, since she was 14, and suddenly she was breaking through, so she did it as a favour, not to become part of it. It turned rough outlines into definite songs, and I had no trouble thinking of the kind of rhythms I wanted to use, with all my experience seeing up close what people loved to dance to. If Deconstruction was Factory as a glossy pop label, the group was UK pop with a Tamla Motown dimension.

The Lisa versions made Pete see that I could come up with songs. For the next part of the plan, we had a meeting with BMG, and he was bullshitting about this project he said I was working on, making it more advanced than it actually was, a sort of northern version of Soul II Soul, with the euphoria of rave as part of the sound. It's how we got the *North* album – talking about some project I had on the go before I even knew what it was, and getting BMG to finance it, and release it on Deconstruction.

He told them, 'Mike's got a host of great singers he's writing songs for.' 'Like who?' they obviously asked, and off the top of my head I quickly came up with Martin Fry and the Undertones' Feargal Sharkey, two of my favourite pop singers. They were names. The label sounded interested, so that got me even more interested. After those first tries at Strawberry, I said to Pete, 'Look, I need a musician to take my rough ideas and give them extra depth and sophistication.' I played the sax and a bit of piano, but I really needed a more technically adept musician to fill out my ideas. He introduced me to a friend of his, Paul Heard, to see if we were compatible.

Paul had been in some jazz outfits, played with Orange Juice and Strawberry Switchblade – he liked fruit – recorded for the Acid Jazz label, and studied classical theory at the Guildhall School of Music. It was still a solo project, M People, with the M being for Mike, but now I had a songwriting partner. My first person, before there were any people. We decided to give it nine months of working together during 1990, because we'd both been in bands and knew it was best to quit if it wasn't working before it became too much of an ordeal. I would come down from Manchester for a few days a week to his place in Hackney in north London, and slowly we started to work each other out. I'd always have my box of records with me, and I'd play ones I had in mind – I liked the bass on this, the drum on that, this bit of melody, that Northern Soul sound, some change in tempo on an old Philly record. A lot of musicians wouldn't have been happy with that way of working, but he liked it and it worked for us. We got on, we fitted together well, and we'd go for a pint of Guinness after working all day. He must have noted the day when our nine months were up because one day we were having a Guinness and he suddenly said – our nine months are up! We'd already had a hit, we said, so we might as well keep at it then.

At first, as we started putting songs together, we would look for vocalists and plan the kind of music we would play. It was a little like how I would structure a DJ set, but I was building an M People world. I'd create a kind of fantasy set of moments from my favourite music over the years, from all over the place, and we'd filter it through a series of techniques we'd developed to turn one melody into our melody, and put it all into our world.

Hot House were supporting Barry White at the Albert Hall, and Pete and Keith got me to come along because I hadn't seen them yet and, to be honest, hadn't really paid much attention to the single they'd released on Deconstruction, 'Don't Come To Stay', which had very much been Pete and Keith's thing. It was a very well-made and beautifully sung British soul song, which hadn't received much attention. My excuse for not paying attention was that I had plenty on my mind when it was released, not least getting out of my mind finding, playing and making house music, and wasn't even looking for singers to work with.

Hot House at the Albert Hall focused my mind. I went along with Paul and Martin Fry, and the Hot House singer was called Heather Small, and it seemed as though it might have been her first ever live show. She was painfully shy, clearly suffering from stage fright, and the vast, grand Albert Hall is a very tough and exposed place to play, especially supporting an iconic act that people are restless to see. She may have come across as timid, looking down at her feet all the way through their short set, but she was a hell of a singer. Driving home I asked Martin what he thought of the support band. I said, 'I think the singer is terrific.' Martin wasn't so sure. He didn't like the band, and he didn't think Heather had any stagecraft.

He couldn't get past the nervousness and the fact she sang mostly staring at the floor. I said, 'Well, forget the shyness, just think of the voice, it's totally identifiable. If she can get over the nerves, there is no one else who sounds like her – she's got power, and she's got subtlety.' Martin didn't seem very convinced. Maybe he was wondering why Barry White made his dolled-up female backing singers sing off stage. 'But Martin', I said, 'the Hot House singer's a star! Her voice!' He shrugged. 'Not for me', he said.

I always remind him of that. Paul, though, heard what I heard.

45
A son of god remix

The next day I asked Pete if Heather might want to sing on a couple of the songs I'd been writing, and she agreed, singing on 'How Can I Love You More' and 'Colour My Life' – two songs that just came to me as I was walking along the street. Walking seemed to loosen ideas in my mind, drawing a certain flavour out from all my favourite music. It was something I needed to do – tap into some resolve that was clearly building up inside me, something outside of The Haçienda. On 'Colour My Life', I'd even slowed the bpm down from 125 to around 94, just to show a little defiance of what might be expected of me, to prove M People wasn't going to be stuck in the house rut.

Heather came along to Hackney, and she sang them like it was meant to be. It came very naturally and the words and the spirit seemed to suit her, and best of all, we got on very well.

I was still thinking of her as one of a number of guest singers, and for the first album, *Northern Soul*, she was one of a few that we used. For some, there was a feeling she was too reserved to lead a band. She was very private and didn't even like singing in the studio if there were people working there she didn't know. We did a lot of vocal recording in Paul's house, very low key, making sure she was comfortable and in the mood. But her tracks were by far the best on the album.

It became obvious that when Heather was singing, it was a group, not a solo project with different voices, and after *Northern Soul*, which was me planning it as me leading a fluid collective, a kind of follow-up to *North*, we started planning the second album as a group – which in a way was a continuation of Quando Quango, the other side of house, the other side of Factory obscurity.

The first album sold quite well, we had a couple of singles that made the lower edges of the Top 30, and it was being looked on as an underground project selling better than expected, something trying to mix the house of The Haçienda with memories of the punchiest Northern Soul. At first, having minor hits was something of a triumph, coming out of Factory, and club music, but I was determined to make it more than that.

Twelve-inch mixes were going to be a big part of what we were doing, and I'd asked Sasha to do one for us. He had been working at The Haçienda under the wing of Jon Dasilva, and was a big hit in the fabulous Blackburn raves at the end of the eighties. In 1990, Sasha moved to a residency at Shelley's Laserdome in Stoke, saving him from all The Haçienda hassle, and I played with him there and other places around the North, which was always a total blast. Shelley's led to Renaissance, and Sasha making it onto the cover of *Mixmag* in 1994, paraded as the Son of God – another sign that DJs were becoming new kinds of stars in a fast-growing scene, getting confident enough to build up the hyperbole.

The Haçienda was like Sasha's university. Before he started to study with Dasilva, he'd been a big fan of the Nude night, the kind of nerd who would queue up to make sure he got in, and then treat the music as a kind of seminar.

He'd work out how we'd first of all test a new record we liked between certain hours, early on at first, part of a warm-up. If it worked, it would move deeper into the set through the weeks to become one of the big end-of-evening epics. He spotted the structure: the new tracks, building up to the more familiar tracks, and then the total bangers, and how you didn't need to fiddle too much with the 4/4 beat because in the end it was the only one that worked in the clubs. It was why house rocked the world and if you wanted to play around with it you'd better not stray too far or you'd lose the crowd.

Sasha was pretty new to mixing when I asked him for an M People mix, and he was finding his way at Shelley's, picking up on the big, anthemic quality Graeme and I had been running with at The Haçienda before it was forced to shut down for a while. The big voice, big piano Friday night style that had led right into 'Ride on Time'.

He did a mix of 'Someday', a Marshall Jefferson/CC Rogers track we'd done a version of, one of my favourite ever house tracks, and it was epic. You could hear he'd hit his moment and was riding it, everything was clicking, but we didn't want 'Someday' to be a single. It might have trapped us as a covers band recycling Haçienda favourites.

Sasha was very precise, even precious, about what he did, quite rightly, and I had to go and see him and carefully ask if he would do 'How Could I Love You More' in exactly the same way. He said, as I thought he would, a little offended, 'I can't do that', but we pushed him a little, the Haçienda insiders' handshake helping, and he eventually relented.

It was a song I'd written for Grace after she was born, with this new surge of positivity I felt, and I had this urge to make it as special and as noticed as it could be. With Haçienda-educated Sasha doing the remix, based around me and Paul creating a kind of Motown version of the house power I'd channelled into the club, with Heather's voice being an element in the rise of 'Ride on Time', the whole thing had come out of the Haçienda.

Made in the Haçienda, made in Manchester, if not released on Factory. At the same time, it was a way of throwing a forcefield of liberation around me as things got worse at the Haçienda, a way of pulling myself clear of the hostilities. I wanted to keep that Summer of Love vibe alive, and for me the best way was to do it through something I could be more in control of than I was as a DJ.

Sacha's mix of 'How Can I Love You More' was the perfect combination of the song's hook and where stirring post-house club rhythms were at that moment in time, and it changed everything for us – it pushed a rerelease of the single into the Top 10 in February 1993, and helped M People become what I had wanted them to be:

a glamorous pop group on 7-inch single, an irresistible dance act on 12-inch. Smart in the charts and smashing it in the clubs. I knew in my heart that the house four-on-the-floor was going to explode, having been a witness to it creating such an impact in the clubs. It was just a matter of time.

We also worked live, which for a dance band wasn't necessarily a given. Initially we were still thinking of it as a concept, not a band, and didn't see how we could do it live, but Pete said, build everything around Heather, which was pretty optimistic considering how nervous she was. She was terrified really, and we always had to gently coax her on stage. And she'd grown up singing soul and gospel, and now we were asking her to get into the 127 bpm house groove, and carry the whole thing as a performance, me and Paul looking like the kind of eager, behind-the-scenes musos who should stay behind the scenes, or at least in the shadows.

In rehearsal, we almost had to choreograph her performance step by step, when she would talk, where she would look. Once the show was up and running, she was fine, and in the flow, dancing all over the stage, but those first few minutes were really hard for her. She did it though, and it took us all the way to arena shows – one of the few dance acts to play arenas – and headlining Glastonbury. Heather grew with it, and became a great front person, but at first it was one step at a time.

The only way to get gigs for M People in the beginning was for me to DJ. I had the name; M People meant nothing. We started to play a few songs inside my DJ sets, so that one ran into the other, using tapes, me playing a bit of sax and some percussion. As soon as we finished, I would be back on the decks. It was three or four hours' work for me, but it got M People out there, if as a PA more than a live show.

We put on some M People songs during one of my Friday night sets at the Haçienda, and Heather froze when she came out on stage and was faced with the intensity of a Friday night crowd hungry for sensation. There was sweat pouring from the ceiling and this incredible cheer that came out of nowhere, as if we were coming home and we hadn't even been anywhere yet.

She almost walked straight off the stage, faced with this torrent of sweaty crazies with their tops off shouting at the top of their voices. Her mic was open so you could hear her say, 'Oh my God', with a little bit of astonishment, and a little bit of fear. That just led to more cheers and more alarm in Heather's eyes. As soon as she started singing, you could see her take control. Once she was singing, she knew what to do.

The next night we played Manchester's Boardwalk, and it was completely sold out – people were climbing in through the toilet windows. It was so different from Quando Quango, where it always felt like a slog, and even in Manchester we didn't seem to belong. It was so encouraging from the very beginning playing to a crowd that had energy and were in the mood, rather than being faced with blank stares.

We did Renaissance and Cream, me as part of the group and then as the DJ. We did a show at the always intensely buoyant Sub Club in Glasgow, another one of those underground clubs that looked like nothing much from the outside, and then you went down some steep stairs, and into a whole world of disorientating pleasure.

There was no stage, because there wasn't usually a band, and so we just played in the middle of the crowd, Heather standing on some beer crates. I would DJ, play the instrumental of 'How Can I Love You More', and then we'd take over as M People, Heather in full voice. I'll never forget tiny Heather with her big hair under a spotlight in the middle of all these outstretched hands and rapturous faces. Once she got going, she was like a woman possessed. Quite scary, actually. It's the Heather you can hear on her 'secret' version of 'Ride on Time', making those three words sound so momentous – it's like heavy metal soul.

I felt then it was going to work. Breaking into the playing of records with a performance can unsettle the mood, but we slipped right in and the crowd didn't miss a beat.

Simon Moran of SJM was another important part of M People, becoming our promoter after seeing us at one of these PAs. I'd first met Simon when he put on one of his first promotions, which was New Order at the Octagon Centre in Sheffield in 1985, after putting on a couple of gigs at Sheffield University when he was studying there, including The Farm. After the show, before I drove Rob back across the Snake Pass, Rob said to Simon, 'You're a great new promoter, best I've ever worked with. You're going to do well!' That was a very accurate prediction, as after being right on the spot for the baggy period and Manchester, Moran went on to be the UK's leading concert promoter and ended up on the *Sunday Times* Rich List. Rob was great at spotting all kinds of talent.

Simon and SJM had a brilliantly worked-out plan to build us as a live act, seamlessly increasing the size of the venues from universities to theatres to arenas, so that we never played to less than a sold-out crowd.

As the venues got larger, we started to make it more musical, with more musicians, getting rid of backing tapes. By the time Sasha had delivered his massive 'Love You More' mix, we were an experienced live band, and everything was in place. We moved quickly from the smaller places to the bigger places, and sometimes we had to upgrade as we were on tour because we were getting more popular by the month.

We took the live group to Ibiza to play at the heady, open-air Ku, one of the world's great venues – an unheard of venture, a folly of almost Factory proportions in how to go against the grain. We were then an eleven-piece band, the first dance band to play live in a fantasyscape of clubs and DJs. We had to transport all our equipment on large articulated trucks, carefully squeezing them onto the ferry from Valencia.

I just didn't want us to do one of those crappy PAs that irritate an audience more than delight them. We thought, well, let's give them the whole revue – and we went on at 2 in the morning. The audience had been flying to the usual sounds on record, and suddenly there was a live band. They took a little time to cotton on to what was happening, but everyone went for it.

It cost us a fortune, but it made me very happy, just for the adventure – and at that point, no one was going to stop us. I was determined to enjoy being in a pop group once it happened. The 'M' in M People definitely wasn't for miserable or moaning, at least not when Simon Topping had left the group after a few months playing percussion, spent mostly grumbling about the food, or his petrol money, or the early mornings. I was taking the party out into the world, feeling the relief that for a while I didn't have to rely on other people's songs. I now had my own.

46
A pair of Woolworths ears

I'd been in music one way or another for years – from fan and dancer, then obsessive fan and committed dancer, to club organiser and Euro-roadie, to Rob's mate, to promoter, to electro band member, to A&R, to DJ – and all that experience channelled into M People. It made me a natural, strategic leader of a group, someone who knew the ropes: what to do and what not to do, in what was just as much a business as an art form, but who also knew the right beats and hooks, the right kind of message, that would get a crowd going.

It happened so quickly, and the money started to roll in – which made a big difference from my slender Factory wages. With the DJ earnings mounting up at the beginning of the nineties, Laura and I could afford to move from the inner-city Cromford Court into suburban civilisation. We'd bought a beautiful house in a smart part of Chorlton next to Longford Park, not far from Rob and Lesley, the kind of house and garden that made sense now I was turning 40. We could just about afford it, on the back of the DJ work. And then I became a pop star, as much as I had always favoured staying in the background.

I remember looking at my tatty, less-than-reliable Renault 5 and thinking pretty much the first thing you think in my circumstances when you suddenly come into money – I've got to get a new car! I got a BMW 5 Series, proof I'd been upgraded and gone all eighties, even if it was in the nineties.

I had an expensive city-centre number 2 cut, sharp as, and I got myself a sleek Prada coat – it was like a posh parka, which you could button up round your neck and pull up over the lower part of your face. Coming into money didn't change my football habits – not yet anyway. A move from the rowdy, standing-only Kippax Street terraces to the more sedate, all-seated Main Stand was a few years off.

Man City was business as usual even in a brand new BMW and Prada parka, and one day I drove to Maine Road in Moss Side, getting older and more woebegone by the day as City helplessly drifted down the divisions, but still a kind of church to me, to get some tickets for a match. I didn't think how I now looked from the outside in my swanky BMW with black coat zipped up under my chin, probably looking a little too pleased with myself.

Tickets got, I'm driving back to Chorlton, and all of a sudden, like something out of a film, there's the weary whine of a siren and some flashing blue lights cutting through the Rusholme urban gloom. The Old Bill was pulling me over. Two cops slowly strolled up to me in my new car and did the usual 'Do you mind getting out of the car, please, sir?' And I'm like, as casual as possible, 'Yeah, sure, but why?'

They said, 'We just need to do a check on you, make sure all is in order.' They kept me for ages as they did whatever they were doing in their car, occasionally glancing my way. Eventually, they came back and said, 'Oh, all okay, yep, you can go. Thanks for your patience.' I asked them, 'Why did you pull me over?' They said, 'You fit a description.' I was like, 'What, drug dealer?' They didn't comment.

I said, 'I've been to Maine Road for some City tickets.' It was only when I was talking to one of the cops that the other suddenly blurted out, 'He's that lad from M People? They're in the charts.' Their demeanour instantly changed – hard-edged, blank-faced Manc cops suddenly melting into goofy fans. They went, 'Oh sorry, sorry to bother you, we just had to check certain things. You know how it is.' I said, 'Is it a look that I have with the car and coat?' and they went, 'Yeah, yeah, yeah, to be honest, it is a bit.' I said, 'Well, I'm not changing it!'

I got pulled a couple of times because I had a flash car and, in the eyes of the police, didn't look the type to own one – unless I was up to no good. It all got sorted quickly, and if M People were playing locally, a couple of concert tickets made a bit of speeding go away.

It gave me an insight into how Tony Wilson always seemed to get away with driving his Jag in and out of the city centre far too fast and often while smoking, even rolling, a joint. I guess I'd made it.

Which didn't go down well in certain quarters. We'd been hip when we were playing the clubs, but that was smashed when we started selling records.

There was definite snobbery when M People tipped over from being a personal conceptual project playing with the idea of pop music to actually being popular – and what some considered to be almost middle of the road. I got a sense at the time from the underground world where I had been that I had sold out the community, and I even felt a little resentment from certain elements at The Haçienda.

The Haçienda manager Paul Mason put out the message that I had left the club specifically to form M People – which wasn't actually the truth. I would have been doing M People if I'd stayed, the same way I did Quando Quango and T-Coy. I'd left because of the violence – because I had a knife thrust into my face – but that didn't suit the new Haçienda regime that wanted to act as though they had all that sorted, and the future was bright. There were those wondering why I was still DJing at Cream, Ministry of Sound and Renaissance, thinking I'd turned my back on The Haçienda, which was something I had given so much to.

I didn't want to make a massive thing about it, because those still working at the club were my friends, but I felt I was being forced to either tell the truth – that I thought it was still a dangerous place, which might have undermined their efforts to relaunch it – or lie, and pretend I hadn't left because it was still caught up with criminal elements. At best, there was an uneasy truce between the club and the intimidating gangland outsiders, but I decided to leave them to it. Perhaps they could have handled my departure better, but then, in truth, you never expected anything like that when it came to The Haçienda. It wasn't my business anymore.

I was concentrating on M People, pulling back from the DJing while it was beginning to happen, and taking the whole idea of being in a successful pop group very seriously. Maintaining momentum was important – keeping up the pressure while we had attention. While you've got an opening, it's all or nothing, and I wasn't going to waste the chance. I was pretty ruthless. I knew it was important to be in people's faces day and night week after week. People forget easily.

As the rereleased 'Love You More' was in the Top 10 – lifted there with the help of Sasha – we started working on our second album, *Elegant Slumming*, the first one we'd made from the beginning as a group album.

It was the real M People debut, and we'd got two singles ready to follow up 'Love You More' – 'One Night in Heaven', which reached number 6, and 'Moving on Up', our serious attempt to make a modern 'I Will Survive', which made it to number 2 in the autumn, keeping the album *Elegant Slumming* in the charts all the way into 1994.

'Moving On Up' would be used later for the theme tune to the BBC's election coverage when Tony Blair's New Labour got into power, which linked the optimism of the late eighties raves with a new political optimism. We got connected with that – the Blairs were fans – and we got invited to 10 Downing Street, which was a bit disconcerting, but I did get to meet one of my favourite film directors, Mike Leigh. I hate show business parties, but you can't really turn down the chance to look inside 10 Downing Street and meet someone who could give you proper lessons about how to look pissed off at a party.

It did get a little show business, which can be hard work – all that mingling with people you have nothing in common with. In general, M People was the hardest I'd ever worked in music, because it wasn't just the dreaming up of the band, dreaming up the look and sound of the band, making and mixing the records, which was the best part, the soul of the group – there was the slog of all the promotion and hanging out at parties. That's where it can all go wrong.

You'd be flung around the world, airport to airport, country to country, answering the same question over and over again. I must have heard the question 'What does the M stand for in M People?' thousands of times. As you're doing this work, appearing on radio and television shows, interviewed by the press, thinking of new poses for photos, you have to find the time to think of the next music, the next tour, without the peripherals swallowing you up. I didn't want to burn out overnight.

We were still considered inventive enough for *Elegant Slumming* to be nominated for the Mercury Music Prize, which was awarded to what the judging panel considered the strongest album of the year in any genre, and which in the early nineties definitely seemed as though it leaned towards indie rock – the two winners in the previous two years since it started were the critically adored Primal Scream and Suede.

This was at the beginning of Britpop, and Blur's *Parklife* and Pulp's *His 'n' Hers* had been nominated, as well as other favourites Paul Weller's *Wild Wood* and The Prodigy's *Music for the Jilted Generation*. We seemed like unfancied outsiders, as much as Take That or Ian McNabb's concept album *Head Like a Rock*.

Much to some people's surprise, including ours, and some people's disgust, we won the award, and the decision really underlined the snobbery large parts of the music industry and the media had when it came to UK dance music. It was very much considered an inferior species.

A lot of critics in the music papers thought it was a disgrace that we won, darkly murmuring about a shallow, anonymous dance-pop band making music to dance around your handbags to, stealing the award from the era-defining and bookmakers' favourites Blur and Paul Weller. We were publicly adored but not critically admired. Essentially, the more popular we got, the more the critics hated us.

Black, working-class, female Heather, who'd recently been working in the dole office in Hammersmith, was somehow turned into an emblem of privilege, victimising poor darling middle-class Blur. To me, it sounded like a great nineties house album made with subtlety and power by a very stylish and conceptually minded UK act – but what did I know?

The Factory Records me that still lingered loved the pearl-clutching shock, loved riling up the indie snobs whose idea of so-called indie integrity was pretty feeble next to what I'd been part of at Factory.

Apparently, it was a very close call among the judges, and it was the chairman of the judging panel, the veteran rock critic and academic Simon Frith, who said the vote shifted towards M People because of the album's 'immediacy' and its uplifting quality. This made perfect sense to me, as that got to the heart of what we set out to do, and that we may not have been fashionable darlings but were, oddly enough, actually fashionable.

I could get pretty angry about it at the time. It was the fact that, after everything that happened during the eighties to demonstrate that dance music could be as intelligent, experimental and certainly culturally significant as any music, there was still this sense that it was lightweight and throwaway. It was almost as though, if you were a dance act, you weren't allowed to make albums. It seemed like the end of disco days, the Disco Demolition Night at Comiskey Park, the idea that dance music was a lesser music.

We were called 'chart friendly' like it was the worst kind of insult. 'Feel good' was another of the insults. One writer claimed that when we came down for the press conference, we were booed. Only in her mind! We got attacked for saying we were going to share the prize money among the four of us, and each give their money to a charity of their choice, like we were just looking for pats on the back, trying to buy some credibility. Paul and Heather had to calm me down. It's just their opinion, they'd say.

They were much better at dealing with it than me, I suppose, because I'd grown up reading the music papers and it was hard to shake off the need to feel loved and respected by them. A few of the music paper writers understood – Stuart Maconie and David Quantick wrote pieces pointing out how we reflected dance culture and the personal transformation that came with it as one of the most positive things offered to young people in the UK. For most, though, the more popular we got, the more they disliked us, and that dislike – even condescension – seemed to extend to our audiences, which didn't seem to fit into any box.

I'd look on enviously at Bjork and Massive Attack, and realised we were seen as being closer to Take That than them. Which did hurt a bit, because, after all, I had my own levels of snobbery. The royalty cheques did help take away some of the pain. We also helped change some things in the music industry, which began taking dance music more seriously and put more money and thought into their dance subsidiary labels. In the following years, the Brit Awards started to award one for the best British dance act, which for the first two years just happened to be us.

Two of the best 'awards' I received weren't really awards at all, just sort of commendations from music industry stalwarts. Deconstruction itself had become a successful dance label, following the template established by 'Ride on Time'. As well as releasing M People and various acts selling millions throughout Europe, including The Grid and Robert Miles, by the mid-nineties we were in a position to sign major acts like Kylie Minogue.

Around 1996, Pete and Keith became too busy with the demands of the label to continue as our managers. The group itself had to look after the more organisational side of things, and at the level we were at, we needed new management. In the same way I wanted the best musicians working on our records, I also wanted the best managers. I asked as many people in the industry as I could who the best manager in the world was at that time, and I got a list of three, all based in New York.

Paul and I flew over, and the one who inspired us the most was Steve Barnett, who, a long time before, had been Elton John's agent and now looked after Cyndi Lauper and AC/DC. I'd been to see AC/DC numerous times and loved the madness of it all, including the pub they would have installed backstage. Steve was so good at what he did that, before we could hire him, he was poached to be the MD of Columbia and then the CEO of Capitol. So, we had to go back to New York to meet another manager we were told was one of the best in the world at the time, if not the very best.

Roger Davies had helped resurrect Tina Turner's career after the miserable breakup with Ike, managed Joe Cocker, Cher, Pink and Janet Jackson, and had looked after Sade since the early 1980s. Those who said he was the best manager in the world didn't think he'd be interested, but one of the things I'd learnt from Rob is that everyone's on the same level really, and you might as well ask. All he could do was say no. The experience alone would be worth it.

To ask Roger meant flying back to New York, which I did, believing in the group enough to think he would be interested. No one could get over the fact I'd even managed to secure the meeting, but we got on great and had a very similar approach to record companies and music. He didn't really commit, and we parted after a few pleasantries. I assumed it was a no.

He got in touch a bit later, and this time he said he was interested in managing us. I asked him why he changed his mind. He said, 'Well, I mentioned M People to all the girls in the office, and every single one was a huge fan.' That definitely made me feel like we were doing something right.

The other virtual honour was something the record producer and one-time Mecca DJ Pete Waterman said to me after I started writing the M People hits. He was all over the charts in the eighties and nineties as the mouthy, opinionated one in the non-stop Stock Aitken Waterman hit machine, producing monster kitsch electropop for the masses.

We'd collided in the most absurd way in 1989, when his tacky, weirdly watchable, low-budget, low-brow dance programme *The Hitman and Her*, filmed in various clubs around the North, came to The Haçienda, creating a crash-up between his show's slapstick disco brashness and our up-to-speed, cutting-edge house culture.

Waterman happily, a little sneeringly, played 'The Hitman' as the ageing fool presenting a show, with youthful 'Her' Michaela Strachan playing the loved-up club goer who couldn't care less about appearing cool and trendy. It was an early hint of reality TV, with real people given a chance to appear on television, as long as they didn't mind being humiliated. It was usually shown at 2 or 3 in the morning, but it was perfect timing to watch ordinary people getting off their heads.

The show landed at The Haçienda because, of course, that was the centre of clubland at the time – even though it was a very different clubland from Pete's gaudy, gruesome version, which actually did play some good, unheralded dance tracks, and broke a few.

The meeting of minds and mindlessness wasn't the best use of anyone's time, and an attempt to bring some authentic Haçienda atmosphere and unstaged club dancing into the Hitman's territory – with me playing a kind of avant-garde Hitman – didn't work at all. It wasn't either The Hitman and Her doing The Haçienda or The Haçienda doing The Hitman and Her. Michaela got obscenely heckled, and it failed to capture the warped wildness of the regular show.

A few years later, Pete and I were travelling on the same train from London to Manchester, and he saw me and sat with me. We chatted on the journey, and he said to me, 'You know what's great about you, Mike? You've got Woolworths ears', referring to the nationwide high street store that only stocked the top seventy-five singles. 'You know what people want to listen to and what they want to dance to. At the moment, you've got it absolutely right.'

To some, Pete was a commercial cynic, but he had his own strange, uncompromising purity. He researched what people wanted by seeing them dance in clubs, and he had an innate understanding that, above all, the point of pop music was that it reached as many people as possible. His attitude was as rooted as mine was in the 1960s idea of working-class people coming home from factory jobs and putting on some Tamla Motown – which, however exquisite the songs, was itself commercialised soul and gospel – and having a good time shaking out the pressure of the day. Pop could give you back to yourself.

M People had taken the shake-up of house and then the triggering energies of acid house and popularised them. DJing had taught me a lot about pace, drive, when to keep things going, when to suddenly drop the rhythm, when to switch direction. It was instant market research – seeing what lifted the crowd, and finding ways to do that again and again, somehow not repeating yourself.

The dream was to put all of those influences and inspirations into a three-minute pop song. The main influence on that was Roxy Music, who didn't appear to have a single on their debut album. So, inspired by the sophistication of the best Motown – which was also my main influence for the kind of pop songs I wanted to write – they decided to see if they could put all their different interests and styles into a song that was less than three minutes long. They wrote 'Virginia Plain', which didn't have a chorus but captured the Motown spirit in different form and was a massive, beautifully unusual hit.

When you popularise something, you often run into a backlash, but I figured it was better that the populariser had been there when Chicago house mutated into acid house and then the permutations that spiralled from there – rather than someone from the outside with no direct experience of the transformation.

Some might have called what we did 'handbag', although no one ever did to my face, especially when I was in an angry place, but it helped create a massive house pop market, and previously faceless dance acts – like The Prodigy and The Chemical Brothers, who I nearly signed to Deconstruction – became as famous as the rock bands like Oasis and Blur.

Eventually, a more experimental dance act, Reprezent, won the Mercury Prize, and I think M People were part of a new dance culture after we showed that dance music didn't only belong on 7- or 12-inch singles – it could work on albums. Those albums could go multi-platinum, as ours did. Maybe it was my revenge on Tony and the number of times he said to me, almost to the very day that Factory went bankrupt, that dance music doesn't sell albums.

It wasn't deliberate revenge. I didn't set out to ignore Factory on purpose – it was simply that there was no interest from Tony in the kind of things I was doing, and there was no point in me banging my head against the wall. He was pleased for me when the *North* album was released and Black Box got to number 1, but there was never any interest in any of it being on Factory.

When the local author and musician John Robb wrote a piece in the *Manchester Evening News* on the day the receivers went into the Factory office to begin proceedings, he mentioned that Factory could have been saved if they'd released Black Box and had Deconstruction as its dance subsidiary. I didn't want people to think it's what Factory wanted and I refused. It simply wasn't meant to be. The truth was, as much as the whole Manchester scene was based around the whole thing being made in Manchester, in those days you couldn't really be an international pop group and be based there. It was boring logistics, really. New Order could get away with being New Order and reach a certain point as legends and innovators, but they had a certain block when it came to the next stage – which involved constant touring and constant recording – and it's not what they wanted to do. I was prepared to go for it. I took what Pete Waterman said to me as a compliment. He was saying I deserved to have hits because I knew what I was doing. It was the best review M People got because it came from the position that having a hit was a good thing – not some kind of sell-out. The hits kept coming, as Pete sort of predicted, and we were straight back into the studio after the award ceremony, more or less finishing the album *Bizarre Fruit*, while we were still high from winning the Mercury.

Elegant Slumming could easily have been the end result of the hybrid we'd put together, climaxing with a Mercury, but the new album included two of the best known M People songs. The three of us had reached a zone where we all knew what an M People track should sound like from our own experience.

It was something as a fan of pop music I'm glad I experienced – that rare, lucky time when you find yourself in a pop group and only you know the secret of how and why the group sounds like it does. For me as a songwriter, I had managed to recreate that feeling when I was running a set as a DJ and one track flowed into another and I knew exactly what track was going to come next, and the one after that, and the one after that.

I'd worked out 'Search For The Hero' while pushing Grace in her pram early one Sunday morning through Longford Park near our house, trying to get her to sleep. I stared at the wheels on the pram as they went round and round and I had these words in my head, and I sang them into a dictaphone matching the pace I was walking. The next day, I played it to Paul in Hackney, and we sorted out the words, made them fit better, worked out an arrangement, and with Heather's voice lifting it higher than even we had hoped for, we had it recorded in a day. Same with 'Moving On Up'; the work to get to it was hard, but once we had the ideas and Heather gave it the drama, taking charge of the rhythm however dominant, the recording and mixing came easy. I always felt Heather was underestimated in the way she mixed her gospel background and dark-tinged Joan Armatrading-like introspection with the group's supercharged music, but don't get me started.

Without Heather, the group might have been simply an extension of T-Coy or Quando Quango, maybe this time with better reviews in *NME*, but having such a distinctive singer who became such a forceful performer made it international. You could see the difference in sensibility between old Factory and where I was after we did our first *Top of the Pops*, when grumpy Simon Topping from ACR was still playing with us.

After we had recorded it we were in the bar at the hotel in Swiss Cottage where we stayed, and I'm marvelling that we'd just done *Top of the Pops*, with all its history – the Stevie Wonder of 'Uptight', the David Bowie of 'Starman', the Blondie of 'Heart of Glass', even the New Order of 'Blue Monday' when they played the song live and sounded like they'd just woken up. I was jumping up and down with excitement, and Simon was fretting about getting his twenty quid per diems the next day. Oh, the glamour.

Shovell, who took over percussion from Simon, and to put it mildly smiled more, knew that the travel and the dreary in-between bits were part of the job of being an entertainer – which is what we'd become. Mostly, compared to everyday life, you were having the time of your life.

We came across Shovell when we played the Brixton Academy in 1992 with Jamiroquai, the Brand New Heavies and a large, ebullient south-east London collective called Natural Life who were bringing Balearic beats into rock. Simon couldn't make it that night for some reason, and during the soundcheck we noticed Natural Life's percussionist, who seemed something of a showman with a fabulous smile – he called himself the drum warrior. He just loved banging drums, and building the perfect groove. Paul and I wanted him in M People almost on the spot, and he stood in for Simon that night and immediately felt part of the group.

His actual name was Andrew Lovell, but that didn't suit his infectious personality, and we said we had a tour coming up and would he like to join us. He didn't need much persuading; it was a chance for him to make sure he didn't have to return to his day job as a plumber for Lewisham Council, and within a few days he was on our tour bus heading to Middlesbrough, and was there with us when we won the Mercury Prize. He was a great percussionist, but also a great, positive personality to have on tour with you. He really made you appreciate the craziness of flying first class to Australia to play three nights at the Hordern Pavilion in Sydney, where Mick Jagger's backstage because his girlfriend at the time was a huge fan of M People. With Shovell, you couldn't take any of it for granted. A few weeks later there was a piece in the *News of the World* where Jagger's girlfriend talked about how she would slip an M People CD on before they made passionate love. Sometimes it was work, but sometimes it was just wonderfully ridiculous, and I can still hear Shovell laughing at it all.

'Search for The Hero' was the fourth single taken from *Bizarre Fruit*, which stayed in the album charts for over two years, released to coincide with an extravagant TV commercial for the new Peugeot 406 car that was directed by James Cameron of *The Terminator* and *Avatar* films. It cost £3 million to make, and was premiered during the entire commercial break during a Friday night showing of *News at Ten* in February 1996. It was like getting a Hollywood director to direct your video, and then have it played repeatedly on television. It didn't concentrate so much on the car, on the product, and there was no dialogue. A line at the beginning suggests that an individual has 12,367 thoughts a day. A young girl in a red hooded jacket seems to have entered the film from Nicolas Roeg's psychodrama *Don't Look Now*, which took it even further away from being an ordinary commercial. Then you hear all of 'Search for the Hero'.

The film focused on the emotions of an ideal Peugeot driver, which also seemed to reflect the emotions of the song – Cameron was responding to the images and impressions of the song as much as the car, so it really did seem like a 'Search for the Hero' video. It was as though there was this emotional short film on the edge of the uncanny being shown on television randomly with a soundtrack by M People, which we'd written to have its own otherworldliness. Of course, the critics decided it confirmed us as calculated soul charlatans making politically correct Peugeot pop, and there was me thinking it was just a tremendous, slightly strange piece of pop culture synergy that got our music out into the world. Yes, like we were going to turn that down.

I never forgot Factory doing absolutely no promotion for their records, especially the Quando Quango ones, so I was delighted to find myself at the other end of the spectrum. As far as I was concerned, no souls were harmed during the making of the ad. Peugeot replaced the ad after a few months of showing with versions edited to more conventional lengths, alongside a new commercial showing a man having fantasies about Kim Basinger. Sales of the 406 dipped, and the Peugeot dealers lobbied to have the Cameron 'Search for the Hero' commercial reinstated. We got a few more months of exposure, which didn't bother us, as it meant more M People, and more of Heather's voice getting through to people.

Later in that summer of 1996, we played a long weekend of shows in front of 100,000 people, all promoted by Simon Moran. We'd warmed up at two shows in Edinburgh at the beginning of June and we were playing Crystal Palace Bowl on the 16th with Gabrielle and Lighthouse Family, and a week later a home concert, alas, at Old Trafford for Euro 96 with Madness and Simply Red in front of 60,000. I had a special sky blue shirt made with a Man City badge and the words 'How Can I Love Blue More'. I wore it for the encore, and I pulled it over my head at the side of the stage ready to go on stage. When my head popped out I found I was standing in front of the Manchester United manager Alex Ferguson and United legend Bobby Charlton. Well, I said, kissing the badge, 'Once a blue ...' they just gave me a stern stare. Maybe they were purists and still mad we'd won the Mercury Prize.

We were riding high, but the day before the Crystal Palace show, on Saturday 15 June, when we were playing Alton Towers, reality suddenly smashed into all the fantasy. I'd called home in the morning, and Laura said it was a bright and sunny morning and she was going to take Grace into Manchester to do some shopping, and head for the Arndale Centre. That seemed nice and normal and all seemed good with the world. The group and a few friends were going to meet in the afternoon in the hotel bar to watch the England v Scotland game in the European Championships, which was kicking off at Wembley at 3 pm. Again, nice and normal – even better than that, as there was a general mood growing that England had a good chance of actually winning the tournament, their first trophy since the 1966 World Cup. The Lightning Seeds and Frank Skinner and David Baddiel's Britpoppy 'Football's Coming Home' had replaced New Order's 'World in Motion' as the England song of the summer.

Around midday, news started to filter through of a bomb that had exploded on Corporation Street outside the Arndale Centre in Manchester. At first there weren't many details, but I immediately started to panic. It was exactly where Laura was heading with Grace. Pre-mobile phones, it was difficult to get any information. After a frantic couple of hours, I managed to get Laura on the phone at home. There had been a warning given before the 1,500 kg bomb went off – planted by the IRA – and the police had about ninety minutes to clear a large area of central Manchester before the massive explosion that destroyed a significant section of the city centre. It was the biggest bomb detonation in the UK since the Second World War, and the largest peacetime bomb. Those that heard the explosion even from three hundred yards away said the sound ripped through their body. Nearly two hundred people were injured, but there were no deaths. Some saw the devastation as the catalyst for a new era of Manchester regeneration, a typical local fight back against adversity, and there were dark mutterings that it wasn't necessarily the worst thing that could have happened, as a dysfunctional city centre re-emerged in much better shape over the following decade.

Laura and Grace had been part of the fantastically organised evacuation by the emergency services of over 75,000 people. I was in a terrible state when there was no news, and it was the sheer relief that they were safe, combined with a little defiance, that got me through the weekend's shows. Many in Manchester, after the shock, watched the football as a welcome distraction from the terrible events.

The Arndale Centre was among the most heavily damaged of the buildings affected by the bomb, and it wasn't long before we had lived above it inside Cromford Court. I read that one old resident stayed put in his home as the evacuation took place, wondering what all the fuss had been about, and somehow most of Cromford Court survived the destruction. I was still glad we'd moved out. We'd been one of the few who lived in the city centre up to that point, and one of the consequences of the bomb and the rebuilding that followed was that, thirty years later, over 60,000 people were living in the centre of the city, although by then Cromford Court, once so modern-seeming, was part of an old Manchester.

47
A Rob by any other name

I did feel that the success of M People caused a rift between me and Rob. We'd been inseparable throughout the eighties, and there were some unrepeatable, unforgettable times. He was never spiky or rude with me like he could be with others. Somehow he could challenge me and take the piss without it being nasty, although that did change slightly as the pressure of it all increased in the late eighties. He'd always been so helpful, but once I started to sell records with M People and became more independent from The Haçienda, things were definitely different. He wasn't jealous – he was part of New Order, after all, and for someone of his sensibility it didn't get better or bigger than that – but you could tell he didn't think I needed his help anymore, and if I did, well, I was on my own now.

I had M People, I was a well-known disc jockey, and the Deconstruction label had a profile and a steady run of hit acts; meanwhile, The Haçienda was becoming a bundle of trouble, Factory went bust, and New Order were beginning to look a little shaky as Bernard and Hooky started clashing over all sorts of things, big and small.

Rob was very attached to Manchester, and to the Manchester indie mentality, which, let's face it, he had helped create. Once M People started, I was literally going around the world all the time and losing my close ties to the city. Manchester was still in my head, but not like it was for Rob. If anything, when he was abroad with New Order, he would become more Manchester, more deadpan and ironic, just to show he wasn't being tempted by the outside world, and, worse, by the money in the outside world.

I didn't have the same zealous attachment to the city that he had. He wouldn't have admitted it, and it would have provoked a sarcastic snigger, but he was more political about his connection. I loved Manchester, and it made me what I was and gave me a platform like no other, but I was more interested in the world out there than Rob was.

Rob was always Rob, until he wasn't anymore. He'd taken a lot on, not as publicly as Tony, but he was incredibly committed to what he was doing, even if he'd never really talk about it. The essential Rob-ness of Rob was particularly visible when it came to following City, even when he was on tour with New Order during the football season, and missing games. This was years before the Premier League would be shown around the world, long before mobile phones. He'd be in some hotel room in America, where it would be breakfast time, or Australia, where it would be the middle of the night, and he'd call me and get me to put the local radio commentary of a City match on the phone. He'd listen to the commentary on *Radio Manchester* or *Piccadilly* for a couple of hours, and I'd sometimes check that he was still there. He always was, usually with an expletive-laden moan about how bad it was going. What was life without a good grumble? God knows how much those phone calls cost, but for Rob they were worth it.

Rob was always Rob, even when he was dealing with Quincy Jones, who signed New Order to his Qwest label in 1985, adding them to a roster that included Frank Sinatra and George Benson, because after he'd made *Thriller*, it was his world and he could do what he wanted.

Rob couldn't resist the idea of New Order entering the kingdom of Quincy. That was true class, and class recognised class, and for Rob, it was still punk – just think of those big band records Quincy made with Count Basie in the 1960s. More punk than signing for CBS, who were one of those labels offering so much money to tempt New Order to the other side. Even though there was never a Quincy-produced New Order album, there was a Quincy Jones remix of 'Blue Monday' in 1988, which reached even higher in the UK charts than the 1983 original. It was almost too wonderful to get your head around.

'They're beautiful people', Quincy said about New Order, meaning Rob as well, genuinely touched that they wanted to sign to his label. The man with the most incredible musical ears thought New Order were perfect, and he didn't want to change them at all. We met him once at a pub on Knutsford High Street because he had flown from LA into Manchester Airport about ten miles away and was probably then flying off to play golf with David Bowie and Tony Bennett in Switzerland or something.

There we were sat with Quincy fucking Jones, Rob grinning away, me thinking this is what it's all about, Quincy asking where the mustard was as he ate a sandwich: 'Yeah, it's in one of those yellow sachets, love.' Quincy then trying to tear one open. I just stared at him, immediately now just one degree away now from Ray Charles, Frank Sinatra, Louis Armstrong, Dizzy Gillespie, Ella Fitzgerald, Michael Jackson …

Quincy seemed to love chatting with Rob, but Rob didn't change himself one bit. He was never starstruck, and I don't think Quincy understood a word he was saying, as slow as he spoke. We didn't really understand what Quincy was talking about, but it was magical, and essentially it seemed to come down to: 'You gotta enjoy life. Hell yeah.' Later, I thought they should put a plaque on the wall of that country pub in Knutsford – Rob Gretton and Quincy Jones met here in 1985. What a meeting of minds.

Rob started to noticeably wobble a bit around this time. At first, that just seemed to be Rob being Rob, which had taken him from the monotonous backstreets of Wythenshawe to summit meetings with Quincy Jones. Every day with Rob was an adventure, and he approached every situation in a unique way, which sometimes was very entertaining to watch, even as he pushed things to the limit.

There was the time around 1986 when the deputy leader of Liverpool Council, the notorious radical politician Derek Hatton, was sacked from his job and removed from the Labour Party for his membership of the far-left Militant group. His colleagues wanted to put on a benefit for him at the Royal Court theatre to show support, and were really keen that New Order would play. Tony, of course, was a big fan of a fellow disruptor, especially a self-professed

Trotskyist doing all he could to stand up to Margaret Thatcher's governmental interference in Liverpool's spending, and wanted to help, but Rob played hard to get.

They took us to a City match at Everton, bought us meals, really did all they could, and it turned out Rob had one condition if New Order were to appear. He wanted Hatton to admit he was a gangster. He kept needling Hatton – 'Say you're a gangster and we'll do it.' Hatton would say nothing, and get a little annoyed, and Rob kept coming. 'Are you a gangster?' Hatton would just shake his head. I don't know what he'd heard about Hatton, and whether he approved of the idea that he could be a gangster or not, but he wouldn't let it go. He was always fond of picking on people, from those he'd just met to those who were quite important in the story of Joy Division and New Order. 'Why', you'd ask him when he was in a particularly prickly mood? 'Summat to do. It relieves the boredom.'

The Hatton supporters would say to me, 'What can we do to persuade him?' I said, 'Well, I think the gangster bit is the clincher.' They must have wondered what the hell was wrong with him. Eventually, Derek and Rob were sat in the Britons Protection pub, and Rob asked the question again. Hatton sighed and said, 'Ok, yes, alright, I'm a gangster.' Rob's conditions were met and he immediately shook his hand and said, 'Ok, we'll do it.' And New Order did, for a few quid expenses, along with The Smiths, The Fall and John Cooper Clarke. Years later, Hatton did get charged with bribery and corruption.

So that was Rob – walking the fine line between genius and madness, or maybe just Rob being Rob with the weed smoking adding extra Rob and sometimes just too much Rob.

He was putting himself through it, keeping New Order on the straight and narrow, which involved a lot of twists and turns and meetings with the tax man, fighting to keep The Haçienda going – without New Order they would have been fucked – and going through the usual fun and games with Tony to make the best sense of Factory Records, whatever that was.

Indie idealism and Manc loyalty was all well and good, but it took an incredible amount of courage to go through all this without just throwing his hands in the air and taking the major label millions.

He wouldn't entertain it even when some of the band were tempted. Tony really appreciated it, but to some extent he also took it for granted. Rob would have his anger flare-ups and wind people up like he teased Derek Hatton, but nothing that seemed too far outside his usual behaviour.

Rob did have a particularly bad time in 1986, and suffered what was then called a nervous breakdown, and needed to spend some time recovering in hospital. Slowly, he came back, but I never thought he was the same after that. When Rob was being Rob after the breakdown, speaking his mind, having a laugh, there was always the sense he might be on the verge of another collapse, and he sensed that others were worried, and maybe he was as well, and it knocked some of the energy out of him. Always laidback, he would sometimes come to a standstill. Sometimes he had too much energy, and would start speaking and he wouldn't stop.

Bernard was always very vocal about it and thought that Rob was never properly diagnosed. Consequently, he was always on the wrong medication. When he was first treated, he filled in a form about other members of his family and their mental health history, and he wrote down that his brother had schizophrenia. After that, they gave him drugs for schizophrenia, but we were convinced that wasn't what he had. Rob didn't seem to be hearing voices or hallucinating; he was always who he was, oddly straight down the line and wonderfully sardonic for all his unorthodoxy.

There were so many drugs he needed to take for something he probably didn't have. By the early nineties, as Factory shut down and New Order signed to, of all labels, London Records, he was becoming more laconic than ever. The group effectively had split apart, Bernard and Hooky fighting for territory, and time was mostly spent maintaining the illusion they were still a unit.

Tony powered on with more plans and even more purpose after the end of Factory. The television career never stopped one way or another, and he replaced Factory with the In The City music conference. That's where I would see him most, when I was invited onto panels or judging committees. Despite, or because of, the end of Factory, he was accelerating into a new role as a kind of unfixed music business executive without portfolio, with public intellectual additions, making sure the music industry in general appreciated that Manchester was now a major centre of activity.

To feel things were as they were when they were building Factory, or even when he was using punk to find a way to make a living through music, after Factory failed, Rob formed Manchester Records, which said it all, and then Rob's Records, which said even more. Like me, he wanted a dance label, and was always frustrated by Tony's dance dogma.

With those golden ears of his that he used to boast about, he had great hit records with Haçienda regulars Sub Sub from Handforth in Cheshire, including a Top 3 hit in 1993 with 'Ain't No Love (Ain't No Use)' – which led to the less house, more indie Doves in 1998. For Rob, these new labels weren't quite the same – it seemed the end of something rather than the beginning. He loved beginning things. In truth, he loved discovering things and making a scene.

Even though we lived near each other, I saw less and less of Rob. It represented how I seemed to have fewer friends in Manchester after the success of M People. It's like people assume you've changed even if you haven't. You're seen as a big shot, however you act.

They somehow think you're happy being in a celebrity world now, and you've got no time for them. After the Arndale IRA bombing, which seemed to mark the end of an era in all sorts of ways, and the start of another kind of Manchester architecturally and culturally, when I mentioned to Laura maybe it was time to move to London, she wasn't bothered. 'No one talks to me anymore anyway', she said.

For Rob, and New Order, if you had money, you still didn't need to leave the North. You moved into the country, or, like the Premier League footballers, into Wilmslow, Hale, Barnes or Alderley Edge. For me, I could leave entirely, and still be the northerner, the awkward Mancunian.

Maybe it was because I had already moved away before, so it didn't seem such a definitive act. I knew the Manchester inside you didn't stop the day you left, but living in 'that London' even in the nineties was like moving to the dark side.

For Tony, it was the ultimate act of betrayal, and it was like you lost his trust overnight if you did it. You were expelled from the 'club'. Things became a little more formal.

With Rob, he seemed most perturbed by a trip to London we took together in 1996, that year when M People were riding high. I'd got some interviews to do, a meeting with the label, he had some New Order business to take care of. There were problems with the trains, so we flew down to Heathrow. On the flight, we mostly talked about City.

It would be a funny old season. We'd end the 1996/97 season having had five managers, including a couple of caretakers, and Steve Coppell, a one-time Manchester United player who signed with much fanfare and resigned after six matches and thirty-three days, driven out by the pressure of managing a fatally seeming worn-out Manchester team. It didn't seem to have much hope of ever being anywhere near as successful as United. Actually, it looked as though we were heading nowhere fast.

After we landed, I asked where he was going, and he said, 'Oh, I've got some meetings in the centre of town.' I said, 'I'll give you a lift', and he thought that meant I'd parked my car. I said, 'No, the label has sent me a car.' That brought out a look of disgust with just a whisper of an approving smirk. 'Ooh, look at you, you've made it, haven't you!'

It got worse. The label always sent Jaguars or Daimlers – this was the nineties, the climax of the record label era, when plenty of money was washing around if you were having big hits. 'Fucking hell', he said as he climbed in, 'this is swanky.' I said, 'Well, they always send a car when I'm doing the promoting. I'll be paying for it in the end, but it's all part of the system. It's how it works.'

He asked what I meant. I said, 'Well, all the royalties from the records you sell have to recoup the advances they have given you and the expenses you incur. You're borrowing money all the time and if you're lucky you pay it back and start to make a profit.' He looked out of the window mulling this over.

I thought it was a bit odd as by now he surely must know all this. I thought, maybe he's just winding me up, now that I've made the very suspicious big time. Or maybe he just was always so indie. He didn't know or want to know how it really worked in the mainstream record industry.

In that sense, I wasn't indie at all. It's like how the hardcore Haçienda people at the beginning were surprised how much pop I would book in the early eighties – which meant The Teardrop Explodes, Echo & the Bunnymen, The Associates, Edwyn Collins – so it depends on your definition of pop. I was comfortable with that, and made it work for me.

As we sat in the posh car, I was in a pop group, playing at being a pop star, so it was awkward that he was being so off about it. But then, he was Rob being Rob, and he was being the awkward bugger now that my job was no longer being Rob's mate. I wasn't driving him. We were both being driven. He didn't know how to deal with how it showed up that we were in different worlds and the world we had shared was gone.

I don't think he enjoyed that ride into London. It was too show business for him, and he never wanted to think that what he did was showbusiness. Maybe he was sad about how it had turned out, and that we were no longer as close as we had been. It was sad, really. There didn't have to be a division, but there was one. He looked at me differently. Music had brought us incredibly close, and now it had got between us. We would still meet up at the football, and there it could seem as though nothing had changed. We could have a good moan together about this player, the manager, even Peter Swales, although he'd stopped being chairman in 1993 and died in May 1996. Years of Swales' mismanagement and poor leadership were hard to reverse.

We'd gravitated into the Main Stand – for old-time City fans wedded to the Kippax Street stand that would have been the sell-out – and some Saturdays the team was so bad, we'd join those smoking weed and watching telly in the lounge, popping back to our seat now and then to check on the latest calamity. Some of the games were shocking, but we were still City fans, because to change that was as impossible as changing your skin. We were going through a difficult phase, and sometimes you had to avert your eyes.

48
A loss and a victory

Laura and I had moved to 'that London' in 1998, and maybe moving away from Manchester had something to do with Manchester City now being in the third tier of English football, the Second Division, which fans of my age still thought of as being the Third Division. I was trying to get away from something I never thought would happen to City, as erratic as they'd been for years.

I was still City though, through and through, often finding myself in cramped, unfamiliar stadiums for away matches, against teams that City seemed too big a team to play, which led to the classic City chant, 'We're not really here.'

After that first long, grim season in the old Third Division, we just missed the automatic promotion back to the old Second Division fans had hoped would happen. Otherwise, it might seem that we were really there. For Good. To rub it in, Manchester United had won a treble that year – League, Cup and the Champions League, something even the most dedicated City fan would never dare dream of achieving.

City did come third in the table, and made the play-offs – four teams battling for the one remaining promotion spot. We were drawn against Wigan Athletic in the semi-finals of the Second Division play-off, with the first match of two legs to be played on 15 April at Wigan's then home, Springfield Park.

I really wanted to go, because City hadn't been involved in a match like this, one that really mattered, for a long time. I couldn't make it because M People were relentlessly touring, the working-class me not wanting to slack off, and me as the pop music lover not wanting to be forgotten. We were also recording the fourth and final M People studio album, *Fresco*, and for some of the recording, Paul and I were using the world-class Chung King studios near Hudson Square in Lower Manhattan. They'd moved there from their original home, where iconic albums by LL Cool J, Run DMC, Beastie Boys and Public Enemy were made.

Spread over two floors, Chung King was one of the best places to be if you wanted to make an authentic, very grown up, American-sounding R&B record. It was a long way from the Wigan Athletic stadium. We were by then the kind of bestselling international group who would be recording there, in central New York, which wasn't the most practical place in the world to park and carry in all the equipment needed. We'd be working with David Sussman, fresh from mixing Mariah Carey, and Warren Riker, an anomalous looking bearded redneck Texan who'd collaborated with the Fugees on *The Score*. That was definitely our template. As fans, who happened to be selling millions of records, it was that sound we were after – sod the cost.

We'd have the most professional backing singers in the world, used to working with Luther Vandross, and we even had Will Downing singing backing vocals on one track. Sussman could call in Lenny Kravitz's bassist when we needed some bass; back home, recording some *Fresco* tracks in our favourite London studio, the Strong Room, we had bass master Pino Palladino. The soul singer's soul singer Danny Madden was creating these amazing gospel vocal arrangements.

Everyone was so on it, totally committed to doing the very best for the session. I can't imagine reaching a more opposite point to being in the studio with the Happy Mondays. The American sound Sussman would get was so big. He'd push the drums and bass as far as they would go into the red without it distorting. Paul and I would watch it all happening from these seats like you were on a private jet, like we were watching a film. Sometimes it would seem as though we were actually in the film.

While we were in one studio, the hardcore Brooklyn rap duo Mobb Deep were next door, Havoc and Prodigy savouring their pungent

Philly blunt cigars – the cheap, go-to hip-hop cigars of the time, packed with weed, beloved by Nas and Notorious B.I.G. Some critics of *Fresco*, thinking it was a little too polished, probably thought we needed a little of what they were having.

Meticulously crafted R&B records were what we wanted to emulate, especially now that Heather was so confident in her singing. We didn't want rough round the edges, we definitely didn't want indie – we were looking for this highly refined strength.

Rock critics heard bland; it's actually anything but bland. The sound is by its very nature commercial – designed to sell records around the world, and so American engineers make everything BIG, even the edgiest hip-hop. We were big in countries around the world now; it was no use pretending we were underground just to please a few critics who thought we'd betrayed our house roots.

Mobb Deep had turned their supersonic studio into party central. They liked having an audience in there with them as they got down to business, even the skinny white guy from somewhere near Merrie England who tried to deal with a smoking Philly blunt and then much to his shame could barely stand up. Once I'd tried a couple of puffs I nearly had to crawl on all fours to get back to our studio.

It would be mayhem in their studio, but I suppose that was the vibe they needed to capture their mood. That's what those kind of recording studios were all about – making an atmosphere and then getting it recorded with added dimension.

'Hey Mike', they'd say, shocking me that they knew my name, 'we're making a dope, dope groundbreaking album, right there, hope you are too!' When it was my turn to speak I found myself sounding like an uptight BBC weather forecaster from the 1950s, but to them I guess that was just English.

Money couldn't buy the experience of hanging out with Mobb Deep when they were ruling New York and smoking the cigars of champions – although now I come to think of it, remembering the size of the bill, so big you had to look at it twice, it did take quite a chunk of cash.

Fresco was our glossy, superstar album, recorded over a few months in numerous studios, needing a whole crew of drum programmers, the list of elite guest musicians including one link with my past, Johnny Marr, who'd become international in his own way, and the cover photograph of Heather by the revolutionary photographer and director of Robert Palmer's 'Addicted to Love' video, Terence Donovan – just a few months before, awfully, he hanged himself.

I loved that using Terence connected M People to his history, the working-class kid making such an impact on the world, and those great photos of Jimi Hendrix, Albert Finney, Elvis Costello, Julie Christie, Sophia Loren, Jazzie B and, God help us, Mark E. Smith.

We'd come a long way from recording in Paul's flat in Hackney, with Heather singing in the nursery with a line passed in from where we were in the lounge. You'd know that Heather was in the right mood to do some singing because you'd hear her practising in the tiny kitchen as she made a cup of tea.

Our fourth album was the kind of expensive, indulgent major label extravaganza Rob would have scoffed at – although he would have loved hanging out with Mobb Deep, easily handling the blunts and loving the drums toppling out of the speakers sounding as though they were getting their power from the city itself. *Fresco* would have confirmed to him that success had sent me soft in the head. When it came to City, though, we were still brothers. Blue blood runs deep.

Even though I couldn't make it to the first leg of the Wigan match, I knew that Rob was going, due to meet up with the usual bunch of friends he'd go with in their regular meeting place in a Chorlton pub.

Rob never arrived, which actually wasn't that uncommon. Even at his youngest and fittest Rob would easily miss a few matches, either being late or lazy. They all headed off, thinking they'd get some call from Rob later, and hear some excuse, or just no excuse at all; in the end he couldn't be bothered.

Rob had died in his sleep on the Friday night into Saturday morning. He was only 46. I was back at home in London after a few days recording *Fresco*, and the news was so weird and unexpected I don't even remember who called to tell me that he had just gone to bed and never woke up.

I went into shock, and sat on the edge of my bed sobbing for hours. I was completely bewildered and couldn't take in the information.

I hadn't seen him much recently, but this was completely out of the blue, and I never saw it coming. At the back of my mind I always assumed that we'd get close again once I'd got this pop group thing out of my system. I hated that when it happened we weren't close.

I went to see Lesley a few days later, and she was incredibly calm and stoical. There was nothing we could say, so we didn't say anything. How could Rob be gone?

All this was going on while Manchester City were fighting to win promotion and head back towards relative civilisation. It was so important but so difficult to concentrate on, like it was happening a million miles away and a million years ago.

City had drawn Saturday's first leg of the Wigan play-off game, which took me a day or two to process after Rob's death. The following Wednesday, 19 April, in the second leg at Maine Road, after a few scares Shaun Goater scored a fluky-looking goal that took us into the final at Wembley. It was a really strange night, being there without Rob, who the week before was still being Rob.

We draped a City shirt over his season ticket seat. It was an important win, giving us a chance to get back into the second tier First Division (which wasn't great, but was better than another season in the Second Division, and the possibility of never getting out of that league). We watched more or less in silence as City started their move towards the big time, or at least the Second Division, finding it hard to get over the weird lack of Rob.

There was a huge turnout for Rob's funeral at St Anthony's church in Wythenshawe, everybody with anything to do with Manchester music turning up to say goodbye. Not bad for a scallywag from the Wythenshawe estate.

They brought the coffin in to Al Green's 'Let's Stay Together', and I was in tears halfway through the song. I remember little of what happened next, apart from a very lovely, moving speech by the writer and close Factory associate Jon Savage, and the other songs that were played – Marvin Gaye's 'Abraham, Martin and John' and Rob and Lesley's special song, Candi Staton's 'Young Hearts Run Free'.

Rob was buried – as Martin Hannett was, and Tony Wilson would be when he died eight years later – in Chorlton's Southern Cemetery, right opposite The Oaks pub where Rob had put on those tremendous early punk gigs, announcing his presence as part dreamer, part activist, and part fucked-up impresario.

Tony said a few words about his old partner, ultimately the one who gave him the space to make up a new Manchester. They were obviously in English but in the state I was in, it all sounded like Latin. *Audaces fortuna juvat* – fortune favours the bold – Tony would say. *Cunnus*, Rob would reply.

There were drinks for the many at the posh Midland Hotel in Manchester, and then drinks for those that were closest at The Britons Protection pub, on the corner by the now defunct Haçienda – soon to become modern loft-style flats, the home of acid house turned into people's homes, now with a Haçienda address, an early part of the new wave of inner-city dwellers.

The Britons Protection had been used as The Haçienda staffroom, so it was a fitting place for some lively remembering, and fittingly the liveliness lasted into the early hours, just as Rob would have wanted.

It's hard to believe now, but Rob's passing continued to be tangled up with the legendary drama of Manchester City and their Wembley play-off final against Gillingham. It was all surreal enough without the surreal addition of it happening in the days after his death.

Rob's City gang were still in shock, and I took Rob's son Benedict and a friend, and I kept thinking, what excuse does Rob have for missing this? There was something a little Factory about it – the idea that if City didn't win, they would be at serious risk of going out of business. If not that, another season in the third tier would have been disastrous for the morale of players and fans.

We were two nil down after eighty-seven minutes, so that seemed to be that. Hundreds of City fans, resigned to their fate, headed out of the ground. Noel Gallagher and his crew, including jungle maestro Goldie and actor and New Order pal Keith Allen, were on their way out. A few days before, Manchester United had scored two goals in the dying seconds to win the Champions League. No way was another Manchester team going to score two goals in the final few minutes of a match.

Those staying to suffer the final minutes couldn't muster up any sounds of encouragement. There was a goal in the last minute of normal time, and the board showed there was going to be five minutes of injury time. The City fans found their voice. Noel and company ran back to their seats. I kept looking round to find Rob, so we could give each other hope.

The five minutes were almost over – the goal, after all that, had been a pointless consolation – and the hopelessness seeped back into the City fans. Then, in the last few minutes, Paul Dickov equalised, meaning utter bedlam, and then the torture of extra time, and then, after no more goals, the torture of penalty kicks.

Something seemed to swing things around, and typical City can mean pulling off the impossible as well as fucking things up, and we beat Gillingham on penalties. Being in the First Division seemed to the City fans beginning their party to be sweeter than the United treble.

I looked up and gave Rob a big smile. Unbelievable that he missed it, and the next quarter of a century when we would become one of the world's richest clubs, worth upwards of £5 billion, transforming east Manchester and bringing the future to a previously unloved wasteland.

He missed moving out of Maine Road in 2003 into a gleaming new stadium, which he would have grumbled about for years; missed us getting taken over by Sheik Mansour bin Zayed al Nahyan and the Abu Dhabi United Group in 2008 – making us one of the wealthiest clubs in the world – which he would have grumbled about for a bit; and missed the last-minute Sergio Agüero goal in 2012 against QPR that won us the Premier League – echoing the Dickov equaliser against Gillingham, bedlam ensues – which he wouldn't have grumbled about for a second.

His friends made sure he knew all about that match, laying down the newspaper headlines about the victory on his grave so he could read all about it. After 2012, eventually managed by the greatest coach in the world, Pep Guardiola, we kept winning trophies, FA Cups, League Cups, Premier Leagues, absurdly the Champions League and then the World Club Cup, to the extent that I did start to wonder if Rob was pulling a few levers wherever he was, or we were all living in Rob's dream.

He's even made Manchester United the laughing stock Manchester team that seems to be mismanaged by Peter Swales while City, whatever the politics, the financial realities, the alleged rule breaking, is one of the best run clubs in the world.

The typical City chants that go along with the glory are very Rob – 'We're not really here' is still going, 'Empty seats at home' is for those that wrongly think that however successful we are we can't fill our own Etihad stadium, and a version of an old Fleetwood Mac song that can go on for minutes gloating, 'We spend all our money on drugs and City.'

Every time we win another Premier League title – four in a row between 2020 and 2024, thank you – or FA Cup, and especially when we won the Champions League in Istanbul in 2023, the first thing I do is look up at the sky and celebrate with him. I hope he's got a great seat. Even if he would think what a soft southern *cunnus* I was for thinking like that. He might yet, if it is indeed him making it all happen from wherever he is, let it fall apart, just to relieve the boredom.

49
A fresh start

Living in London at the end of the nineties, I could feel that M People were coming to an end. If I had written out some sort of plan at the beginning, rather than relying on instincts I never really properly articulated, I think I would have said, 'We'll get ten years, over half of them at the top, finish with a greatest hits album, and then that's that. Don't overstay your welcome.' It felt natural. I'd tried writing songs for other people and it never seemed right, and now, after eight or nine years, it started to feel the same writing for M People.

Everything I had at the beginning of the nineties and powered into M People was running out. Maybe deep down I knew the reviews for *Fresco* whining that it was tipping into the middle of the road weren't entirely unfair. I felt I was becoming detached from what I was good at, which was responding quickly to shifts in music, in youth culture fashion.

We all needed a break after years of record, tour, record, tour. It was time to move on, maybe temporarily, but who knew. It was a shame because Roger Davies had only just started working with us. I'd had enough, and he was the manager of Pink, Janet Jackson, Tina, and Cher, so he knew his divas, and he was happy to take on a solo Heather.

Heather, the star of the group for most of our audience, was more than ready to go solo, even though she was a little nervous to mention it. It would give her the chance to begin again, and free herself from the responsibilities of being in a group. She had proved herself, and now she could be free.

It felt like that for me as well. I could go solo, which meant a return to DJing, and also something new I really didn't see coming.

I'd bought a house in the south of France, a ramshackle place in Languedoc, and for a while, post popstar, I'd sit there and think. For a while it was good to have nothing to do. No songs to write, no interviews to do, no meetings. Drink the local wine, smoke weed, stare into space.

After a while, I started to twitch a little. I did need something to do. What the hell did a fresh start consist of for an ex-pop star of my age? Maybe I could become a behind the scenes song writing duo with Paul.

There was another street-smart City fan from a Catholic family in Wythenshawe that I knew who lived near me in Primrose Hill, north London, where I'd become an unlikely part of some celebrity set – I seemed to be a neighbour of comedians Harry Enfield and Ben Elton, 1980s pop punk idol Adam Ant and film director Jonathan Glazer. Having managed Paul Young and Alison Moyet in the 1980s, Ged Doherty had joined Epic Records in the early nineties, and by the early 2000s he was managing director of Columbia, before taking over Sony BMG in 2006.

He was quick to see how for record companies things were blurring into new shapes in the early twenty-first century, and was making some unusual appointments to work in what he was seeing as different kinds of departments. To stay in touch with a rapidly developing new world, record labels needed to adapt, discover new income streams, new ways of finding and selling talent. That was the aim, anyway.

He came over to my house one day, and said, 'I want you to work for me.' I didn't understand what he meant. Doing what? He said, 'Well, for want of a better label, A&R, signing talent, organising studios.' Me work for a record company? I was laughing my head off, totally incredulous.

How not Factory would that be, working for a major label, for bloody Sony. I said, 'Fuck, no. No way!' He wasn't fazed at all. He said he really wanted to have a dance label, and he'd give me the chance to create it with all the freedom I needed.

He gave me a load of demos and said, 'No pressure, have a listen to these, and if you like anything, let me know.' I said, 'Sure, yeah, absolutely', having no intention of listening to them.

After a bit I thought, actually, working for a major label in the twenty-first century might be a very Factory thing to do, and not necessarily an act of treason. I talked with Laura about the idea, and as I talked about it, I realised I liked the thought of it more than writing songs as part of some anonymous songwriting team.

In the end, as a so-called songwriter, I was more likely to sit around in France missing the old times, struggling for ideas and drinking myself to death. Working for Ged might work if I didn't think of it as working for a villainous major label, if I didn't think of it as being an A&R man, which had all kinds of unsavoury associations, and simply thought of it as a chance to work with new artists, and work in the world that I knew well and had helped set up.

I listened to the tapes and CDs Ged had given me, and they were all ordinary at best, truly awful at worst, and my heart sank. There was one called 'Process Beats' by a group called Kasabian that stood out, obviously at first because it rang out with some Stones Roses swagger, but mostly because it lifted off from there in a way the Roses never did.

I still wasn't sure. I went for a couple of walks with Ged and he said, 'Well, we have a development deal with Kasabian, why don't you look after them?' I asked a friend of mine, Rob Stringer, who was also high up at Sony, and he said, 'You should do it. You've done it all your life anyway – you signed James, the Mondays, Black Box, you put together the *North* album, the defining document of northern acid house, you were hanging around New Order for a decade, you won the Mercury Prize. You were really doing A&R at Deconstruction and for M People. Just carry on doing that with some money to spend that you don't have to pay back.'

I had met Rob through Mark Farrow, who did all the artwork for Deconstruction, and the cover for *Elegant Slumming* – we were getting drunk one night in the Atlantic Bar in Piccadilly Circus, and even though we had a lot in common through music all we talked about was football. Rob's a mad Luton Town fan, and he's now on the board, and ever since then we've become really close. So as soon as Sony and BMG merged they came into the building in Putney; Rob and I had never worked together – we only knew each other as football mates. We saw each other in the corridor and we were laughing and giggling.

He became the English CEO of Sony and now he's CEO of Sony Worldwide, but we're still football mates and he comes over for the Luton matches and unfortunately I have to go to Luton games with him. There are those who know I am friends with him, and they'll ask me what he thinks about some music business thing, about indie digital distribution companies or the influence of TikTok on the music industry, and I'll tell them I haven't got a clue, but I do know what he thinks of Luton Town's left back or Man City's number 4.

I said to Ged I'd come in as some kind of A&R consultant working on an act by act basis, and we could relaunch Deconstruction as part of the arrangement, which might be the dance label he was looking for. We agreed terms and conditions, and it was time for another costume change.

The first month was really weird. Did I have a boss now? Did I have to work out of an office? I told Ged there was no way I was going to sit in any business meetings. Unless I could bring in some Philly blunts.

Ged said, 'Just do what makes you feel comfortable.' It wasn't easy to work out how it would work. First of all, I was a really well-known artist who had sold over 10 million albums, and secondly, I had absolutely no idea how it all worked in a record company. Maybe I was too old to learn.

I didn't know how to work the computer system. I would find myself just sitting in an anonymous glass-walled office with a stereo in it, listening to demos. I asked another of the A&R guys, 'What do you do with your time?' He said, 'Well, we're out most of the time looking at bands.' So I mucked in and went out with them and got into the swing of it.

Maybe still not the real job my dad always wanted for me, but it was something new, and it was still all about music, and I had enough experience as an artist to know what artists wanted from a record label. I could be pretty awkward myself, so I quite looked forward to dealing with awkward artists and finding a way to be the connection between them and one of the world's biggest labels.

The person looking after Kasabian left, so I started working with them, became part of their team, and they reacted to me being unlike anyone else working at their label. I wasn't the usual record company type, but I knew how to hang out with artists, mavericks and hedonists, and with my experience I knew a lot more about the science of mastering a record than a lot of the other members of the A&R department.

I knew how a great song makes a great record, whatever the era, and that seemed a skill the great A&R men had – thinking of people like Seymour Stein, Chris Blackwell, Daniel Miller and Rick Rubin.

I felt with Kasabian that I could finish off what I didn't get a chance to with James and the Mondays. I'd tell them, and I'd tell all the artists I worked with, 'I don't work for Sony or BMG, I work for you. I'll get you what you want and need, and if you're happy, you're going to make great music, and the label will be happy. Think of them as an ATM. When you need a bit of money, they're there. Don't take the piss. Don't throw tantrums. Just make sure you get the room you need to make the music you want to make.'

Kasabian all lived at a farm just outside Leicester that they'd rented – a freezing hovel of a place. There were five of them living in sleeping bags or on mattresses on the floor, totally dedicated to the band and to making it.

They were real Leicester City lads and for me it was like going back to the Mondays. They liked me because of the Mondays – they figured, well, if he's worked for the Mondays he must be alright. We had them play 200, or 250 gigs over eighteen months – any kind of venue – to work on getting a distinctive band sound. They were very much a live rock band and had to sound immediately themselves, and they were good but I wanted them to be great. They had to be the perfect rock band, or why bother? They were up for it.

We finally found the right drummer, the final piece of the puzzle, and it all started to gel. One night they were playing in the Half Moon in Putney, and this guy who worked with me at Sony couldn't believe how powerful – and wonderfully cocky – they were. It was sending shivers down my spine. I went backstage afterwards and I said to them, 'That's it, it's done, you're a complete band, you've got an amazing front man. Now let's get going.'

My daughter Grace when she was about 14 started to come to Glastonbury with me, and in 2005 we had Kasabian on the Other Stage on Thursday, that opening 12 o'clock slot that can be hard work.

They had this amazing artwork of an Ultra football fan, and overnight Grace and her mates went around all the tents and put Ultra-flags by the tents. We knew it would be on TV and there would be thousands of Kasabian flags. They were ready for action, and the crowd was filled with people holding their Ultra flags. We wanted to create something like a gang of Kasabian supporters, and their songs had these terrace-like chants that were made for crowds to sing along with.

Ten years later they headlined Glastonbury's Pyramid Stage, and deserved to be there. They had seven number 1 albums. I was there for the whole ten years until I stopped working at Sony. Job done.

Another of my favourite signings was Gossip. I was at the 2008 South by Southwest music festival in Austin Texas, and fucking hated it. I was a fish out of water, there were so many tattoos and rockers, and I wasn't seeing anything that meant anything to me.

The festival would put gigs on in different spaces, like stores and car parks, and one night I was walking past a car park after another hopeless night seeing no hoper bands, and I thought I just have to get out of here. I wanted to go home. And then I heard this woman's unbelievably soulful voice singing, really going for it at the far end of the car park. People were streaming out and I thought wow that sounds good – is that a record? It sounded like some Brooklyn disco-punk that might have been on ZE Records or some mash-up of Gang of Four and Janis Joplin.

The A&R in me kicked in and I fought through the crowd flowing out to get to the stage, and it was me and I guess about twenty lesbians watching this really gutsy trio with a massive, totally committed singer, and my first thought was, they were better than the White Stripes.

That girl could really sing, and it was punk really, with house insistence, minimal, scratchy and feisty with loads of space for the incredible voice. It took me back to Rotterdam, to The Ranch and the Electric Circus. I managed to find my way into the dressing room after they'd finished, a bit nervous. They didn't know who the fuck I was, and were not very outgoing. I was telling them how amazing they were like an excited kid.

They were like, 'Oh, ok, thanks', but not thinking it meant much coming from this skinny guy with a funny accent and no tattoos. I thought right, go for it, they were obviously seriously indie, and that wasn't a foreign language for me even if I was working at Sony. I introduced myself to their multi-instrumentalist Nathan, and I mentioned the golden word: I used to work at Factory Records. Whoosh, their entire demeanour changed, they certainly knew their A Certain Ratio, and I was straight in, part of their inner circle for the night.

We became quite good friends and they said, 'Well, we're coming over to England in a couple of weeks', and they played the Elbow Room in Islington. I was selling them to the British branch of Sony, and it was greeted with all-round incredulity – they just seemed like a noisy outsider punk band from nowheresville with a lead singer essentially at the opposite extreme to what would be considered a traditional record company-designed female singer, which to me meant she was provocative, strong and sexy. They stared at a picture of a 16-stone lead singer and thought I was mad. I thought they were mad for even questioning it. I hated that side of the record industry that was always suspicious of anything that didn't fit the usual boxes.

The band had done well in the UK with the track 'Standing in the Way of Control' after it was featured on Channel 4's comedy teen drama *Skins* and released on a small indie label. I got a call from Sony America, who'd eventually spotted them on their slightly faulty radar screens, picking up on Beth as a provocative celebrity being seen in all the right places more than anything. They said they were trying to sign this band Gossip, but they wouldn't sign unless I was involved.

They were dead underground in America, even if they were hanging out with Kate Moss over in England – one of those great American bands that make more sense in Britain before they do in America. They were worried that making that move from the underground to a big label would be dangerous, and I would be a friendly face, someone they knew wouldn't want to knock off all their edges but make more of a virtue of them.

I clapped my hands in delight. Rob, who was then head of Sony, came to see me and said 'What the hell have you done now!' I said, 'Well I told everyone here, they're fantastic. I told them we needed to sign them.'

I ended up being their A&R point of contact. Rick Rubin wanted to make their first album for the label when he was Co-President of Columbia, part of Sony. The thought of him making their record was mind-blowing, couldn't be better. He'd been brilliantly reinventing grand old timers like Johnny Cash and Neil Diamond, and his list of iconic productions was never-ending – Public Enemy, Run-DMC, Beastie Boys, Red Hot Chilli Peppers, The Mars Volta, Rage Against the Machine, Jay-Z, Metallica. Whatever he's got, he's really got.

I flew over to LA and we set up a meeting with Rick at this little breakfast place on Santa Monica the morning after they'd play at the Troubadour, sounding incredible.

Even after the pop star decade I still looked like a wiry Manc scally, and Rob Stringer always said he would have loved to have seen that meeting – me and Rick Rubin, loads of crystals round his neck, an immense God-like beard, wearing a complicated smock, like a vision of some mighty guru, and me where six weeks of not shaving would still only mean a reluctant scattering of bum fluff. He said it must have been the meeting of all time.

Oddly, we bonded over Worldwide Wrestling because it turned out we were both passionate about wrestling, and he had connections with the company that produced the shows. He saw it as some kind of performance art, all human life was there, but he didn't want to talk about it in front of Gossip – he wanted to be a bit more mysterious.

The album *Music For Men* was Gossip entering the mainstream, trying to bring the fame of the group up to the fame of Beth – the drummer Hannah was on the cover on her own, which squashed any thoughts they were going to labelwash Beth and use her fame to sell the band. They were still as unfettered and defiant as ever, but reaching so many more people around the world – they sold millions of records in Europe.

When they took a break for a while in 2009, Beth came to me when she wanted to make a record. She said she wanted to keep it in the family and 'Avoid the label bullshit.' I signed her to the relaunched Deconstruction, thinking of Decon as much as anything as a surreal home for definitive dance divas, and the Beth Ditto EP she made with Simian Mobile Disco was one of my favourite achievements in what turned out to be a twenty-year stint disguised as an A&R man. I think Ged was a little surprised I'd managed to smuggle into Sony twice, even temporarily, such a fluid, loose-lipped character speaking such a challenging musical language, making such fabulously fucked-up disco, but as I said to him, 'She's the real fucking deal, she's the real Madonna. You said I could do what I wanted!'

Such an attitude led me straight to The Ting Tings, a spiky Salford duo, Katie White and Jules De Martino, who'd had a bad label experience when they were called Dear Eskiimo. They knew exactly the kind of group they wanted to be, had hundreds of ideas about their style and presentation – which a great group always should do – but their first label was more interested in pushing Katie as some kind of nineties-style ladette willing to strip off for the lads' magazines.

Katie naturally resisted, with a few expletives thrown in, and within months they were let go. Their second coming, as an uncompromising art pop unit mixing Spice Girl pop with cosmic underground German sounds and Japanese noise, required careful handling, and I liked their electro-pop energy on the demo I'd played in the office – for me it was Vice Versa plus Talking Heads with a dusting of Cyndi Lauper.

I left the office as soon as I heard their new demo, which had 'That's Not My Name' on it – a man on a mission. I had some weird plan I would just turn up wherever they were. I rang a Sony scout in Manchester and asked if he knew where they were based. They were living in Islington Mill, the arts centre in Salford. I immediately jumped on the train north at Euston – I had no overnight bag. I was on the hunt. I'd get like that when I found something I thought was going to hit.

Three hours later I was in Salford. I gave them a call actually standing outside their place, the other side of this massive black gate. Jules answered and was a bit nonplussed to hear me beginning the conversation by raving about their demo. I said I want to meet as soon as possible. He asked where I was? I said, well I'm outside your place.

And he went, oh, right, sounding like he thought I might be a wrong'un, but they let me in and they had an apartment and a studio where they lived and worked. They played some more tracks, and they told me other record companies were interested and they were going to do a showcase in their studio in a few days' time. They'd released 'That's Not My Name' themselves on a tiny indie label, and because it sounded like an adrenaline rush of a hit, like something from the early eighties, and also a timeless, fuck off manifesto for teenage freedom, lots of labels were keen on them.

I said, 'I'll be there.' I put my work in first – took them for fish and chips in the Northern Quarter, had a few drinks. I could play at being the artist's view of a typical, know nothing record company A&R man, but I was anything but, and they knew it really.

At the show they put on in their studio, it was bean bags and loads of other record companies milling about, a bit of a bunfight, not my cup of tea at all. I just stood against the wall taking it in. As they were being chatted up by all the record companies offering their versions of the world, I said 'Right Jules, I'm off.' He asked, 'Where are you going?' I said, 'I don't swim in these waters' – I don't know where that came from, it came out of nowhere. 'I'll speak to you later', I said, heading out.

He said later that was the clincher. While he was talking to all these other labels, he was thinking we have to go with the one who said, he doesn't swim in these waters.

All the representatives from the other labels made them nervous. I sidled in and made it clear that we could make it work inside Sony as its own self-contained art project, and they could look after their own image. I appeared to not make them nervous, and their snippy Salford teasing didn't unsettle me at all, and I was happy to give some of it back.

The plan definitely worked for the first album, and the intensely infectious simplicity of 'That's Not My Name' was a number 1 single – at the same time as a number 1 album – not least because that's exactly what it sounded like, as if it was built for 7-inch vinyl. Fifteen years later it also proved itself a perfect fit for the unfathomable algorithmic spaces of TikTok and Netflix. It's become a modern pop classic that never runs out of steam.

The plan didn't work so well for the second album, and I recognised how their success had set them on a treadmill that they weren't necessarily prepared for. What had emerged out of pleasing themselves and a few friends was now hard work, and conceptually needed a different approach.

It was like with M People – when you start out, it feels like you have all the time in the world to work yourself out, and then after a hit record or two you have no time at all, and even if you've been promised complete creative control – as The Ting Tings were – you lose control in other ways.

They're happy now. They live in Ibiza as a couple, have a family and make their own records together. 'That's Not My Name' did give them some freedom. We're still close and I still offer advice, but their world reminds me how lucky I was to sneak into pop music in the nineties with M People. It was a last gasp cash-rich Babylon before the whole record business turned inside out, and selling a million singles became generating a billion streams, and having hits and being pop stars became a completely different thing from what it was in the twentieth century.

Doing what I wanted, what felt right, also led to coming across a young lad called Adam from Dumfries. Sony was based in Putney at the time, and around 2006 there was a sad little second wave of Britpop thing going on, which depressed the hell out of me. We were dribbling to the end of that, and there was a lot of really awful, plain, white rubbish about, sort of Britpop without the pop and without much Brit. One of the other A&R guys asked me to come down to the Half Moon nearby to take a look at some band he was desperate to sign.

The thought of another trip down to a pub to see a guitar band made my heart sink – this was when the dance of The Chemical Brothers, Fatboy Slim and Daft Punk was running out of energy, but other dance music, EDM especially, was beginning to go mega, and DJs like David Guetta and Tiësto were mapping out a future based on different sorts of numbers. The last place to look to the future was guitar music. For me, even as the highs of the nineties seemed over, I still fancied dance as being where things were heading.

I asked him what his Britpop band were called. I've wiped it from my memory for the sake of my mental health, but it was something like Jolene and the Jing Jong Jangs. I felt like screaming. Was he having me on? He said no, no, and as though he had found the new Arctic Monkeys, played me the demo. It was miserable, not even the new Monkees.

I went to meet them, and they were very posh and limp, and possibly the band that most sounded like other bands I had ever seen. I was honest to the A&R guy – no more middle-class guitar bands lethargically jingling up the world PLEASE!!

While I was simmering in my office the next day, going through one of my 'maybe this is a mistake' moments, Kasabian's publisher at EMI, Kenny McGoff, gave me a call about some detail or other. I wasn't paying much attention to what he was saying because there was some music he was playing in the background that sounded interesting.

Some distorted male voice was blankly reading out a list of girl types he liked and maybe liked him. Could be corny, but it was lifted up by it knowing about the fact it could be corny. I couldn't help but think LCD Soundsystem, and that wasn't a bad reference at the time.

The beat was the real hook, and the whole thing sounded nutty but infinitely clubbable. The technical term was: as catchy as fuck.

Sometimes that's a slippery slope into novelty, and sometimes it's a slippery slope into world conquering.

'Yeah', I said to Kenny about his little technical problem, 'I'll sort that out, but what's that you're playing?' My intuition had kicked in. The DJ in me was on alert, hearing something new with the right bpm come my way. 'Sounds fucking great.' To me, a day after witnessing the last tortured breath of Britpop, it sounded like a breath of fresh air. It sounded like the next track I wanted to play in one of my sets.

'Hang on', he said, 'I think it's something we've just signed.' He said 'It's someone called Calvin Harris.' Sounds made up, I thought.

He gave me the number of his manager, and when I called he said, 'That's funny, because Adam' – Calvin *was* made up, his real name is Adam Wiles – 'is from Scotland, but he just happens to be in London today, because we're close to signing to Gut Records.' Disappointed he was about to sign to a label, I said, 'Well, can I have twenty minutes before he catches his train?' Sure, he said, sounding intrigued, and sounding like he knew who I was.

A bad Friday had turned into a good Friday, and the kind of adventure I liked. I'd only heard him down the phone, but for some reason I was convinced he had some sort of difference, and knew how to make a song to go with a rhythm. I also sensed he had something a lot of dance music makers didn't have – a sense of humour.

I jumped in a cab and headed straight to the station. Another mission! I had a little time before he caught his train back home. I was waiting outside Costa and noticed this very tall, very geeky and unassuming looking kid nonchalantly walking towards me. I'd already made my mind up I was going to sign him. Sometimes you just know. And when you know, you know.

50
A contribution from Calvin Harris

I saw him standing outside Costa looking a little furtive and I thought, he doesn't look like a Sony A&R guy. Whatever that looks like. It was a Friday and I was going back home to Dumfries that day on the train, so Mike had rushed to the station. It was a good sign he'd come so quick. I'm not sure what he'd heard, maybe a cassette with a few songs on, but he seemed to have a plan when we met. He didn't bullshit me, or make the usual false promises, but he could see a way forward for a dance act and seemed totally knowledgeable about dance genres and trends, and how I put my songs together. It was still quite rare to meet a record company executive or publisher who knew much about dance and electronics, so this was another good sign.

My manager knew all about him, and he was excited Mike wanted to sign me and thought it would be a good fit. On the way to meet Mike he filled me in a bit. He'd come from DJing and from a group that played dance music with strong melodies and sold millions of records, so he'd turned club music into pop music, which was what I was interested in as well. He had the kind of experience you didn't often get from your usual A&R man.

Mike was offering me an album deal, and there was a smaller label, Gut, offering me a basic one-single deal before Mike got in touch, so it was almost at the last minute. I was going to sign the Gut deal because someone was showing interest. Mike actually called as my manager and I were going through the contract in my lawyer's office, thinking that we were going to do it.

We sort of put things on ice with Gut, because Mike sounded so keen and was talking about making an album. He had ideas and plans. I was worried Gut wanted to do the one-single deal with a few options, nothing really solid, because I had this track called 'The Girls', and felt they might want to do it as some cheesy novelty song.

If the next track bombed, that would be me done. Mike had a different strategy. I think he could see something I hadn't seen, but could also see 'The Girls' wasn't just a novelty – it was more knowing, and it was part of a bigger picture.

At that point I'd become a bit cynical about the whole thing. I'd been sending demos out to people for eight years, since I was 15, and it seemed like I was going nowhere. Sometimes it felt you were getting close, and then it would fall apart over some silly detail.

Mike was very straightforward, and he talked like a musician and someone who went to clubs, not like a record company. And when he talked like a marketing man, which he clearly also was, it sounded interesting, not the usual predictable shite. I was also interested in finding new ways to communicate my music. There were new ways to do it, and record companies were already struggling to see these new ways.

I was using MySpace as part of who and what I was. The visuals were important – not like Lady Gaga or something, but simply to be seen, to be active, communicating with your audience. That was still in its early stages, and record companies were very slow to see it as the future. You're following your instincts and presenting an image, and moving in a world beyond record shops and radio plays.

I was doing videos and chatting, sometimes just messing about, like people do now, but back then it was in a different medium. Same principle though: building up your numbers, a community, your own scene. Basically, you're getting supporters.

Record companies were still stuck in the twentieth century. They didn't understand how much things were changing. In that sense, in some ways I didn't need a record company, but it was that in-between period before streaming really kicked in.

Mike seemed up to speed, or at least very open to trying new channels. He didn't see any reason why dance music couldn't make it into arenas, and he'd had experience doing it himself. Also, he got the humour, and very few others at the time did.

I didn't want to make a mistake. I had the Gut deal. I said to Mike upfront, 'I need to see the money.' I needed to see some money hit the bank. I was putting sandwiches on shelves at Marks & Spencer's in Dumfries. It was doing my head in, but I wasn't going to leave that job until I knew this was real. I wasn't in a position to give up my steady job based on some fantasy, as persuasive as Mike was. Where I lived I would never get another job. I wanted to see the number. I wanted to get my tunes out and I wanted to make sure I could keep doing that.

Mike could see I was in no mood for a delay, especially when I had a deal ready to go, and it turned out he had an offer ready by the following Tuesday. Which was yet another good sign. There was no worry from him that I wanted to play all the music and produce myself, and even sing it, when I didn't really have a voice. For him, that was punk. Nothing to worry about. There was none of the usual hesitancy when you were dealing with record companies, always looking for problems, for why something won't work.

I called the first album *I Created Disco*, obviously not because I had, but sort of imagining a world where I had. I was playing around with the idea of being someone who would release an album with that title that had these particular songs on it.

Mike got it – the whole concept about making an album in my bedroom on a Commodore Amiga computer that sounded like it wanted to be a radio-friendly number 1 album. He'd had experience with M People of coming out of the clubs with an ambition to make Top 10 pop music, so he could see the route I wanted to take.

You don't get love from the critics but they absolutely are not your audience, and they're reviewing the wrong thing. It's more than music. You're creating excitement, and experiences, and hopefully events, and they don't know how to review that.

I was also creating a character, like an alter ego, and I had always used other names for myself – Jimmy Bones, Stouffer, after the cat on Harry Hill's comedy show – and then there was Calvin Harris – after Calvin Richardson the R&B singer and Andre Harris, the producer.

No one got it after the first album, how I was playing roles. So I moved on, but kept the name.

I realised I was a bit stuck when I started to become successful and everyone began to call me Calvin. That freaked me out a little, because in my head I'd left him behind, the one wearing the goggles on the cover of *I Created Disco*, the one singing in a band with

Calvin, Cabaret Voltaire

his mates from Dumfries, but even my manager who always knew me as Adam started calling me Calvin. Then there was a girlfriend I was having an argument with, and she suddenly started calling me Calvin. She'd met Adam, she was going out with Adam, and now she was calling me Calvin.

The reviews from the beginning would frustrate me, but they didn't make me change anything. I changed when I wanted to change into what I wanted to change into – like when I stopped singing it was because I wanted to write songs for female voices, because they have the right frequencies for clubs: it lets the bass find its place. At first I had the band, but pretty soon the singing, touring, doing interviews thing got boring. I just wanted to make tracks, write them, record them, mix them, because that was my favourite thing, and then the band became less interesting to me as a way to perform them. It was holding me back.

The band sounded shite and if you played on the same night as a DJ, they would sound so fantastic playing records with their powerful sound, whereas we were all muffled and out of synch and I was never going to be able to sing on really big hits. If I sang, whatever I did would still be seen as some kind of novelty, or a bit lo-fi.

I saw Mike play a midnight DJ set in Manchester, and the response was absolutely incredible. I said to him afterwards, sort of joking, 'Wow, maybe I should just DJ.' A band is just so old-fashioned.

And then as a band we did a show about 10.30 pm, opening this show, and we got a very lukewarm response. All that trouble getting there, sixteen people on a tour bus, setting up, soundchecking, hanging around, for not much reward. Steve Angello follows us. He sticks in his USB and he's ready to go. The sound is fantastic and blows us away. He's playing amazing tunes, known and unknown, that sound brilliant. We are just a band with another lead singer looking for new poses, slogging our guts out.

After seeing Mike and Steve get an audience going wild, I started thinking more seriously – I want to do that. Mike told me I should start mixing DJing in with playing with the band. I wasn't sure at first, but the idea became more attractive. I taught myself how to DJ, and it changed how I wrote songs. I'd write them conscious of how they'd fit into my DJ set. If I needed a type of track – a banger, a house track, something EDM – I'd write it. And it developed so that as a DJ I would only play my own records. I ditched the band.

I'd shapeshifted really into another fantasy, and if it had been the seventies, I might have used another name – like Ziggy becoming Aladdin Sane becoming the Thin White Duke. It's theatre. What I've learnt though is that when you're being slagged off on the internet or there's gossip about you and your latest girlfriend, it doesn't matter what name they use. They're still talking about you.

After the song with Rihanna, which to some made me American but with a Scottish accent, I worked with Ariana Grande, Katy Perry, Nicki Minaj, Lil Yachty, Future, Dua Lipa, Young Thug, Busta Rhymes, Kylie Minogue, NeYo, Florence Welch, Snoop Dogg, Dizzee Rascal, Ellie Goulding, so I was always building my set.

I got a better reaction as a DJ then I ever did in a band – there was that whole thing about, well, you just press a button and the music plays, but putting on a show is more than that, and being the person responsible for the music, playing the music as a DJ, reading a crowd to work out when and where the music fits, felt as much musical as it did when I was fronting a band. Maybe even more so.

I was used to waving my arms in the air because I used to do that in the band. That seemed like something you had to do as a DJ. I think Mike might have to take some of the responsibility for that.

He was also there for me when I lost my Ableton software just before a show, and didn't know what the hell to do. I rang him from New York in a right state, and he was as calm as usual, told me to buy some CDs and burn them onto the computer. It meant being on more of a knife-edge than doing it all relying on the computer, where it's more pre-done, but it was a lot more fun. There was more freedom, because with the computer you're so locked in, there's no room for spontaneity. Without the computer, it's like playing an instrument.

I got the Ableton back, and played a few more gigs that way, but I missed using CDs and being able to mix more in the moment. Mike said that was when I became a proper DJ, but in a unique position, because as he says, no one else has the library of self-made hit songs I have. It's a DJ set and an artist performance at the same time.

The crowd, performing with me, collaborating with me, do the rest. And then I have all these guest artists, and none of them have to turn up.

***

When Calvin plays, all the tracks that everyone is going crazy for, with different superstar voices, he made them. He's not a club DJ, because he plays arenas, festivals and even stadiums. It's a unique experience watching him play and I never get fed up with it, because I love all the songs, and they all come from his mind.

You have this big production with this little silhouette in the middle. It's about as far as the pop music that began in the early sixties can go as a spectacle, and it can seem as though he is disappearing into the music, and the audience are losing themselves in the music.

The great illusion is that he doesn't need to have the performers on the record with him. Now and then he'll have one of them guest, but if there is an appearance, it had to be of the Rihanna level, because ultimately he's the star, and it's not practical to do all the shows he does with a series of guest vocalists.

It almost didn't happen, at least not with me, and not with Sony. The first single in March 2007 was his wonky remix of the 1980s itself, and a tribute to what then seemed like ancient electro pop, 'Acceptable in the Eighties'. It was the kind of song you could sing along with even if you didn't know the words, and it made the Top 10. In June, 'The Girls', the one I'd heard down the phone, made number 3, and the same month the album debuted at number 8 and was selling pretty respectably.

This all seemed very solid for a new act, except this was Sony, and there were regular meetings to discuss which artists weren't passing muster and perhaps needed culling. It was often nothing to do with the talent and commitment of the artists whether they were selling or not, and it could be brutal.

It was the part of my job I hated the most, if I had to tell a group or singer that we were letting them go. I wouldn't get any sleep for days.

At the big meeting we were having with all the Sony departments about whether to keep Calvin or not, I sensed doom. The album had sold 150,000 copies by then, and because Calvin had more or less done it all himself it didn't cost that much. But for Sony, this was not good enough. I knew I was going to have a fight on my hands.

Ged, who had lured me in with the promise of doing what I wanted, would have his Sony boss face on. No City fan solidarity today. This was serious stuff. It was like some big policy meeting in the Houses of Parliament. It was about as far away from a Factory meeting as you could get. They were two very different 'war' rooms, although both could resemble the war room in Dr Strangelove.

Ged had been saying a lot lately about the need to radically alter the Sony business model, as the music industry faced up to the new world of downloads and the incoming Apple iPhone, which was going to be the iPod for everyone, and something new called Spotify.

Luckily for me, while getting ready for the meeting I bumped into a high-level Sony executive, William Rowe. He was the main man in the finance department. He had all the sales figures, but also the other figures in terms of where revenue was coming from outside of record sales.

William said to me, 'Hey, that Calvin Harris is making us a lot of money.' I said, 'What do you mean?' He said, 'His PPL revenue is massive' – public performance licensing, where businesses and organisations paid for licences to play recorded music. Calvin's music was being used for lots of ads and TV shows, and in the hitherto mysterious Eastern European countries he was generating more money than just about anyone else at the label. He was getting used for loads of things – it was part of Adam's very digital era sensibility that he had an instinct that making pop music wasn't about records. It was part of a bigger entertainment landscape. Songs were reaching the world in diverse new ways.

When it came to discuss Calvin Harris in the meeting, those against said, 'Well, he's only sold 150,000 copies of the album, and the novelty is wearing off. He's going nowhere.' I got up and said, 'Well, if you're looking to change your business model, Calvin is the future – I've just spoken to William in finance', making it seem like we'd had a specially scheduled meeting, 'and Calvin is our second highest PPL earner this year, making money in all sorts of places – ads, films, games.' Not trusting me on the money, they checked with William, who looked the part of the sensible and reliable guy you trusted with the money. 'Yes', he said with much formality and understatement, 'he's earning quite a lot of money.' He gave them the figures, and that was that. The whole atmosphere in the room changed. Calvin Harris was not being dropped. The novelty was not wearing off; he had plenty of plans.

The model for a while was for him to work with singers who were significantly more well known than he was, and each time he did, it lifted him a little higher, brought in a whole new audience – until he absorbed their collective star power, and it became difficult to find anyone with a bigger name than his, anyone making as much money.

It was part of how he marketed himself. It was Madonna in reverse – she chose the right producers; he chose the right featured artists at just the right time. He was a pop art marketing man as much as anything. He made the fly goggles with the diamonds he wore on the neon covers of the *I Created Disco* album. When one of his singles was struggling in 2009, he disrupted a live *X Factor* performance by the Jedward twins in protest, holding a pineapple on his head to poke fun at their hair, which boosted airplay for his single. The stunt got the pissed off attention, and eventual grudging respect, of Simon Cowell, who admitted to me, even though publicly he was furious, that it got Calvin some good publicity. Obviously, Cowell wasn't so forgiving when we took 'We Found Love' from Leona Lewis and gave it to Rihanna.

As big as he got, as ridiculously famous as his girlfriends were, for me he was still the gangly kid I saw walking towards me as I stood outside Costa Coffee at King's Cross Station. When Adam went on a health kick and quit drinking he suddenly went all sex symbol on me, but it was still the low key, often quite sickly lad from Dumfries treating me as a kind of uncle.

I knew a socially awkward music nerd hijacking pre-existing cultural elements with a meticulous attention to detail when I met one. I had absolutely no idea he would become a chart-topping Adonis

A-lister who could transform his image and lifestyle as much as he could his music, playing with dance genres and dream singers as though he was still making it up in his bedroom on a computer he'd built himself.

Even in 2007 it was hard to envisage a world ten years on where electronic music would be completely commercialised and where he would be the highest paid DJ in the world, playing regular season-long residencies in Las Vegas at $400,000 a night. Being connected to it was somehow the perfect place where everything I had done over the past thirty years had led.

I was sort of the DIY pre-superstar, cash-in-hand house DJ of the 1980s living through him without having to go through all the pressure and chaos. I could get a hint of a world of fame and riches I was twenty years too early for, and certainly not pretty enough or temperamentally adept enough to deal with all the fuss and scrutiny.

The £50 million a year when he was the richest DJ in the world for a few years would have been nice, but it was great to experience his life in short bursts. I couldn't live it. He's got the temperament to take it in his stride.

Calvin and I laugh about it. I used to hump around my record boxes, travelling up and down the motorways in my wheezing old Renault 5. He's got his little USBs and he's flying into his shows on sleek, sparkling private jets, being picked up straight off the plane in important looking blacked out SUVs, and whisked straight to the stage door. A good gig for me was a couple of thousand. For him its 200,000. I had my night in one club. He's all over the world.

He topped the bill at Coachella in 2016 and did 'We Found Love' with Rihanna. He was on top of his riser staring out at all the phone lights on thousands of cameras, and he saw Katy Perry at the front, crowd-surfing. He said he knew that would never happen again, so made sure to remember it for all time.

I had similar nights at The Haçienda – no phone lights, maybe it was Rowetta doing the crowd-surfing – but it was great to feel that somehow I was part of the chain that led from one to the other. Calvin Harris is like the mega version of the original idea for my *North* album and then M People – getting certain singers at the right time in their careers to perform different songs, getting the most appropriate and infectious rhythms and coordinating a mix of genres.

Watching him, this epic, aroused production of energy, melody and frenzy, a roaring, jubilant audience, it does seem like the end of something that began with The Beatles. I feel like I was there at the beginning as a teenage world took shape, and now I was there at the grand finale and a series of encores that will last until the nostalgia for it runs out.

Weirdly, 2007, when I was beginning a new collaboration with Calvin Harris, was the year when Tony Wilson died, at just 57. Another far too early death for a Factory man – to some extent, *the* Factory man – another sad, draining Catholic funeral, another service with the maximum of fuss and another burial in the Southern Cemetery, where Tony was laid to rest close to his fallen comrades, Martin Hannett and Rob Gretton.

Factory, The Haçienda and the Dry Bar, and their contribution to the making of a new post-industrial Manchester took their toll. It was funny for me, as I always thought that later in life Tony and I would meet up regularly, in a world where Rob lived and we made up and I'd be Rob's mate again. They'd forgive me for living in the south for twenty-six years. We'd roll a spliff, swap stories, make plans, argue for fun, and against our better instincts remember the great, mostly unacceptable madness of the 1980s.

I would be able to say to Tony, remember when you always used to say to me, darling, dance music will never sell, and I'd stick on a pair of Calvin Harris goggles and marvel at how we found love in a hopeless place.

With Calvin I felt it was the climax of everything I had done over the past thirty years. All the experience I had over those three decades led to signing and working with Calvin and watching what happened to him. And that seemed like a good end to my place in music.

I was there as the music industry started to turn into something else. I'd had my time, it was filled with an incredible music, a lot of which will last a long time. But how it happened back then will never happen again. When I finished I felt there was no place for me in the new type of record companies mostly servicing the streaming sites and managing their catalogues. I couldn't progress.

I left around 2022 because the balance of acts that Sony were signing was becoming determined by TikTok. That's where most of the new music was coming from. Over 50 per cent of their output was stuff that had gone viral online. It hadn't been developed or signed because it was unique and setting a new trend. In A&R meetings decisions were made about signing something based on twenty seconds of music. A few months later, the twenty seconds of music could lead to arena sized venues. Everything was speeding up.

Large amounts of money were being offered not because of the strength of the songs or the potential, but because of the numbers the music was getting on various platforms. It was all about the numbers. It was all safety first market research really. That was totally alien to me and it was no use me pretending to go along with it. It wasn't for me, and if I moaned about it, thinking it all sounded the same, well that just confirmed I was too old for whatever was now going on.

My kind of record company, of signing and releasing records, was rooted in the twentieth century. Those pioneering decades after The Beatles came along when music on records shifted from being entertainment to being life itself. By the 2020s, pop music had gone back to being pure entertainment. Record companies were more obviously entertainment companies now, supplying streaming sites, and I didn't want to work for what was solely an entertainment company.

They were too impatient to invest in or develop talent. It had to happen immediately, because everything else did thanks to social media and Spotify. The new used to be year to year, and now it was almost day to day. And record companies started to leave out the part I liked best, the setting up of things, the early work, to become management companies. There are no real departments any more where you can work with a band on their sound and style. This was the era I came through, and there were different battles and struggles but it changed my life.

There are other battles now and lives will be changed in different ways, and I'll watch it happen but it's a different world. I don't want to dismiss it just because I am old, like I've become my dad, but you have to look at how it is with a little concern. Not because the music is getting weirder or more dangerous, but because it's become made up of the same patterns and poses.

This is how it is, there is no use fighting it. Labels as I knew them are now fundamentally defunct. The entertainment companies keep them because there is a kind of nostalgic kudos about being on Island, the original independent-minded home of Bob Marley, Grace Jones, and Roxy Music, or Columbia, the oldest record company in the world. But it's more about branding than anything. Those labels have got nothing to do with the original Island or the great history of Columbia, except they bought up the company that bought the company that bought the company that originally bought the label back in the day. And the money that came into Columbia for a new act, after a couple of years it all passes into central Sony, as heritage music, to be packaged into legacy compilations and reissues.

I was into music because of everything else that came with it – the fashions, the urgency, the uniqueness, its connection to a wider culture and community – and TikTok makes music that exists inside TikTok and that's changed the business, and lives are now inevitably changed in very different ways from when I was a lad.

51
A new city

Because Martin died at 42, Rob at 46, and Tony at 57, there's been no real guide to how an ex-Factory insider moves through their sixties – and God help me, beyond.

The two remaining main Factory figures, Alan Erasmus and Peter Saville, do not offer much in the way of advice on how to age – or 'come in to land', as Erasmus would say – unless you happen to live the lives of Alan Erasmus and Peter Saville.

Alan remains in shadowy places, leaving few traces, a post-Situationist monk keeping in touch with a unique past, sending regular gnomic texts to his former cohorts on special occasions. Peter Saville was somehow always ageless even in his twenties, and deals in ideas and concepts as a graphic design icon, where it doesn't matter how old you are. In fact, like an important, innovative architect, you somehow get cooler and more revered the older you are.

That's a difficult trick to pull off as a DJ, although now and then I give it a go, and I can still get a crowd going and feel pretty ageless myself. I'd probably do more if my DJing hours could be in the late afternoon, finishing about 6 pm – time to get home for a cup of tea and a Netflix binge.

The Manchester we helped to make through not knowing what we were doing and just following our instinct is not my Manchester now. It's changed beyond belief – not only because of the music, and the clubs, the hotels, restaurants and bars, the sport and universities, the inner-city population boom, and what became a considerable cultural history with the unspoilt version of The Haçienda at the centre.

A new Manchester emerged because of the consequences of the IRA bomb, and the Manchester Arena attack at an Ariana Grande concert in 2017, along with the rise of Manchester City as a world-famous and innovative, forward-looking football club that needed a modern city to grow around it – and for various reasons, got one.

The older City fans, those around my age still moaning after all these years and all these trophies, find this new, more complicated City, an international Manchester City, difficult to deal with. It seems less and less their City. But then it was never really their City, even when City most closely resembled a failed, old-fashioned team rummaging around in the lower divisions with failed manager after failed manager.

To have the success we've had, and the players we sign, and, miraculously, Pep Guardiola as manager for ten years, means we have become a very different club with a variety of fans, and mysterious sources of money and backing. It's a world game, and we're a world team.

Like me – and Noel, Johnny and Kevin Cummins, for whom a home City match is now an awayday – the new Manchester City are part Manchester, part something else altogether, so I can be comfortable with what they are, a hybrid of analogue tradition and digital transcendence. I can accept the new so-called 'plastic fans' coming in from all over the world, even if they do take bloody selfies after the match has started.

We're more ready for the rest of the twenty-first century than most football teams, and at one point it looked like we might not make it through the twentieth century, so I'll take it, as far-fetched science fiction as it sometimes seems.

For a while, after Rob died and Tony died, I would feel alienated in my own home city. The changes – the big city centre developments and twenty-five-storey and higher tower blocks that changed the skyline into a kind of Manhattanchester – made it clear to me I didn't belong any more. Even as a City fan I could feel like an interloper, as though moving south had erased over forty years of suffering and shivering in the often calamitous dark ages.

Things started to change when Garry Cook took over as CEO of Manchester City in 2008, transforming the infrastructure and direction of the club, which led to the beginning of the Abu Dhabi years and becoming a world superstar club. He'd come from Nike, and brought some new-fangled marketing ideas, linking the club with its past but mostly imagining a sophisticated future.

Under Cook, they pulled City fans like me, Noel and Johnny into the club as a reflection of the image of the surrounding city. We were the new show business, which might have looked a little privileged, but made me feel connected to the club again. Not necessarily through family and tradition, although that would come back, and I would pass it on, as should be the way, to my son Charlie, but through some sort of reward for being a Manchester music figure.

The fans didn't sing any M People songs – apart from a brief time when 'Moving on Up' was sung as we dragged ourselves back up from the Second Division into the Premier League – but Garry wanted to get some local history and a sense of its fashion and music culture into a club that was changing fast and needed some sense of Manchester. It obviously worked most obviously with Liam and Noel, especially Noel, but I found myself doing things with and for the club.

Through City, Kevin and I got involved with some sponsorship scheme organised by Umbro where we gave funds to local start-up businesses, and we helped Rob Gretton's son Ben with a reggae record label he was launching. Lesley was stunned and Umbro were a bit puzzled, but we just said, 'It's Rob Gretton's son. If anyone deserves some money for a Manchester project, it's Ben.'

We felt it was a way for the club Rob loved so much to help Ben, although it didn't do too well. Ben went into catering and hospitality, and had a nice Rob-like way of responding very drily to one star reviews online of his restaurants.

My son Charlie was a year old when we played Gillingham in the play-off finals in 1999, which had saved us from possible oblivion, and I took him to his first match on 28 December 2004 – City against West Brom. He was only 6 and I was trying to find a way to bond with him, find something that was ours.

Grace and I took him and it was at the new stadium, then called the City of Manchester Stadium before it became the Etihad Stadium. It was going through the conversion from being the Commonwealth Games athletics stadium to being City's home, and City were going through managers very quickly. It was the hope as always that was killing us as one manager after another turned up – this was the Kevin Keegan era, who'd taken over from Joe Royle in 2001 and got us back into the Premier League.

It had started off optimistically, because Keegan seemed a good choice and had done well when he was managing Newcastle. He had a bit of passion about him, but by 2004 it was beginning to become the usual story, another false dawn. There were still 47,000 in the crowd, but the hope was killing us, again.

The weather was horrible, relentless sleet and ice, and after a visit to the souvenir shop Charlie was a picture, drowning in his brand new City scarf and hat. The game was really frustrating. Nicolas Anelka scored after half an hour and then we just couldn't score another, even after West Brom went down to ten men following a sending off.

I thought we were just about going to get away with it and then, with five minutes to go, our captain Richard Dunne scored a freak own goal, one of quite a few he scored.

How typical City was that? The crowd was deflated. It was the worst possible day to take Charlie. We came out into the freezing cold and we had to get the train back to London, and I thought he's never going to want to come again after that. It just didn't seem magical enough. But I was seeing it through the eyes of a fan who'd seen too much disappointment.

When we were on the train he was reading the programme and he suddenly said, 'We're playing Everton on New Year's Day – can we go to that?' So I brought him back up – and we won 2–1, Dunne got two assists ... and the roller coaster goes back up again. And that was that. He's been fanatical ever since. For the next few years he always wanted to go to the Etihad, and I was really energised about City going to the matches with Charlie, which coincided with the unbelievable turnaround in fortunes. Ten years later he was wanting to go to every away game, and then when we started qualifying for Europe we would travel all over Europe together. After the Sheikh had just taken over Charlie came to America with me when I DJ'd on a pre-season tour thanks to Umbro, and then we were together in Istanbul when we won the Champions League, celebrating into the early hours like life couldn't get any better. We were the best team in all the land and all the world, in my lifetime.

It went from my grandad to my dad to me to Charlie. We are all just links in a chain. It must be something in the blood. All of that has made me much more Manchester than I felt in the first years after Rob died and I moved to London.

I also felt taken back into the Manchester fold when Sacha Lord and Sam Kandel, who'd revived the Sankeys nightclub in 2000, started the Warehouse Project in Manchester, which kicked some energy into Manchester's nightlife as a pop-up club. With the help of Kirsty Smith from Sankeys, they started out in 2005 with some raves in the old, abandoned Boddington's Brewery in Strangeways, a twelve-week series of club nights running from September to New Year's Eve, aiming to fill a gap left by The Haçienda closing, but trying something different.

The difference was based on their experience at Sankeys, which tended to peak for the last three months in a year, maybe because of the inrush of students. The project didn't intend to be around for ever. It would represent a moment in time before it became something else, and somewhere else.

I would play there – it was about the closest experience I'd had to The Haçienda nights twenty years earlier, and it had that same feeling: it was always on the edge of either disaster or absolute bliss.

The brewery had one big, cavernous space and a warren of smaller spaces, and a fabulous sound system. But the parties quickly outgrew the place, and the bass vibrating into the nearby prison caused some issues. In 2007, they moved the site to Store Street, an old air raid shelter turned car park directly under Piccadilly Station, near what is now Motel One, which was built on the premises of the Twisted Wheel.

A couple of days before they were due to throw their first night, where I would be playing, the fire department came down to check that it was safe to host an event. They said there weren't enough fire doors for the amount of people we were expecting.

We asked them where we would need to put a fire escape to bring it up to scratch, and they said, 'That wall there'. If we didn't get a fire door in that wall the venue couldn't open. Luckily, we never had that kind of scrutiny in the early days of The Haçienda, or we would never have opened in the first place.

We found out it was Railtrack that owned the wall we needed to put a door into. I said, 'Well, you're never going to get an answer from them in two days.' The solution was to secretly bore a big hole in the wall and cover it with a couple of doors. I stood there with Sam and Sacha watching the drill piercing the wall for hours, and it broke through at about 5 in the morning. There were a few tired cheers, as this meant we could go ahead. We were still clearing the rubble away and getting the doors put in hours before people were allowed in for the opening night.

That's what I loved about the Warehouse Project. It was the next stage on from Factory, and they did what it took to make sure that Manchester would get its party, and get its night out. That's Manchester: whatever it takes. I still smile when I see those doors. To this day Railtrack haven't noticed that we did it.

It was where Calvin Harris played when he was beginning to think he liked the idea of being a DJ. They put him on as a favour to me because then he was just a name – not A Name – and they didn't know him from Adam.

He played at 10.30, before the evening had warmed up, and he didn't set the place on fire. It's part of his origin story, part of how he moved from being a sort of singer in a slightly ramshackle band to being the world's number one DJ, and it's part of the Warehouse Project origin story.

The Warehouse Project has moved venues in Manchester a few times, warehouse to warehouse, with Store Street its spiritual home, and its line-up of DJs, collaborators and new and classic acts is always world class. Everywhere you are inside their venues something is happening, each space an event, an intoxicating not-quite-reality, the perfect mix between old and new, then and now, and, of course, what's next. It's become a transient venue for transient people, with a name, like Factory, that says 'This is Manchester'.

It's become one of the best clubbing experiences in the world, and I especially love it because I can play there and not feel I'm just being nostalgic for The Haçienda and rocking the house one more time. We can take The Haçienda to the Warehouse Project in 2025 as one of its internal modular festivals, with the old gang – Hewan Clarke, Greg Wilson, Jon Dasilva, Marshall Jefferson, Graeme, me and many others – and become part of the contemporary action. It doesn't feel like a sentimental act, a bunch of old timers waving their arms in the air yearning for an illusory golden age where it's always 2 am in the morning and everyone's nutted and necking pills.

Manchester has moved on. There's a place for me and what I bring, but it's also very much the new Manchester. The Warehouse Project, and other clubs like The White Hotel and Hidden, things happening in fly-by-night basements and back rooms, capturing moments in time, seals Manchester as a world-renowned club destination where the best parties never stop.

My old partner at Nude, Graeme Park, works in Manchester regularly and he says there are so many clubs, you could work there seven nights week and there would always be an audience. You can see it just walking around the city centre, with all the posters advertising nights and clubs and places to go.

Dancing and the rhythm, involvement and togetherness that comes with it, going for it and going for it hard, became an essential, distinctive part of the identity of the city. A city used to dealing in their own way with the unease and uncertainty of the world, using drums and songs – as well as the comedy and stoicism – to create their own certainty, one night at a time.

If clubs and nightlife as I knew them are dying out, as I read they are – too expensive, too predictable, too corporate, too sweaty, a post-pandemic, social media-era lack of enthusiasm for going out and mixing with other strange bodies – Manchester, driven by music, will still find places and ways to make something happen under cover of the night. Manchester will push people to find their madness and their freedom, get high on hope, and see their efforts help create new global cultures. Manchester has to do what it has to do; the rhythm either survives, or it stops.

I suppose I have taken on that ambassadorial role for the city that Johnny talks about me having. I can go on about the great restaurants there now are, the galleries and art centres, the numerous fabulous hotels, MediaCity helping to shift emphasis away from that bloody London, a constant sense the city is evolving and moving somewhere.

There's a lot of money about, and also there's those with little money, and there's also a clear definition between a north Manchester and a south Manchester – so the city still has a very Manchester tension, between those who've made it and those on the make, those getting high and those stuck in a rut. That tension is part of its soul.

When Rob and I used to drive around a hollowed out city in the early 1980s, checking the outside of the sad-looking boarded up building that would become The Haçienda, through dead end places that now hum with life and action, it was like there were no street lights and you'd be in no-man's land just a few yards outside the city centre. Maybe just a few dodgy pubs full of wrecked blokes in the mood for a skirmish. Then we put The Haçienda on Whitworth Street, and the street lights started coming, and the city began to come to life.

In the 2020s it's definitely become a city for the young. It's exciting in a different way from when I was there. People move there now rather than move away. I have friends whose kids have come to the city to study and they tell me they're having the time of their life. For them, it's the best city in the country. It's where you can feel that things happen, people always trying to do something different, and it's more cosmopolitan than in my day.

It's not my Manchester any more, but my Manchester is part of it. I don't recognise it, but it's very familiar. Full of ghosts, and full of what made me what I am and what made me love the music that I do.

Would I live there again?

No way.

I can't stand the fucking weather.

Illustrations

FIGURES

COLOUR PLATES

From left: Me, Mark Kamins, Simon Topping, recording the Quando Quango album at Strawberry Studios Stockport, 1984

Donald Johnson and me in a studio somewhere, mid-eighties

Simon Topping, Gonnie Rietveld, Mike P, Barry Johnson, Chinatown Manchester – chosen to look like New York, mid-eighties

Martin Prendergast, Mike P, 1985

T-Coy: Richie Close, Simon Topping, Mike P after Granada Studios gig in Manchester, 1987

Me on my rave balcony, Cromford Court, Manchester, 1988

Mike P, Haçienda, 1988

Graeme Park, Mike P, 1988 on tour in Australia. The hats were standard Summer of Love uniform

Rob Gretton, Mike P, downstairs at the Haçienda, mid-eighties

Live the Dream rave, Tockholes, Lancashire, 1989

M People: Mike P, Paul Heard, Heather Small, Shovell, winning the Mercury Music Prize 1994. That ruffled some feathers

With Heather Small, Amsterdam mid-nineties

Mark Kamins and Mike P, Havana, Cuba, 2004

Our annual pilgrimage. Grace Pickering, Mike P, Glastonbury Festival 2005

Mike P, Haçienda live, Albert Hall 2015

Charlie Tadman, Calvin Harris, Burns, Mike P in private jet, not sure when

Scully, Pep Guardiola, Mike P, Noel Gallagher, Charlie Pickering, Wembley dressing room. Can't remember the year because we won it so many times

Mike P, Calvin Harris, The Brit Awards 2019

Playlists

PART I: LEARNING

https://open.spotify.com/playlist/70Mp7yrft7DSyV5xewCYUR?si=ZloHBpXYQrqqF5PuXhZPxg&pi=JSgMxMF_TDKef&pt_success=1&nd=1&dlsi=78aa9226b9e643b5

TITLE	ARTIST
How Long Will It Take	Pat Kelly
Long Shot Kick De Bucket	The Pioneers
Do I Love You (Indeed I do)	Frank Wilson
Get Up Offa That Thing	James Brown
Try A Little Tenderness	Otis Redding
Heaven Must Have Sent You	The Elgins
Breakin' Down The Walls Of Heartache	Johnny Johnson and The Bandwagon
Everything's Tuesday	Chairmen Of The Board
The Tracks Of My Tears	Smokey Robinson and The Miracles

A Day In The Life	The Beatles
Inner City Blues	Marvin Gaye
Let's Get It On	Marvin Gaye
Tired Of Being Alone	Al Green
TVC15	David Bowie
Suffragette City	David Bowie
Vicious	Lou Reed
Coney Island Baby	Lou Reed
Nightclubbing	Iggy Pop
Land/Horses	Patti Smith
Stranger In Blue Suede Shoes (Live At The Rainbow Theatre)	Kevin Ayers
Baby's On Fire	Brian Eno
Dream Baby Dream	Suicide
The Black Angel's Death Song	Velvet Underground and Nico
Femme Fatal	Velvet Underground and Nico
You Know More Than I Know	John Cale
Paris 1919	John Cale
Boredom	Buzzcocks
What Do I Get?	Buzzcocks
Train In Vain	The Clash
Dot Dash	Wire
Venus	Television
She's Lost Control	Joy Division
Being Boiled	The Human League
A Forest	The Cure
No Tears	Tuxedomoon
Der Mussolini	DAF
Contort Yourself	James White and The Blacks
Los Niños Del Parque	Liaisons Dangereuses
1969	The Stooges
Virginia Plain	Roxy Music
Pyjamarama	Roxy Music
Roadrunner	The Modern Lovers

PART II: PLAYING

https://open.spotify.com/playlist/4OrfupZiVVSrfYOcV9aONE?si=lUakszLwTdGOhGH8bUm0RQ&pi=Q4oRC09hQ5edh&pt

TITLE	ARTIST
Do You Believe In The Westworld	Theatre Of Hate
Reward	The Teardrop Explodes
Tell Me When The Light Turns Green	Dexys Midnight Runners
Tears Are Not Enough	ABC
Hymn From A Village	James
Blue Monday	New Order
Temptation	New Order
Set It Off (Vocal)	Strafe
Dirty Talk	Klein & M.B.O.
Love Tempo (Mark Kamins Mix)	Quando Quango
This Charming Man	The Smiths
There Is A Light That Never Goes Out	The Smiths
Hip Hop Be Bop	Man Parrish
(We Don't Need) This Fascist Groove Thing	Heaven 17
Never Too Much	Luther Vandross
Moody	ESG

Trapped	Colonel Abrams
I Can't Turn Around	J.M. Silk
Jump Back (Set Me Free)	Dhar Braxton
Hallelujah (Andy Weatherall Mix)	Happy Mondays
Ride On Time	Black Box
Promised Land	Joe Smooth
No Way Back	Adonis
Voodoo Ray	A Guy Called Gerald
Dream 17	Annette
Carino	T Coy
Strings Of Life	Derrick May, Mayday
Your Love	Frankie Knuckles
Bassline	Mantronix
King Of The Beats	Mantronix
Confusion	New Order
E = MC2	Big Audio Dynamite
Passion	Gat Decor
Track With No Name	Forgemasters
Let It Roll	Doug Lazy
Bela Lugosi's Dead	Bauhaus
Keep On Movin'	Soul II Soul, Caron Wheeler

PART III: WORKING

https://open.spotify.com/playlist/1zkYuVgSApVUJ9nYaVW1uV?si=gOUuRyzoSqKIboEa-fRU-g&pi=Z-BGnnQ-T_mbK&pt_=&nd=1&dlsi=84d48689730c4f6a

TITLE	ARTIST
Don't Come To Stay	Hot House
Colour My Life	M People
How Can I Love You More (Sasha Mix)	M People
Don't You Want Me	Felix
7 Seconds	Youssou N'dour, Neneh Cherry
Rhythm Is A Mystery	K- Klass
Everybody Everybody	Black Box
Time Will Pass You By	Kylie Minogue (M People Production)
I Found U	Axwell
Nothing But Love	Axwell
Au Seve	Julio Bashmore
Fire	Kasabian
Club Foot	Kasabian
Standing In The Way Of Control	Gossip
Heavy Cross	Gossip
Acceptable In The 80s	Calvin Harris
I'm Not Alone	Calvin Harris

Slide	Calvin Harris (Feat. Frank Ocean, Migos)
Live Forever	Oasis
I Wrote The Book	Gossip
That's Not My Name	The Ting Tings
Molly's Chambers	Kings Of Leon
Ms. Jackson	OutKast
We Found Love	Rihanna (Feat. Calvin Harris)
Moving On Up	M People

Index